THE INTERNATIONAL
PSYCHO-ANALYTICAL
LIBRARY

NO. 47

PORTRAIT OF BERKELEY AS DEAN 1728
by John Smibert

THE INTERNATIONAL PSYCHO-ANALYTICAL LIBRARY
EDITED BY ERNEST JONES, M.D.
No. 47

THE UNCONSCIOUS ORIGIN OF BERKELEY'S PHILOSOPHY

John Oulton Wisdom

LONDON
THE HOGARTH PRESS
AND THE INSTITUTE OF PSYCHO-ANALYSIS
1953

PUBLISHED BY
The Hogarth Press Ltd.
LONDON

★

Clarke, Irwin & Co. Ltd.
TORONTO

PRINTED IN ENGLAND BY
HAZELL WATSON AND VINEY LTD
AYLESBURY AND LONDON
ALL RIGHTS RESERVED

CONTENTS

v

33419

CONTENTS

PREFACE

THIS book has complementary aims. It is concerned both to interest psycho-analysts in philosophy, which is perhaps the strangest of all the creations of the human mind, and to interest philosophers in psycho-analysis, which they may find illuminating in their own field. For I attempt not only to analyse Berkeley the man, but also his philosophy and philosophical conceptions. To throw light on philosophy in this way is the chief aim.

The book has also a further philosophical aim. There is no full exposition of Berkeley's metaphysic that utilises the results of recent scholarship. This is a serious gap and I have made a serious attempt to fill it.

The researches of Dr. A. A. Luce and also of Professor T. E. Jessop make it reasonably certain what Berkeley's philosophy actually was. Part I contains a detailed account of this, together with some critical discussion. Dr. Luce's work has also cleared up many points about Berkeley's life, various aspects of which are considered in Part II. It is highly necessary to dwell closely on Berkeley's life and philosophy, especially on his philosophy; otherwise it would be impossible to give the detailed psycho-analytical interpretation of his philosophical conceptions presented in Part III.

There has been some spasmodic writing on the relations between philosophy and psycho-analysis. On the Continent the first work of this kind appeared in 1913, written by Hitschmann and by von Winterstein; they were followed by a few other analysts. In this country a few philosophers have quite recently turned their attention to the subject. I can find no writing in this field here earlier than 1936, when I attempted, in a paper on ethics, to use psycho-analytical considerations in dealing with a philosophical problem. The first draft of the present analysis was written in 1937. The idea of psycho-analysing the writings of a philosopher arose, not from the work done on the Continent, of which I was then unaware, but from a theory I had formed about the nature of metaphysics;

it was also inspired by the celebrated applications of psycho-. analysis made in other fields by Dr. Ernest Jones.

Some readers may find it of interest that even at the time the first draft was made the central interpretations concerned projection and introjection, although I was then unaware that these concepts were assuming an increasing importance in psycho-analytical theory and technique. I used them simply because they seemed to fit the Berkeley data. Though the material of that draft is now greatly re-arranged, the substance of it is almost all retained. Considerable additions have since been made, carrying the analysis further in certain respects. Some of the further elaborations I have made were rendered possible by the new contributions on projection and introjection by Mrs. Melanie Klein; other developments owe much to Dr. Clifford Scott's recent work on the 'body-scheme'; but not all the newer psycho-analytical views have been adopted. Another addition is a theory of psychosomatic disorder, a field in which Dr. M. Ziwar's work first aroused my interest. I arrived at this theory in quite a different connexion, but found it to have an immediate application to Berkeley. The theory is reproduced here together with the application made of it.

For helpful comment on the book in general I am indebted to Dr. Ernest Jones and Mr. Roger Money-Kyrle. For useful criticism or comment in respect of Chapter 22 I wish to thank Dr. Clifford Scott, Professor Karl Popper, Dr. H. Ezriel, Dr. John Hambling, and Dr. Dennis Scott.

"An Outline of Berkeley's Life" appeared in *The British Journal for the Philosophy of Science*. It is here reproduced, apart from a few paragraphs, as Chapter 9; the chronological outline appended to that paper here appears at the beginning of the book. "A General Hypothesis of Psychosomatic Disorder" appeared in *The British Journal of Medical Psychology*; it is reproduced in Chapter 22. These papers are reprinted by permission of the Editors of the respective journals.

J. O. Wisdom

The London School of Economics
     and Political Science, W.C.2
   August 1953

BERKELEY'S LIFE

Chronological Outline, including Major Works

1685   March 12. Born near Kilkenny

1696   Entered Kilkenny College

1700   Entered Trinity College, Dublin

1707   Elected Junior Fellow

1707–8 Wrote *Philosophical Commentaries*

1709   Published *An Essay towards a New Theory of Vision*

1710   Published *A Treatise concerning the Principles of Human Knowledge*

1713   January. Left Dublin for London

1713   May. Published *Three Dialogues between Hylas and Philonous*

1713   October. Accompanied the Earl of Peterborough to Italy as chaplain

1714   August. Returned to England

1715   October 13. Malebranche died

1716   Autumn. Went abroad as travelling tutor to St. George Ashe; went as far as Sicily. Co-opted Senior Fellow in his absence

1720   Autumn. Returned to London

1721   Early. Published *De Motu*

1721   September. Returned to Dublin. D.D. conferred during following term

1722   Presented by the Crown to the Deanery of Dromore; this contested by the Bishop

1722   About May. Conceived project of founding a College in Bermuda

1722   December. Visited London; nearly wrecked on a thirty-six-hour crossing to Holyhead

1723   March. Returned to Dublin

1723   June. Legatee of Esther Vanhomrigh

1724   May. Resigned from T.C.D. to become Dean of Derry

1724   September. Left for London to raise funds for Bermuda project and get Royal Charter

1725   March 15. Report on Bermuda project by Law Officers (Attorney-General and Solicitor-General)

1726   May 11. House of Commons voted a grant for St. Paul's College, Bermuda

1728   August 1. Married Anne Forster

1728   September (end of first week). Sailed for America. Arrived Newport, January 23, 1729.

1729   June. Birth of son, Henry

1731   September 21. Embarked for return to England. Arrived October 30.

1732   Published *Alciphron*. Nominated Dean of Down; not appointed

1733   Published *The Theory of Vision Vindicated and Explained*

1733   September 28. Birth of son, George

1734   May. Back to Ireland as Bishop of Cloyne, where he remained for eighteen years

1734   Published *The Analyst*

1735   Took part in Mathematical Controversy

1735–7 Published *The Querist*

1736   December 10. Birth of son, William

1737   Made his only speech in the Irish House of Lords

1738   October 15. Baptism of daughter, Julia

1739   Famine and fever at Cloyne

1741   Declined offer of nomination for Vice-chancellor-
         ship of Dublin University

1744   Published *Siris*

1745   Offered Bishopric of Clogher

1748   May 1. Death of Percival

1751   March 3. Death of son, William

1751   October 21. Death of Tom Prior

1752   August. Went on prolonged visit to Oxford

1753   January 14. Died. Buried at Christ Church, Oxford

NOTE

In order to distract the reader's eye as little as possible, footnotes merely containing references are indicated by numbers, while those containing comment are distinguished by an asterisk or other sign.

Quotations are printed in smaller type than the rest of the text, and without quotation marks. When a section number precedes a quotation from Berkeley, this does not necessarily mean that an entire section is quoted. Double quotation marks are used when words, phrases, expressions, or statements are spoken about. Single quotation marks are used, not to speak about an expression but to draw attention to it, to indicate that it is technical, obscure, or noteworthy for some reason.

The text of Berkeley referred to will be mainly that of A. A. Luce and T. E. Jessop, *The Works of George Berkeley*, Edinburgh, 1948. This being the definitive edition will be referred to as *Works*. Since the whole of this edition is not yet in print it will be necessary sometimes to refer to other editions; these will also be cited as *Works*, but the editor's name will be appended in brackets.

PART ONE

PHILOSOPHY

Chapter 1

INTRODUCTION

THERE is a widespread belief that Berkeley was an idealist who denied the existence of the natural world. The interpretation traditionally accepted by philosophers has been a refinement of this belief. Berkeley was supposed to have asserted that objects, such as trees or tables, could not continue to exist without being perceived by, or without being 'in the mind' of, some human being. Philosophers have held, of course, that he was not satisfied with this position and that he tried, though unsuccessfully, to overcome its obvious absurdity by means of an *ad hoc* device, but that, since this attempt was a failure, his basic assertion remained unmodified.

The works that are supposed to bear this construction are the famous ones, written before Berkeley was twenty-eight. But what of his later writing? For the past eighty years or more commentators have claimed that this depicted a very different philosophy; and it seemed to them that Berkeley recognised the inadequacy of his early views and changed his mind. Some neglected commentators took a different view. Mabbott gave the first closely argued case against the traditional interpretation of Berkeley's philosophy. More recent research, in agreement with Mabbott's basic contention but wider in scope, has put a new complexion upon the problem.

Luce and Jessop have restored the texts of Berkeley's writings and found forgotten manuscripts, including letters. Luce has established a vital historical link between Berkeley and Malebranche. He has also scrutinised the dates of later editions of the early works that were issued by Berkeley himself, and in connexion with this the changes made in these editions. The presumption from the link with Malebranche and the changes made in later editions is that Berkeley did not recant, but held in his youth the philosophy that is attributed to the later works

—that this in fact was his 'considered' philosophy.

In Part I the rival interpretations of Berkeley's metaphysic are reviewed in the light of this work of scholarship, and an attempt is made to clarify and resolve the issues they raise. It seems desirable to begin by presenting the metaphysic along the lines of the new interpretation: it is then possible to show very briefly in what way the traditional construction differed from it. We shall thus be in a position to consider whether the new construction is fully established or whether the traditional one contains an important element of truth. No attempt will be made to read into Berkeley's philosophy the thought of some other metaphysician, or to discuss academically any pros and cons concerning the truth of his system, or to develop it into a form that might be more acceptable; for the first would seem to be undesirable, the second misdirected, and the third unrealistic.

Berkeley made contributions to psychology, mathematics, the philosophy of physics, and economics, the importance of which is seldom recognised; indeed they may even have more permanent value than the metaphysic on which his fame rests. In this volume there will be no space to deal with these contributions in detail; a brief statement of contents and achievements must suffice.

I begin with the philosophy because it is this that arouses our interest in the man and raises the questions I try to answer. It is from this that we pass in Part II to the man himself and his life.

The aim of Part III is to present a psycho-analytical interpretation; and it will be an interpretation of the man. But it will also be a psycho-analytical interpretation of his metaphysic, to explain its genesis, purpose, and modification; and an attempt will be made to explain the psychosomatic disorder from which its author appears to have suffered. For this purpose I have included in Part III a new theory, as yet untested, of the nature and genesis of psychosomatic disorders, which seems to apply aptly to Berkeley's complaint.

Psycho-analysis is a clinical method governed by theoretical conceptions and a theory moulded by clinical findings. Illuminating applications of it have been made in many fields, but to pure philosophy it has hardly been applied at all; and of the handful of such writings, some do not carry the analysis of philosophical conceptions far. This book rarely mentions the significance of such analyses; it is concerned rather to carry one out.

The analysis here presented cannot have the certainty that the analysis of a living patient can have, for we lack Berkeley's responses to the interpretations. Despite this, the analysis is by no means purely speculative, for the interpretations, even though not phrased in a form suitable to use with a patient, are in general of a well-recognised clinical type.

Berkeley was an admirable and great man and a great philosopher. The maturity of his work, the presentation of his ideas, his standards of argument, and lucidity stand out. He could shoulder much responsibility. He was realistic. He was highly esteemed by many of high standing. He was a devoted father. Yet his metaphysic taken as a whole is a fantasy, though one of charm, as was his belief that tar-water was a divine panacea.

To understand him we must draw on the resources of modern science.

Chapter 2

BERKELEY'S CONSIDERED PHILOSOPHY

THE two philosophers who had the greatest influence on Berkeley were Locke and Malebranche. To Locke he was totally opposed in doctrine and in spirit, and his philosophy, regarded negatively, is a refutation, or an attempted refutation, of Locke. His relation to Malebranche is more complex. Many writers have noticed a connexion, but fairly recent work by Luce[1] has firmly established it. Luce's argument cannot be summarised, but his method can be described in a sentence: he compared the ideas, arguments, illustrations, and the very phrases of the two thinkers, and thus reveals an extraordinary identity between them. Thus, as Luce says, Locke taught Berkeley but Malebranche inspired him. We must be cautious, however, about the conclusions we draw. What this work of scholarship shows is that Berkeley studied Malebranche with intense care. While he found in Locke a stimulus to thought and a doctrine to oppose, he found in Malebranche ideas that particularly attracted him, and illustrations and phrases that he found apt and could use. But it does not follow that he fully accepted Malebranche's teaching. In fact he expressly disavowed holding Malebranche's philosophy. In the *Three Dialogues* Hylas asked Philonous (*i.e.* Berkeley):

Are not you too of opinion that we see all things in God? If I mistake not, what you advance comes near it.[2]

In reply, Philonous stated a considerable number of important doctrines in Malebranche which he could not accept, and he was consistent with his own philosophy in rejecting these; but he ended by saying:

I entirely agree with what the holy Scripture saith, *that in God we live, and move, and have our being.*

[1] A. A. Luce, *Berkeley and Malebranche*, Oxford, 1934.
[2] *Works*, II, *Three Dialogues between Hylas and Philonous*, Dial. II, p. 214.

4

This may seem to be much the same as the Malebranchean 'seeing all things in God'. But Berkeley would not have liked this way of putting it, because, as we shall see, it could bear a construction to which he was totally opposed and which would constitute a misunderstanding of his position that he was at pains in his correspondence with Johnson to correct. If we ascribe this doctrine to Berkeley, we must remember that in his early years at least he would have interpreted it differently from Malebranche. In short, he found in Malebranche a philosophy that appealed to him as being near the right lines but not itself quite right; and he found a central doctrine which, as he interpreted it, he whole-heartedly accepted.

This link with Malebranche is important in that it enables us to read Berkeley's early philosophical works in a new light. We can see in them a philosophy different from the one traditionally ascribed to him. The discovery of the historical link plays a peculiar rôle, however; it does not *supplement* the philosophical writings; it simply enables us to see in those writings what is actually there, to see what we should have been able to see for ourselves by reading them. Luce's work has thus reoriented the study of Berkeley. Joussain[1] and Mabbott,[2] however, succeeded in seeing what was there without the aid of elaborate research.

Berkeley's position has been described as "Panentheism", a name given to the doctrine that God is neither the world, nor separate from the world, but that the world is in him[3]; and, carefully interpreted, it can be described in this way. It is not the kind of doctrine that could be tacked on to a piece of metaphysics as an extra tenet; it would be primary and would animate the whole. Accordingly the setting for Berkeley's philosophy is the existence of God and the dependence of all else upon that. Thus his philosophy must be understood as a theocentric interpretation of the natural world. For Berkeley, the existence of God, of course, was a piece of intuitive knowledge, for he was an orthodox Anglican (if this description of a clergyman of the Church of Ireland may be allowed), but in unfolding

[1] André Joussain, *Exposé critique de la philosophie de Berkeley*, Paris, 1921.
[2] J. D. Mabbott, "The Place of God in Berkeley's Philosophy", *The Journal of Philosophy*, London, 1931, Vol. VI, No. xxi, pp. 18–29.
[3] Baldwin, *Dictionary of Philosophy and Psychology*.

his philosophy he did not treat it simply as an unproved axiom. On the contrary he wished to demonstrate the existence of God by means of his own new philosophical principle, which he believed the world would recognise as true.

Within this theocentric framework, the body of Berkeley's philosophy is developed in the *Principles of Human Knowledge* and the *Three Dialogues*: he must show in detail the theocentric relation between the natural world, which human beings perceive, and God, by whose will and continued action it exists. Because of the nature of his view, these works are devoted mainly to *sense-perception*, and it is therefore easy to make the mistake of supposing that his chief purpose was to give from an empirical standpoint a philosophical account of this theme for its own sake—in fact he did not treat it for its own sake, nor was his philosophy a form of empiricism.

The presentation that follows owes much to the work of Luce, but it would not be in all respects in agreement with his interpretations.

(1) Berkeley opens by expounding his doctrine of perception known as "*Immaterialism*". We shall in the main follow the *Principles*, but occasionally note points from the *Three Dialogues*.

(a) The various bodily senses furnish us with the various sensory qualities, such as colours, noises, and so on. These Berkeley calls "*ideas*".

§ 1   And as several of these are observed to accompany each other, they come to be marked by one name, and so to be reputed as one thing. Thus, for example, a certain colour, taste, smell, figure and consistence having been observed to go together, are accounted one distinct thing, signified by the name *apple*.

This is paralleled in the *Three Dialogues*:

A cherry . . . is nothing but a congeries of sensible impressions, or ideas perceived by various senses: which ideas are united into one thing (or have one name given them) by the mind; because they are observed to attend each other.[1]

Thus natural objects are collections of ideas. For the present, "idea" is to be regarded as a technical term in the absence of a

---

[1] *Works*, II, *Three Dialogues between Hylas and Philonous*, Dial. III, p. 249.

better one, and no preconceived notion of philosophical speculation is to be read into it: in saying that an apple is a collection
of ideas, he is simply saying it is a collection of sensory qualities.
Now Berkeley also called such collections themselves ideas: thus
not only is the greenness of an apple an idea, but so is the apple
itself. His view would perhaps have been clearer if he had used
two terms rather than one. In what follows it will be convenient
to use "sensory-ideas" for individual sensory qualities and
"thing-idea" for a collection of these; thus an apple is an example of thing-idea.

The use of the word "idea" at all must seem strange, but it
does not lead to confusion. It would have led to fallacious
reasoning, if he had drawn his conclusions from the use of the
term. But he did not do this; he used the term simply because it
was appropriate for expressing his conclusions.

(b) Berkeley finds it evident that ideas of the imagination do
not exist outside the mind, and no less evident that sensory-
ideas can exist only in a mind (§ 3). He supports this, for example, by arguing that *great* and *small*, *swift* and *slow*, are
relative conceptions, existing only in the mind (§ 11).

(c) Since thing-ideas are collections of sensory-ideas, it follows that they, too, must be in a mind. Here he gives a particularly important account of what is meant by "exist":

§ 3   The table I write on, I say, exists, that is, I see and feel it; and
if I were out of my study I should say it existed, meaning thereby
that if I was in my study I might perceive it, or that some other
spirit actually does perceive it.

This is closely connected with, or actually contains, the doctrine currently known as "Phenomenalism", according to
which the existence of an object is expressed in terms of possible
sense-data such as round patches of colour. Berkeley attaches no
meaning to the "existence" of objects in any other sense.

§ 3   Their *esse* is *percipi*, nor is it possible they should have any existence, out of the minds or thinking things which perceive them.

Thus the *esse* of all ideas, thing-ideas as well as sensory-ideas,
and hence of all natural objects, is *percipi*:

all the choir of heaven and furniture of the earth, in a word all those bodies which compose the mighty frame of the world, have not any subsistence without a mind, that their being [first edition, *esse*] is to be perceived or known.

This is a fundamental part of Immaterialism and "*Esse* is *percipi*" is Berkeley's famous expression for it. In a corresponding way, the *esse* of a spirit or person is *percipere*.

(*d*) Berkeley considers that the prevailing opinion that natural objects exist without being perceived in the way described rests on the Lockean doctrine of abstract general ideas. He had devoted the entire "Introduction to the Principles" to attacking the conception of abstract general ideas, which Locke had held. Berkeley agreed that one could imagine the head of a body separated from the trunk, but denied that one could imagine, say, colour separated or abstracted from shape. The application here is that existence could not be abstracted from perception (§§ 4–5).

Berkeley's attack on the doctrine of abstract general ideas is of considerable philosophical importance, but it cannot be discussed in this volume.

(*e*) Considering the possibility that things like ideas, things of which ideas are copies, might exist outside the mind,

§ 8   I answer, an idea can be like nothing but an idea; a colour or figure can be like nothing but another colour or figure.

If these things are supposed to exist outside the mind, *i.e.* unperceived, then a colour would resemble something invisible, which is absurd. In short, what is sensory cannot resemble what is non-sensory.[1]

(*f*) Berkeley's next weapon is of a different kind: it is the famous 'inconceivability argument'. An objection to Immaterialism is imagined: surely trees can be supposed to exist in a park unperceived; to which Berkeley dialectically replies:

§ 23   you conceive them existing unconceived or unthought of, which is a manifest repugnancy.

This as it stands is entirely specious and not worth a moment's academic discussion. What should be noticed, however, is that

---

[1] *Id.*, Dial. I, pp. 205–6.

Berkeley has shifted his ground, and replaced his doctrine of *Esse percipi* by *Esse concepi*. Now there was no need for him to do this. He would have done better to have said that an unperceived tree was an unperceived collection of ideas or an unperceived collection of *percipi*, which *is* a contradiction. But even this would have given a false impression of his view, and it would in fact have been at variance with (c). The proper course for him to have taken with the objection would have been to admit it—for he had already admitted it in (c). Thus a tree exists in the park unperceived, or as in (c) the table in my study exists though I am not present, for this means that if I or some other person went into the park (or study), the tree (or table) would be perceived.

These arguments for Immaterialism may be summarised as follows. (a) claims that natural objects are composed of sensory-ideas. (b) argues that there is an analogy between ideas of natural objects and those of the imagination. (c) extends the first claim to unperceived natural objects, so that these are composed of *possible* sensory-ideas. (d) is negative; it attacks the notion of a mind-independent thing as being an abstract general idea. (e) is also negative; it denies that there is a mind-independent thing of which some thing-idea is a copy. (f) is the 'inconceivability' sophism.

The first conclusion is that sensory-ideas cannot exist without the mind, *i.e.* they depend on being perceived—their *esse* is *percipi*.*

In this doctrine there is nothing to imply that an *esse* depends upon being perceived solely by the person perceiving it; it could not exist outside every mind—that was his only restriction (§ 48). This is plain also from the argument (c). The position is perfectly reasonable, for what he has shown is that *perceiving is an indispensable condition of the existence of sensory-ideas, without, however, being a sufficient condition*. Berkeley did not explicitly make this distinction between necessary and sufficient condi-

* The reader will notice that the word "idea" suited Berkeley's purpose very well, because it could express the immaterialist and mind-dependent aspect of his philosophy. The reason he gave for using it was that it implies a necessary relation to the mind (*Id.*, Dial. III, pp. 235–6). It will later appear that the word had other satisfactory features too.

tions; had he done so he would have created a less bizarre impression, and he would not yet have gone beyond the bounds of reasonableness. Another way of putting this is that *esse* was not regarded as identical with *percipi*: *esse* logically contains *percipi*, but must contain something else as well.

This first conclusion concerns sensory-ideas; the second concerns thing-ideas. Berkeley did not overtly separate these and he writes as if *Esse percipi* applies to both, but it is quite plain that it applies somewhat differently to thing-ideas. He certainly held that a thing-idea is a collection of sensory-ideas, but we have to be careful how we interpret this. When an observer sees, feels, and tastes an apple there is a collection of three sensory-ideas. But Berkeley is in general concerned with another point. From his associationist phrasing—sensory-ideas that are "observed to go together"—we realise that an apple does not consist merely of a collection of sensory-ideas being perceived at any one moment, but has to do with associated sensory-ideas, those the observer could have if he used his other senses. Thus if he is seeing a visual sensory-idea, the apple is the collection of this together with the tactual idea he could have if he moved his hand appropriately. Now the ideas he could have are not actualised, but they are possible—they do not exist until perceived. Thus when perceived their *esse* is *percipi*, but otherwise there is only the possibility of perception, only the possibility of *percipi*. Hence for thing-ideas, as opposed to sensory-ideas, Berkeley's doctrine is not *Esse percipi* but *Esse percipi posse*.[1] This is the doctrine of Phenomenalism. According to this doctrine, to say that a natural object exists is to say that certain sensory-ideas are obtainable, or possible, or perceivable; it takes the form of hypothetical statements, for to say that there is a table in the next room is to say, as Berkeley himself expressly pointed out (quoted above), *if* an observer went into the room he *would* perceive certain sensory-ideas.

It is important to stress that the *esse* of a thing-idea is not the same as the *esse* of a sensory-idea but is a different 'level' of existence: that is to say, thing-ideas and sensory-ideas exist in

[1] *Cf.* Rudolf Metz, *George Berkeley*, Stuttgart, 1925, S. 118; A. A. Luce, "Berkeley's Doctrine of the Perceivable", *Hermathena*, Dublin, 1942, No. lx.

different senses, *i.e.* the "existence" of a thing-idea is derivative and to be defined in terms of the more fundamental sense of "existence" in which sensory-ideas exist.

Now when Berkeley asserted his doctrine of *Esse percipi, i.e.* that nothing exists outside the mind, he did not preclude the above distinction from being drawn; he was concerned to stress, not different 'levels' of existence however important this might be, but the dependence of existence at every level upon being perceived. Hence, as with sensory-ideas, he held that per-ceiving was an indispensable condition of the existence of thing-ideas. But now we see that, whereas the indispensable condition for *sensory*-ideas was their being *actually* perceived, the indis-pensable condition for *thing*-ideas was the *possibility* of their being perceived. And here, too, the condition though in-dispensable was not sufficient.

(2) In fact, perceiving is *not* a sufficient condition; nor did Berkeley hold that every kind of perceiving was sufficient. He held that image-ideas can be produced by the imagination, so that here perception could be a sufficient condition. But he pointed out clearly that sensory-ideas come and go indepen-dently of one's will:

§ 29 When in broad daylight I open my eyes, it is not in my power to choose whether I shall see or no, or to determine what particular objects shall present themselves to my view.

Thus being perceived is a passive condition of the existence of ideas and their origin must be sought elsewhere. Are they, for instance, due to material causes?

(3) Now begins Berkeley's great attack on the conception of Matter, which played a large part in the thought of Aristotle, the Scholastics, and Locke, and a certain rôle also in Male-branche. This conception was of a material substratum in which sensory qualities inhered, itself devoid of all qualities and formless; its function was to assume particular forms or support particular qualities, and to be the seat of powers such as the power of producing movement or sensory-ideas. Brought up on Locke's *Essay*, Berkeley was opposing him at the very outset of his philosophy; the attack on Matter was the negative side of his Immaterialism. The conception comes in for repeated attack.

(i) The first argument was framed in terms of the distinction between primary and secondary qualities. According to Locke, the primary qualities are extension, figure, motion, rest, solidity, impenetrability, and so on, which he held were powers inhering in Matter and resembled the ideas we have of them. So far as Berkeley's argument is concerned we may ignore certain complexities that arise over secondary qualities. His point was simply that shapes, movements, and so on depend on being perceived; for a coin is said to look sometimes circular and sometimes elliptical, so that the shape it appears to have is relative to being perceived.* Now Matter is inert and incapable of perceiving, and hence cannot contain these qualities (§ 9). It should not be supposed, of course, that all Berkeley's arguments are cogent.

(ii) Since great and small, swift and slow are relative conceptions, Berkeley was concerned to attack the conception of extension-in-general and motion-in-general, which would characterise Matter. Such ideas he considered to be absurd abstract ideas; and he held that every argument to show that colours, for instance, exist only in the mind must apply equally to size and motion. Hence there could be no Matter possessing size-in-general and motion-in-general (§§ 11, 15).

(iii) Enquiring further into the received opinion that Matter is a substratum that supports various sensory qualities, Berkeley finds it acknowledged that no other meaning is attached to the notion but that of being-in-general, in which qualities inhere, and maintains that of abstract ideas it is the most abstract and incomprehensible of all (§ 17).

(iv) If, *per impossibile*, there were such an entity, we could only know it by the senses or by inference. But by being stripped of all sensory qualities it cannot be known by the senses; and no necessary connexion can be found between Matter and sensory qualities, so that the inference is impossible (§ 18).

(v) Since those who assert the existence of Matter cannot explain what part it plays in the production of sensory-ideas,

* Berkeley tacitly assumes that, because the apparent shape is the only shape that appears, we cannot perceive any one shape as being the real shape. He is implicitly denying that an object possesses one shape with many appearances.

then these are equally inexplicable with or without the conception. There is therefore no need to assume the existence of an entirely useless entity (§ 19).

(vi) If Matter does not exist we could still have our present reasons for supposing that Matter existed. Hence our present reasons are inadequate (§ 20).

(vii) Again, concerning the Lockean proposal that ideas are *representations* or *copies* of something outside the mind, Berkeley asks: How can what is sensible resemble what is insensible? How can what is fleeting and variable be a copy of what is fixed and constant? (§ 8).

These refutations of Matter may be summarised as follows. (i) The primary qualities cannot inhere in Matter, which is inert and not *percipere*. (ii) They are mind-independent along with the secondary qualities, so that extension-in-general is devoid of all qualities and hence is an abstract general idea. (iii) Matter means only being-in-general, which is the most abstract of all ideas. (iv) It can be known neither by the senses nor by inference. (v) It is an 'explanation' that does not explain. (vi) Existing reasons for believing matter are necessarily insufficient. (vii) It is absurd to postulate an unknowable resembling what we know.*

Berkeley himself did not separate his exposition of Immaterial-

* On the one hand Berkeley argued that Matter was not revealed in experience (and could not be established by reason) and that it was useless as a postulate; here he used the *esse-percipi* principle. On the other hand he argued that the very conception was absurd. Did he hold that the conception was self-contradictory or did he hold that "being-in-general, devoid of all qualities" was meaningless? Most often his phrasing suggests the latter; quite probably he would have said that when philosophers try to use the conception they contradict themselves at some point. It is difficult to establish an interpretation of this kind in a writer for whom the distinction between self-contradiction and meaninglessness had not yet become common coin. One can say only that, had his attention been drawn to the distinction, his writing suggests he would have agreed that there is such a distinction and would have said that "being-in-general, devoid of all qualities" was meaningless. On the other hand it would seem that *Esse percipi*, appliedt o sensory-ideas, was an analytic principle or tautology, the denial of which was self-contradictory. But is there not something strange in holding that "Matter" is meaningless and that "*Esse percipi*" is a tautology, for if the latter is a tautology then it would be contradictory rather than meaningless to speak of anything such as Matter existing unperceived?

ism from his attack on Matter so sharply as I have done, for
many of the arguments adduced are equally relevant to both.

(4) Since the cause or condition of ideas cannot be Matter,
there remains only spirit.[1] It is necessary, therefore, to establish
the existence of other spirits, in the first place of the finite kind.

Berkeley holds that they are known not directly, like natural
objects, but by inference and analogy:

§ 145 We cannot know the existence of other spirits, otherwise
than by their operations, or the ideas by them excited in us. I perceive several motions, changes, and combinations of ideas, that
inform me there are certain particular agents like myself, which
accompany them, and concur in their production.[2]

In the second edition of the *Principles* Berkeley uses the
curious expression that we have *notions* of spirit, finite persons,
human action, and relations.[3] He explicitly denied that we can
have *ideas* of these. This is obscure and has never been clarified.
I therefore venture the following remarks.

Berkeley would seem to be asserting that a person becomes
known as some kind of co-ordinated behaviour, a co-ordination
of actions and responses. A co-ordination is not, of course, a
percept recognised by the senses, but a pattern of past, present,
and expected happenings. Similarly with empirical relations:
when, among a number of perceptual observations, such as
noticing that the sensations felt by turning on one bath-tap are
different from those felt by turning on the other, it becomes
noticed that one produces water *hotter than* the water that flows
from the other, then a relation has become known. The relation
hotter than is not an abstract general idea in the sense Berkeley
decried, but something wherein all the experiences of turning
on both taps agreed. It becomes known through perception of
natural events but is not itself a percept. If the verb "know"
may appropriately be used of persons and empirical relations in
such contexts, the word "notion" is equally appropriate as a
noun. Perhaps this will clarify to a small extent Berkeley's tenet
and be consistent with the rest of his epistemology. It might be
objected that Matter could be readmitted, because *knowable*, on
these grounds; but this is untenable, since the only sense in

---

[1] *Works*, II, *The Principles of Human Knowledge*, §§ 26, 29.
[2] *Cf.* §§ 140, 142.   [3] *Id.*, § 142, *et passim.*

which Matter would be knowable in this way would be as an active co-ordination of sense-experiences; but Matter was inert, whereas persons are active. The most important point to stress is that we cannot have *ideas* of persons or of any of the things of which we can have notions. Presumably anything of which we can have a notion (apart from the doubtful case of relations) is an actively induced co-ordination of sensory-ideas.

If, therefore, other persons can be inferred and known, then natural objects, when they do not exist in Berkeley's mind, can exist in the mind of some other created spirit. But other spirits will have no more power than he to create sensory-ideas or to determine what particular objects shall present themselves to their view. Thus the cause or condition of sensory-ideas and thing-ideas does not lie in any finite mind.

(5) Natural objects must therefore "subsist in the mind of some eternal spirit", or else "have no existence at all".[1] It is therefore necessary to establish the existence of infinite spirit or God.

Three distinct arguments to this end are to be found in Berkeley: (*x*) an argument from design, in which God is inferred from the harmony or co-ordination that pervades the natural world[2]; (*y*) human beings are cognisant of God in the same way as they are of other finite persons[3]; and (*z*) God is necessarily presupposed by our sensory- and thing-ideas.[4]

The harmony of the world implies the existence of a spirit with the characteristics of being "one, eternal, infinitely wise, good and perfect".[5] Just as Berkeley infers the existence of other persons from their operations, so he infers that of God from his operations, namely the co-ordinated processes of nature; just as he does not claim to perceive other human beings but only a certain collection of ideas, so with God he claims only to perceive "manifest tokens of Divinity".[6] Interestingly enough, the argument (*z*) cannot be found in the *Principles*; but it occurs quite explicitly in the *Three Dialogues*, deliberately detached

[1] *Id.*, § 6.
[2] *Id.*, §§ 30, 146; *Works*, III, *Alciphron*, Dial. IV, § 5.
[3] *Principles*, §§ 147–8; *Alciphron, loc. cit.*
[4] *Works*, II, *Three Dialogues between Hylas and Philonous*, Dial. II., p. 212; Dial. III, p. 232.
[5] *Principles*, § 146.   [6] *Id.*, § 148.

from questions of harmony. He thought it self-evident.

It is true that Berkeley argued for the existence of God by elimination of other alternatives: sensory-ideas cannot exist in Matter; finite minds cannot produce them; hence there must be an infinite mind wherein they exist. But he goes on at once to interpret this conclusion in the crucial passage in the *Three Dialogues*. What we find there is that, while men commonly believe there is a God and infer that he perceives all things, Berkeley puts this the other way round:

sensible things do really exist: and if they really exist, they are necessarily perceived by an infinite mind: therefore there is an infinite mind, or God.[1]

And Berkeley makes it clear at once that this argument did not need to be supported by a premiss about the order to be found in the world; he believed he had shown that "an infinite mind" was "necessarily inferred from the bare existence of the sensible world". As an inference this is unintelligible. Possibly he did not regard it as different from his second argument: that we know God through the operations or processes of the sensible world. This, after all, is the important one for Berkeley, for it connects with his doctrine of the 'language of nature' explained in (8) below. In effect it is not an inference but an interpretation: God is an interpretation, and one that is indubitable, of the operations of the sensible world.

(6) Here a certain difficulty of interpretation must be pointed out. We wish to know whether sensory-ideas in the mind of God were *perceived* or *caused* by him. If sensory-ideas perceived by finite minds exist because they are perceived by God, awkward academic problems arise. Suppose that God perceives sensory-ideas (since he is not an embodied spirit, divine *perceiving* must be taken to be somewhat like human *imagining*). If human beings perceived different sensory-ideas from those perceived by God, an insoluble problem about the relationship between the two sets of ideas would confront us; a human being could not get outside the circle of his own ideas, and the traditional interpretation of Solipsism would hold good; and the interpretation of God as manifested in the processes of the sensible world

[1] *Works*, II, *Three Dialogues between Hylas and Philonous*, Dial. II, p. 212.

could not be made. On the other hand, if human beings perceived the same sensory-ideas as those perceived by God, then sensory-ideas would not be dependent upon being perceived by finite beings, and therefore the central arguments involving *Esse percipi*, which show exactly this dependence, would be pointless. It is precisely these difficulties that arise from the Platonic doctrine of 'archetypes'; and the care Berkeley took to avoid this doctrine suggests that he was fully alive to the difficulties mentioned.[1] If he held that sensory-ideas were perceived *and* caused by God, the same difficulty would arise.

It would therefore seem that he did not hold that sensory-ideas were perceived by God. But then his third proof (*z*) of the existence of God was out of place. Here Berkeley himself was evasive.

God knows or hath ideas; but His ideas are not convey'd to Him by sense, as ours are.[2]

Moreover, when we inspect the passages in the *Principles* or the *Three Dialogues* teaching that things do not exist unperceived, we never read that they must be *perceived* either by a human being or by God, but always that they must be *perceived* by a human being or else *exist in the mind of* God, or some such phrase that avoids the issue. In the passage just cited from the *Three Dialogues*, however, he does appear to commit himself:

God . . . who perceives nothing by sense as we do, whose will is absolute and independent, causing all things . . . God is a pure spirit.

This strongly favours the interpretation that our sensory-ideas are caused by God; and it is supported by a much later writing, *The Theory of Vision Vindicated* (1733):

§ 29   Perhaps I think that the same Being which causeth our ideas of sight doth cause not only our ideas of touch likewise, but also all our ideas of all the other senses.*

---

[1] See below, pp. 57–9.   [2] *Loc. cit.*, Dial. III, p. 241.

* Luce has argued, on the other hand, in favour of asserting that sensory-ideas are perceived by God: "The *esse* of the perceivable is *posse percipi* (if I may adapt Berkeley's phrase), and man's *posse percipi* is God's *percipi*" (Luce, *Op. cit.*, p. 4). But the paper in which this occurs aims at showing that Berkeley believed in the perceivable as opposed to merely momentary *percipi*; and this contention does not require that an *esse* should be *percipi*, rather than caused, by God.

It is striking that the only place in which Berkeley actually attributes perception to God is in the proof of the existence of God, considered above. This suggests that he did not himself like this interpretation but felt he had to use it in that context. (Possibly he need not have done so: it would be hardly less intelligible to argue that 'if sensory-ideas exist they are necessarily *caused* by God' than to argue that 'if sensory-ideas exist they are necessarily *perceived* by God'.) If it is true that Berkeley used the interpretation of 'perceiving' in this one place only because it seemed to suit his immediate purpose better, we can find almost no parallel to such a course; but there is one—the 'inconceivability' argument against Matter was one in which he allowed himself to be trapped into using a verbal trick.

Mabbott has argued with considerable force in the same strain. He denies that Berkeley can be correctly interpreted as holding that God perceives sensory-ideas;* he gives textual grounds[1] for asserting that for Berkeley the *esse* of mind was not *percipere* but *velle* or *agere*; and he suggests that the existence of sensory ideas is due to a 'resolve' by God (which is the same as the view here taken, that they are caused by God). This interpretation has also been given by Metz[2] and Joussain.[3]

It seems to me, therefore, that much the more likely interpretation, though it cannot be regarded as absolutely established, is that God does not perceive but causes our sensory-ideas.

It would be natural to express this construction, as Metz has put it, by *Esse est causari*.

(7) We have now to enquire further into the relation between

---

* Mabbott's main reasons are: that the problem of relating God's ideas to ours would arise, a problem of a type that Berkeley regarded as absurd; that Berkeley's theory would no longer be one of direct perception but of indirect perception of archetypes; and that God would have as part of the contents of his mind something passive (Berkeley insists on the passivity of ideas), which he considered was impossible.

[1] *Principles*, §§ 29, 30; *Works*, I, *Philosophical Commentaries*, 429a, 829, 831.

[2] Rudolf Metz, *George Berkeley*, Stuttgart, 1925, S. 101, 130.

[3] André Joussain, *Exposé critique de la philosophie de Berkeley*, Paris, 1921, pp. 46–7.

percipi and *causari*.* *Esse* is not identical with *percipi*; where dreams and where images generally are concerned *Esse* does equal *percipi*; but for *esse* to be part of the order of nature something more is required. Thus *percipi* is part only of what is needed in order that there should be an *esse*. And the additional factor is that of *causari* by God. Hence for sensory-ideas an *esse* is both *percipi* and *causari*. This conjunctive mode of expression, however, has misleading implications, for it is not a combination of predicates that is meant. In fact it is not the *esse* at all that is caused, but the *percipi*. Hence the proper way to express Berkeley's philosophy of sensory-ideas would seem to be: "an *esse* equals a *percipi* that is theistically caused" or "*Esse* is *percipi causari*".†

From this we pass to the nature and rôle of causation.

(8) The 'regularity' interpretation of *causation*, which was held by Hume and Mill and is held to-day by many philosophers and scientists, though often attributed to Hume, was originated by Berkeley, and constituted a large part of his thesis of causation.

From what has just been expounded, it is clear that natural objects could not be causes, since their nature was to be inert thing-ideas; moreover these were caused by God and God alone. Thus Berkeley's thesis contains two sides: (i) spirit—*i.e.* primarily God but in a secondary way finite persons—is the sole cause, and (ii) interaction between thing-ideas is not properly speaking causal. (i) God is the creative cause; but in a sense all spirits

* It is worth noting that, on the present exposition of Berkeley, he is not open to Hume's criticism; his position is not reducible to Solipsism. His beginning with sensory-ideas would in fact have this consequence only if it is assumed that the mind owning sensory-ideas was a sufficient cause of them; and this Berkeley not only did not assume but expressly gave an argument to disprove.

From this presentation it is also clear that he did not beg the question by deducing his philosophy from ordinary associations of the word "idea"; he introduced this word to express his new and special conception.

† From the above paragraph it should be evident that none of the meanings suggested by Moore for "*Esse percipi*" is appropriate to Berkeley. Moore considers in effect two possibilities, one in which *esse* is identical with *percipi* and the other in which *esse* is equated with a conjunction of *percipi* and something else. We have seen reason to believe that *esse* is more than *percipi* without being made up of a conjunction of this with something else. (G. E. Moore, *Philosophical Studies*, London, 1922, "The Refutation of Idealism".)

as active beings are causes, for they can create ideas of imagination. They are also causes not in creating the natural world but in initiating change in it, by willing, by acting, and so on. (ii) Though we may "speak with the vulgar"[1] and call such interaction causal, there is in fact no connexion between what is vulgarly regarded as a cause and what is vulgarly regarded as an effect, beyond one of *regular recurrence*, maintained by God (for human benefit). To express this in Berkeley's way, the relation of *cause* and *effect* is replaced by one between *sign* and thing *signified*.

§ 65 The fire which I see, is not the cause of the pain I suffer upon my approaching it, but the mark that forewarns me of it. . . . That a few original ideas may be made to signify a great number of effects and actions, it is necessary they be variously combined together: and to the end their use be permanent and universal, these combinations must be made by *rule*, and with wise *contrivance*. By this means abundance of information is conveyed unto us, concerning what we are to expect from such and such actions, and what methods are proper to be taken, for the exciting such and such ideas.*

Berkeley has thus one fundamental kind of causation, that due to God; what is ordinarily regarded as causation between natural events is of a secondary kind, which he interprets as a relation between sign and thing signified. With this in mind, he interprets the regularity that constitutes the laws of nature metaphorically as a *language* by which mankind can read how to effect his ends:

§ 108 the steady, consistent methods of nature, may not unfitly be stiled the language of its *Author*, whereby He discovers His attributes

---

[1] *Works*, II, *The Principles of Human Knowledge*, § 51.

* Here we may notice another reason why the word "idea" served Berkeley's purpose: for him—and in the usage of the time—it stood for something passive and inert, the very antithesis of a cause (*Id.*, § 39; *Works*, I, *Philosophical Commentaries*, 644). Luce mentions this and adds that ideas would have *immediacy*, an important feature of Berkeley's philosophy, and *significance*, *i.e.* they form a language. Luce omits the reason given earlier, that an idea represented the immaterialist or mind-dependent aspect of the philosophy, but he may have thought it covered by *significance*; he also mentions *givenness*, but I fail to see that in the field of Berkeley this differs from immediacy (A. A. Luce, "The Berkeleian Idea of Sense", *Hermathena*, Dublin, 1940, Part lv).

to our view, and directs us how to act for the convenience and felicity of life.

A great number of arbitrary signs, various and apposite, do constitute a Language. If such arbitrary connexion be instituted by men, it is an artificial Language; if by the Author of Nature, it is a Natural Language.[1]

(9) The purpose of this doctrine of nature as constituting a language by which we read the details of the divine regulation of nature was no doubt to lead men to God and to show the religious significance of the New Principle. But in the metaphysic it played a metaphysical rôle. Having established the existence of God, Berkeley was first of all enabled to use this result to show that God causes sensory-ideas in us, *i.e.* that God causes our *percipi*. But another step has to be taken. The world is orderly, sensory-ideas are observed to go together, there is a regular concomitance between the sensory-ideas perceived by different senses, and there is a regular concomitance between 'causes' and 'effects'. This means that there is regularity in our *percipi posse* or thing-ideas and also in the relation of cause and effect between one thing-idea and another. Berkeley's theory that nature was a language enabled him to account for both regularities in exactly the same way, *i.e.* the regularity of sensory-ideas forming one thing-idea and that of causes and effects. Thus this conception would enable Berkeley not only to explain our sensory-ideas as caused by God but also our thing-ideas or *percipi posse*.

Thus God is the cause of sensory-ideas or *percipi* on the one hand and the cause of thing-ideas or *percipi posse* on the other. This last reveals Berkeley's doctrine as being not simply Phenomenalism but Theocentric Phenomenalism. It is necessary to stress this, for commentators are divided into those who interpret Berkeley as holding *Esse percipi posse* and those who interpret him as holding *Esse causari**, but the truth of the matter would seem to be that he—quite consistently—held both.

---

[1] *Works*, I, *The Theory of Vision Vindicated and Explained*, § 40. *Cf. New Theory of Vision*, § 147; *Works*, II, *The Principles of Human Knowledge*, § 149; *Works*, III, *Alciphron*, Dial. IV, § 11; *Works*, V, *Siris*, §§ 252, 254.

* Attempts to interpret him in terms of *Esse concipi* are not worth taking seriously; they will be referred to briefly in Ch. V.

What, then, is the relation between the two? We have seen that for sensory-ideas, Berkeley's principle was *"Esse is percipi causari"*. Now here, where thing-ideas are concerned, a *percipi* is possible only and not actual, but when a sensory-idea of it becomes actualised, this is brought about by God. We may therefore say of thing-ideas that *"Esse is percipi posse*, where the actualisation of a *percipi* is *causari* by God", or, if we prefer, "A natural object when unperceived exists if and only if it is perceivable, *i.e.* if and only if its possible sensory constituents, when actually perceived, are caused by God".

(10) We have to enquire lastly whether within the framework of Berkeley's principles the problem of identity can be solved; it is a problem that any account of perception must deal with.

On returning to a room an observer sees the *same* table as when he was there before; and two people in a room can see the *same* table. That is to say, natural objects or thing-ideas *persist* through time and possess a certain *unity* in space—they do not, as in a dream, flicker or appear in sections like the grin without the Cheshire cat. On Berkeley's principles it is necessary to enquire how to account for this, or to enquire how one person can see the same thing at two times or two people see the same thing at one time. For, how can a thing-idea, such as a table which is simply a collection of sensory-ideas perceived here and now by an observer, be the same as the table that was in the room previously, which was a collection of a different set of sensory-ideas perceived here and then? How can the table that is one collection of sensory-ideas perceived here and now by one observer be the same as the table that is another collection of sensory-ideas perceived here and now by another observer?

Berkeley devoted little space to this problem, but the few remarks he made are striking and foreshadowed an approach widely adopted in the present century:

we never see and feel one and the same object. That which is seen is one thing, and that which is felt is another.[1]

Strictly speaking, Hylas, we do not see the same object that we feel; neither is the same object perceived by the microscope, which was by the naked eye . . . when I examine by my other senses a thing I have

[1] *Works*, I, *New Theory of Vision*, § 49.

seen . . . my aim is only to know what ideas are connected together; and the more a man knows of the connexion of ideas, the more he is said to know of the nature of things.[1]

If the term *same* be taken in the vulgar acceptation, it is certain . . . that different persons may perceive the same thing; or the same thing or idea exist in different minds. . . . But if the term *same* be used in the acceptation of philosophers, who pretend to an abstracted notion of identity, then, according to their sundry definitions of this notion . . . it may or may not be possible for divers persons to perceive the same thing.[2]

Or suppose a house, whose walls or outward shell remaining un- altered, the chambers are all pulled down, and new ones built in their place; and that you should call this the *same*, and I should say it was not the *same* house: would we not for all this perfectly agree in our thoughts of the house, considered in it self? and would not all the difference consist in a sound?[3]

The points he makes are these: (i) sensory-ideas that are regularly connected are classed together to form *one* thing; (ii) things are one and the same in the ordinary English usage of the word; (iii) this is appropriate "where no distinction or variety is observed"; (iv) the philosophical conception is an abstract general idea, devoid of meaning; (v) men with the 'same' faculties, he mentions, would have the 'same' perceptions; (vi) when several parts of a house are renovated, it is a matter of indifference whether or not we call it the 'same' house; and, he adds, (vii) sameness is maintained by God.

That there was doubt in his mind is clear; for on the one hand he asserted, as the points (i) to (vi) indicate, that there was no problem or that "identity" must be understood not in the vulgar but in a non-literal sense, while on the other he claimed in (vii) that the problem was solved by the theocentric side of his philosophy, according to which a natural object possessed a literal identity in God.*

---

[1] *Works*, II, *Three Dialogues between Hylas and Philonous*, Dial. III, p. 245.
[2] *Id.*, p. 247.   [3] *Id.*, p. 248.
* Though he had little to say about the matter in his philosophical works, Johnson, an American philosopher, drew something further from him in correspondence (*Works*, II, pp. 271–94). Here, too, the result is disappointing. Johnson asked him eleven numbered questions, of which the seventh, eighth, and ninth concerned identity. Berkeley

But was the problem so difficult, assuming Berkeley's view of theocentric causation or even without this? To say that one person saw the same table on two different occasions would mean that God caused the existence of two groups of sensory-ideas having the same mutual relationships. (He would, of course, have had to discuss structural identity.) The situation in which two people are said to see the same thing is more difficult, but it could perhaps be described in terms of the mutual observations of two people each appearing to look in the same direction, and in terms of their actions and verbal responses. Broad has worked out a procedure of this kind[1] which may be sketched as follows. The observer sees a certain sensory-idea—of a table-like kind—in his visual field; on experiencing certain kinaesthetic sensations—of a walking kind—this sensory-idea becomes slightly changed, resembling the former one but larger. As this process continues he sees a whole series of sensory-ideas which bear a continuous resemblance to one another and which undergo a continuous change. But there comes a point when the series ceases and at the same moment a tactual idea is experienced—the sensation of bumping into a table. Now, though the sensory-ideas seen at different moments are not the *same*, their association with sensory movement and touch may be said to constitute a natural object; and to say that it remains the same is to say, for Berkeley, that God causes the series of sensory-ideas in the visual field, causes their association with the final tactual idea, and causes this also at a certain place in the tactual field. When two observers look at a table, they can obtain in this way two series of visual ideas; they can observe one another looking in the same direction; and when they obtain the tactual ideas

answered the first six only; they were easily answered, since there was nothing novel about them not already covered fully in his books; but he stopped short just at the delicate issue. He mentioned illness as the reason why he had not replied sooner and to excuse his "hastily thrown together" "hints"; and it would, of course, be a good reason for not tackling a difficult and unsolved problem. Johnson was not to be put off, however, and wrote again about the five unanswered questions, the last two of which were answered easily like the first six. But what of the three dealing with identity? Berkeley's brief reply (*Id.*, p. 292) leaves the matter very much where it was.

[1] C. D. Broad, *Scientific Thought*, London, 1923, pp. 303–21, 422–30, 438–51.

of bumping into the table they also obtain those of bumping into one another. Thus God causes the two series of visual ideas, causes the associated tactual ideas, and maintains the association between them. Hence, once it is granted that he sustains the regularity of the laws of nature, a more fully developed solution of the problem of identity should have been within Berkeley's reach.

This concludes the exposition and further elucidation of Berkeley's considered system. A summary of it will be found in Chapter IV. It remains to touch upon two possible misunderstandings.

If thing-ideas are eternally in the divine mind, what did Berkeley understand by the "creation" of the natural world? From the foregoing account it follows that he could not consistently have spoken of an actual *esse*, an actual *percipi*, or a sensory-idea in the universe before human beings arose; there would have been *percipi posse*, however, which would have become actual *percipi causari* if a percipient should have been present. This astute question was put to him by Lady Percival. A letter from Percival, describing how the *Principles* was being received on its first appearance (1710), contains it: "My wife ... desires to know if there be nothing but spirit and ideas, what you make of that part of the six days' creation which preceded man."[1] Berkeley treated the question with respect and answered it, from his own standpoint, perfectly consistently:

As to your Lady's objection, I am extremely honoured by it. . . . In order to which I must beg you will inform her Ladyship that I do not deny the existence of any of those sensible things which Moses says were created by God. They existed from all eternity in the divine intellect, and then became perceptible (*i.e.* were created) in the same manner and order as is described in Genesis. For I take creation to belong to things only as they respect finite spirits, there being nothing new to God. Hence it follows that the act of creation consists in God's willing that those things should be perceptible to other spirits, which before were known only to Himself.*

[1] Benjamin Rand, *Berkeley and Percival*, Cambridge, 1914, p. 81.

* *Id.*, pp. 83–4. Berkeley added that her Ladyship "is the only person of those you mentioned my book to, who opposed it with reason and argument". It will be noticed above that once again Berkeley speaks of things not as being 'perceptible' but as 'known' to God.

In short, before the creation, a human spirit, if he had in any sense existed, would not have perceived the thing-ideas already known to the divine mind, but after the creation would have done so. Berkeley considered this matter important enough to insert in the *Three Dialogues* a few years later.[1]

Berkeley was most insistent that his philosophy conformed with common-sense beliefs, and he made any number of statements to this effect.[2] There were bound to be superficial critics to say that "it sounds very harsh to say we eat and drink ideas, and are clothed with ideas"[3]; he was, on the contrary, adopting a view more nearly corresponding to that of "the vulgar" than that of most philosophers: he believed in the direct perception of natural objects, and he held that the senses were trustworthy. But, if his philosophy is expounded according to the interpretation of this chapter, it should not occur to the reader to make the objection mentioned in the *Principles*.

§ 34 all that is real and substantial in nature is banished out of the world: and instead thereof a chimerical scheme of ideas takes place. . . . What therefore becomes of the sun, moon and stars? What must we think of houses, rivers, mountains, trees, stones; nay, even of our own bodies? Are all these but so many chimeras and illusions on the fancy?

Berkeley was evidently forestalling another interpretation of his work. His point was that in attacking the conception of Matter he was not denying the existence of tables and chairs but only a philosophical speculation about their nature: he was denying not that tables and chairs were material things in the ordinary English usage of "material things" but that they were composed of Matter, the Lockean conception of Matter, the *materia prima* of Aristotle, the formless Matter of the Scholastics. Berkeley's own statements are admirably clear and, at the risk of duplication, must be given:

§ 35 The only thing whose existence we deny, is that which philosophers call matter or corporeal substance.

[1] *Works*, II, *Dial.* III, pp. 250–6.
[2] In addition to passages in the *Principles* and *Three Dialogues* see *Works*, I, *Philosophical Commentaries*, 98, 312, 392, 405, 408, 429, 444, 517, 517a, 518, 535, 740, 807.
[3] *Works*, II, *The Principles of Human Knowledge*, § 38.

§ 37 If the word *substance* be taken in the vulgar sense, for a combination of sensible qualities, such as extension, solidity, weight, &c. this we cannot be accused of taking away. But if it be taken in a philosophic sense, for the support of accidents or qualities without the mind: then, indeed, I acknowledge that we take it away, if one may be said to take away that which never had any existence, not even in the imagination.[1]

Lady Percival's perplexity about the creation of the world and the sense that his philosophy is far removed from commonsense both have their appropriate answers from Berkeley's own writings. Nevertheless it is difficult to escape the feeling that the furniture of the earth is very tenuous. When no one is about, what is an apple? No more than a possibility of sensory-ideas actualised by God when an observer is present. What is a fire? Again the same answer. Yet although no one is about, the fire burns brightly, goes low, burns out, and leave ashes behind. What, then, as has been asked, did Berkeley suppose was going on? Berkeley's answer might be constructed thus. In the interval between perceiving the fire and the ashes, the possibility of sensory-ideas was undergoing change; God's volition was altering; hence the actual sensory-idea perceived, the implementing of the volition, would vary according to the moment when the percipient appeared on the scene. If the reader finds that this is a very tenuous process which does not correspond to our ordinary conception of the process of incineration, the answer seems simple: if you accept the conception of God imprinting sensory ideas on percipients, you have no right to object to the Berkelian interpretation of a fire burning; if you are dissatisfied and regard it as tenuous, it is evidently the conception of God imprinting sensory-ideas on human percipients that you cannot accept.

Mention should perhaps be made of Berkeley's hopes for his philosophy. He believed it would counter atheism and simplify mathematics and physical science by removing from them assumptions that were untrue and unneeded, that were in fact distracting lumber; a considerable part of the *Principles* was devoted to this theme.

[1] *Cf. Works,* I, *Philosophical Commentaries,* 517.

A word should be said on the importance and validity of Berkeley's philosophy. He introduced a standard of clarity and argument into philosophising that had not often been equalled before his time and that was hardly equalled for a long time afterwards. The theocentric form of his metaphysic has had no influence, but the detailed work he put in on the philosophy of perception had made itself strongly felt in current discussions of the subject.

Concerning the validity of his Theocentric Phenomenalism, or even of his doctrine of *Esse percipi*, we may recall that philosophers have striven unconvincingly to refute him; yet their failure has not led to the opinion that his philosophy must be true. But is it so difficult to refute? What Berkeley did was to explain the orderliness of perceptual experience by making God responsible for it; he nowhere explains, however, the mechanism or nature of divine causation; so that his explanation amounts to no more than the assertion that some explanation exists. It does not constitute an explanation to assert that there exists an entity, not clearly specified, which operates by an unknown method to produce what we set out to explain. It is interesting to find that Bradley's comment of views of this kind was to the point and shattering[1]: "It is possible that some follower of Berkeley may urge that the whole of Nature, precisely as it is perceived (and felt?), exists actually in God. But this by itself is not a metaphysical view. *It is merely a delusive attempt to do without one.* The unrationalized heaping up of such a congeries within the Deity, with its (partial?) reduplication inside finite centres . . . —this is an effort surely *not to solve a problem but simply to shelve it.*"

[1] F. H. Bradley, *Appearance and Reality*, London, 1916, p. 282 n, italics mine.

Chapter 3

BERKELEY'S *PHILOSOPHICAL COMMENTARIES*

A VERY remarkable manuscript of Berkeley's was found by Fraser. It consisted of two quarto volumes, with entries mostly on the right-hand pages, and many of these entries had mysterious signs placed against them in the margin. Fraser found that these notebooks were compiled by Berkeley in his College days, and, supposing that Berkeley recorded his philosophical thoughts, made jottings, and wrote aphorisms, he named it the *Commonplace Book*,[1] thus doing less than justice to what is undoubtedly an outstanding warehouse of the raw materials of philosophical ideas. He published it in both his editions of collected works, but transcribed the manuscript inaccurately and placed many entries in a wrong order. G. A. Johnston published a new edition, unaccompanied by other works[2]; he improved the order, without getting it right, but left a considerable number of inaccuracies in the text, lists of which have been given by Aaron[3] and by Luce.[4] These editions did not distinguish between entries written on the *verso* and on the *recto* pages—a serious omission because Berkeley often put second thoughts and corrections on the left—and the marginal signs were not printed.

It would be much to be regretted if there were no satisfactory edition of such a work; but fortunately Luce has produced a beautiful *editio diplomatica*,[5] reproducing every detail, including erasures, keeping the *verso* mostly blank as in the original. The book is printed and does not reproduce Berkeley's handwriting;

[1] A. C. Fraser, *Life and Letters of George Berkeley*, Oxford, 1871, p. 419 n.

[2] G. A. Johnston, *Berkeley's Commonplace Book*, London, 1930.

[3] R. I. Aaron, "Locke and Berkeley's *Commonplace Book*", *Mind*, London, 1931, N.S. Vol. XL, No. clx, pp. 455–8; and "Dr. Johnston's Edition of Berkeley's *Commonplace Book*", *Op cit.*, 1932, Vol. XLI, No. clxii, pp. 277–8.

[4] A. A. Luce, *Berkeley and Malebranche*, Oxford, 1934, pp. 206–7.

[5] George Berkeley, *Philosophical Commentaries*, ed. by A. A. Luce, Edinburgh, 1944. In this chapter I cite the *editio diplomatica*, but the entry numbers are the same in *Works*, I.

that is the only difference. An enormous amount of care has been lavished upon it to make the text accurate. The editor's notes occupy twice the space of the text; they are fully cross-referenced; and they reveal the meaning of many a cryptic entry. The unsatisfactory title of the work put upon it by Fraser Luce has changed to *Philosophical Commentaries*.

So much for its framework; but what about its date, purpose, marginal signs, and contents?

Luce gives good grounds for thinking that Berkeley wrote it in the interval between June or July 1707 and August 1708, just after he had been elected a Fellow of Trinity College at the age of twenty-two,[1] a time previously suggested by Aaron.[2]

The purpose of the notebooks was authorship; they did not, as Fraser supposed, consist of jottings and occasional thoughts, but of entries connected in a very methodical way with two or three works which Berkeley was thinking of writing—sometimes whole sentences were copied almost *verbatim* into the works he soon published.

The evidence for this lies in the marginal letters and signs. About the letters—E for existence, G for God, M for Matter, and so on—there is no difficulty, because Berkeley wrote the key himself, though he did not adhere consistently to his meaning for S. He gave no clue, however, to the marginal signs, "×" and "+". Luce has found that "×" referred to mathematical entries—mathematical, that is, in a broad sense that covered optical questions. Some of the ×'s had a more specific signification: they contained the numbers 1, 2, or 3 in the angles of the ×; Luce has shown that the number 1 on the left referred to Berkeley's first book, which was on vision, and that the numbers 1, 2, and 3 on the right related to the three natural divisions of that work.[3] These again merely show the design for authorship. The sign of prime importance is the "+". This, according to Luce, denoted in the large majority of instances entries that

[1] Luce, *Op. cit.*, pp. 188–92, 200–3; A. A. Luce, "The Purpose and the Date of Berkeley's *Commonplace Book*", *Proc. of the Royal Irish Acad.*, Dublin, 1943, Vol. XLVIII, Sec. C, No. vii, pp. 280–5; Berkeley, *Op. cit.*, pp. xxvii–xxxii.

[2] Aaron, *Op. cit.*, pp. 442–5.

[3] Berkeley, *Op. cit.*, p. xxiv.

Berkeley was *not* going to adopt.[1] Its use is important, because it indicates that Berkeley changed his mind and where he did so. Luce rightly holds that if the apparatus of signs is not understood and Berkeley's withdrawals not appreciated, indiscriminate quotation from the *Commentaries* may be misleading.[2]

Luce does not, however, regard his general diagnosis of purpose as wholly adequate: "it does not explain why literary spade-work should have taken this particular and highly peculiar form."[3] Not only does the work contain relevant material, opinions, references, and the like, useful for the preparation of treatises, but with all its variety the work when closely studied is seen to be methodical.[4] Luce concludes that the *Philosophical Commentaries* was a half-way house, not the starting-point, an intermediate stage in Berkeley's literary preparations, not the first stage, as has hitherto been assumed; and he suggests that Berkeley must first have written a draft work on Immaterialism, now lost, and subsequently have written the *Commentaries* (or at least the earlier notebook) as a critical commentary on that draft work.

The confirmation he finds for this ingenious suggestion is extremely strong; it is based on internal evidence.[5]

It is partly for this reason, though not wholly, that Luce has changed the name of the notebooks to *Philosophical Commentaries*.*

---

[1] *Id.*, pp. xxv–xxvi; A. A. Luce, *Berkeley and Malebranche*, Oxford, 1934, pp. 186–8.

[2] Luce, *Op. cit.*, p. 188.

[3] A. A. Luce, "The Purpose and the Date of Berkeley's *Commonplace Book*", *Proc. of the Royal Irish Acad.*, Dublin, 1943, Vol. XLVIII, Sec. C, No. vii, p. 273.

[4] *Id.*, p. 274.

[5] *Id.*, pp. 275–8; *cf.* Berkeley, *Op. cit.*, pp. xxxv–xxxix.

* Granted that the old name for the work, *Commonplace Book*, is wholly unsatisfactory, does *Commentaries* meet its requirements? "Notebook" would be too prosaic for such a work. In proposing his new title, Luce is not thinking merely of a modern commentary on a text, but of many older kinds, some of which contained new knowledge. In view of its history, therefore, the use of the word is justified. It suffers from the disadvantage, however, that nowadays, when far fewer philosophers have a classical background and almost none is versed in theology, the word will suggest mere exposition and criticism without originality of the kind that is especially characteristic of the work. Apart from this, the word is justified even if the supposed manuscript did not exist, for the work was

As one of the most outstanding original works, the *Commentaries* merits all the attention it has received. Each time one reads it, or even glances at it, one finds things one has previously overlooked—though this may in part be due to lack of deliberate arrangement of the entries. Luce has shown that it contains development: that natural objects cease to be described as thoughts and become ideas; that the passive conception of the mind as a congeries of perceptions settles into something more active and substantial; that the subjectivism becomes less extreme[1]; and that the important word "idea", which began with a small *i*, in the middle is spelt indiscriminately with a small letter or capital, and ends with a capital—thus revealing Berkeley's growing realisation of the significance of the word in his philosophy.[2]

The notebooks discuss the theory of vision, mathematics, abstract ideas, Immaterialism, morality, and personal points. One cannot help being struck by the power of Berkeley's thought and by the similarity many of the entries bear to his published works. Nearly all the important thoughts were used sooner or later; the only ones he did not develop were a few of those concerned with mathematics. The mathematical entries consisted mostly of attacks on infinite divisibility; so far as these had to do with Newton's fluxions, they found their place in *The Analyst* or in the mathematical queries attached to it (1734); but there are a few unused ones, which are of the greatest interest in view of present-day approaches to the foundations of mathematics. Thus he can attach no meaning to the geometrical criterion of equality by congruence,[3] which is an undoubted difficulty in

a commentary on Berkeley's first thoughts—not to mention its being a commentary on other authors as well. "Meditations" might serve, though it too bears misleading implications; its meaning of sustained thinking is appropriate and suggests originality. Nor would this word rule out the existence of a manuscript to be meditated upon. No word is exactly right, and no other suggestion so far made seems in the least satisfactory. Be these things as they may, the new edition of the *Works* has established *Philosophical Commentaries* as the title from now on.

[1] A. A. Luce, "Development within Berkeley's *Commonplace Book*", *Mind*, London, 1940, N.S. Vol. XLIX, No. cxciii, p. 43.

[2] A. A. Luce, *Berkeley and Malebranche*, Oxford, 1934, pp. 194–7.

[3] Berkeley, *Op. cit.*, 514, 526, 528–9.

Euclidean geometry, for whereas ostensibly it deals with *concepts* of lines and figures, the test of congruence requires us to place one line or figure upon another one as if they were *physical* entities. Again, his finitist approach is to be seen in his denial that lines are infinitely divisible[1]; and in accordance with this he denies Pythagoras' theorem, which implies that the hypotenuse is incommensurable with the other sides of a right-angled triangle, on the grounds that lines not infinitely divisible must contain a finite number of points, so that the hypotenuse is commensurable with the other sides:

264. The Diagonal is commensurable with the Side.

500. One square cannot be double of another. Hence the Pythagoric Theorem is false.[2]

He makes the acute observation:

322. Mem. to prove against Keil y^t the infinite divisibility of matter makes the half have an equal number of equal parts with the whole.

This is a well-known property of infinite numbers, but Berkeley used it to show their absurdity. His interest in the basis of the subject is also marked by his desire to unravel the mystery of imaginary roots in algebra.[3]

In addition, many entries reiterate his claim that in his philosophy the world is as commonsense takes it to be: he notes he must "show how the vulgar notion agrees"[3] with his own.

It throws more light on Berkeley's personality to consider entries under the following headings:

(1) personal, (2) contempt for mathematicians, (3) nominalism, (4) subjectivism, (5) apparent scepticism, (6) morality, and (7) God and Matter, most of which bear the marginal sign +, indicating that they were not to be used in his books. Moreover, the subjectivism contradicted his considered philosophy and commonsense.

(1) Of the eight hundred and eighty-eight entries over a dozen are personal. This one is famous:

266. Mem: that I was distrustful at 8 years old and Consequently by nature disposed for these new Doctrines.

[1] *Id.*, 236.   [2] *Cf. Id.*, 469–70.   [3] *Id.*, 764.

And soon after it:

279. I wonder not at my sagacity in discovering the obvious tho' amazing truth, I rather wonder at my stupid inadvertency in not finding it out before. 'tis no witchcraft to see.

This almost certainly refers to the principle of *Esse percipi*. Independence of mind is the note. The next form of this is repudiation of mere authority, which he repeated years afterwards[1]:

465. I am young, I am an upstart, I am a pretender, I am vain, very well. I shall Endeavour patiently to bear up under the most lessening, vilifying appellations the pride & rage of man can devise. But one thing, I know, I am not guilty of, I do not pin my faith on the sleeve of any great man. I act not out of prejudice & prepossession. I do not adhere to any opinion because it is an old one, a receiv'd one, a fashionable one, or one that I have spent much time in the study and cultivation of.

He intended to be very careful about offending those in authority:

209. Mem: to correct my Language and make it as Philosophically nice as possible to avoid giving handle.

715. N.B. To use utmost Caution not to give the least Handle of offence to the Church or Church-men.

716. Even to speak somewhat favourably of the Schoolmen & shew that they who blame them for Jargon are not free from it themselves.[2]

He decided upon calculated modesty and self-restraint in presentation:

633. Mem: upon all occasions to use the Utmost Modesty. to Confute the Mathematicians wth the utmost civility and respect. not to stile them Nihilarians etc:

634. N.B. to rein in y^r Satyrical nature.

His relation to previous philosophers he depicts thus:

682. I must acknowledge my self beholding to the Philosophers [who] have gone before me. They have given good rules tho perhaps

---

[1] *Works*, IV, *A Defence of Free-Thinking in Mathematics*, § 13.
[2] Also 725.

they do not always observe them. Similitude of Adventurers who tho they themselves attained not the desir'd Port, they by their wrecks have made known the Rocks & sands, whereby the Passage of aftercomers is made more secure & easy. Pref: or Introd:

This entry was not marked with a + but with an I for the Introduction to his principal work. Parallel with it is his superiority to the mathematicians, as will appear.

(2) The following entries speak for themselves:

313. What shall I say? dare I pronounce the admir'd ακριβεια Mathematica, that Darling of the Age a trifle?

361. Newton's Harangue amounts to no more than that gravity is proportional to gravity.[1]

372. I see no wit in any of them but Newton, The rest are meer triflers, meer Nihilarians.

373. The folly of the Mathematicians in not judging of sensations by their senses. Reason was given us for nobler uses.

368. I'll not admire the Mathematicians. tis w^t any one of common sense might attain to by repeated acts. I know it by experience, I am but one of common sense, and I etc

375. Mathematicians have some of them good parts, the more is the pity. Had they not been Mathematicians they had been good for nothing. they were such fools they knew not how to employ their parts.

371. A Great Genius cannot stoop to such trifles & minutenesses as they consider.

407. Newton begs his Principle, I Demonstrate mine.

409. The Schoolmen have noble subjects but handle them ill. The Mathematicians have trifling subjects but reason admirably about them. certainly their Method & arguing are excellent.[2]

385. I'll teach any one the whole course of Mathematiques in 1/100 prt the time that another will.[3]

395. I can square the circle, &c. they cannot, wch goes on the best principles

Even national feeling[4] is involved:

[1] *Cf.* 618.   [2] *Cf.* 449, 492, 642.   [3]*Cf.* 383.   [4] *Cf.* 392, 398.

393. The Mathematicians think there are insensible lines, about these they harangue, these cut in a point, at all angles these are divisible ad infinitum. We Irish men can conceive no such lines.

394. The Mathematicians talk of w* they call a point, this they say is not altogether nothing nor is it downright something, now we Irish men are apt to think something & nothing are next neighbours.

(3) The nominalism and positivism of the notebooks is interesting chiefly because he opposed it in *Alciphron*[1] twenty-five years later, and in the *Principles*[2] which was soon to appear in print.

422. No word to be used without an idea.[3]

497. . . . I can by no means conceive a general idea. . . .

—the modification of his published work admitted general ideas but denied *abstract* general ideas.

(4) That Berkeley should have written subjectivist entries is of the utmost importance, since they are opposed to his considered philosophy. They include:

24. Nothing properly but persons i.e. conscious things do exist, all other things are not so much existence as manners of y* existence of persons.

121. Blind at 1st would not take colours to be without his mind, but colours would seem to be in the same place with the colour'd extension, therefore extension would not seem to be without the mind.

(5) Now follow an astounding set of entries; they may appear to be Humean, behaviourist, positivist, or sceptical:

83. Men die or are in state of annihilation oft in a day.

651. Certainly the mind always & constantly thinks & we know this too In Sleep & trances the mind exists not there is no time no succession of Ideas.

---

[1] *Works*, III, *Alciphron*, Dial. VII, §§ 5–7, and § 7 of 1732 editions.
[2] *Works*, II, *The Principles of Human Knowledge*, Introduction, §§ 10–20.
[3] *Cf.* 378 (1, 2), 551, 638.

577. The very existence of Ideas constitutes the soul.

578. Consciousness, perception, existence of Ideas seem to be all one.[1]

580. Mind is a congeries of Perceptions. Take away Perceptions & you take away the Mind put the Perceptions & you put the mind.

This last foreshadows Hume closely.

779. I approve of this axiom of the Schoolmen nihil est in intellectu quod non prius fuit in sensu. I wish they had stuck to it. it had never taught them the Doctrine of Abstract Ideas.

This is not so extreme, but it rules out knowledge of non-natural objects such as God and other finite spirits. Finally comes the very antithesis of the Platonic tradition in philosophy:

735. Qu: w⁴ becomes of the aeternae veritates? Ansʳ they vanish.

873. Qu: whether Veritas stands not for an Abstract Idea.

In his note on entries 576–82, Luce contends that Berkeley was never a sceptic.* But his argument cannot be decisive, for the sceptical Humean view must surely be attributed to 83 and 651; and it does nothing to minimise the subjectivism of 24 which denies physical reality to the natural world. Moreover, Luce has admitted that Berkeley "had come to the edge of the precipice and was looking over".[2]

(6) There are a few entries about morality, but not many, seeing that Berkeley was going to write a work on the subject. Some of them, which have the appropriate marginal letter,

[1] *Cf.* 590.
* The argument turns on a point of terminology. In the early part of the *Commentaries*, Berkeley used "soul" or "mind" in a passive sense for what was conscious or perceived and used "person" for what would ordinarily be called the "soul"; only later did he adopt a more usual terminology, making the soul or mind active and giving up the word "person". Luce's point is that the early terminology masks Berkeley's meaning: that there is nothing sceptical about these entries if "soul" or "mind" does not refer to person but simply means consciousness. This construction is supported, for instance, by entry 577. But the argument, whether or not it is cogent, does not cover the other sceptical entries.
[2] A. A. Luce, "Development within Berkeley's *Commonplace Book*", *Mind*, London, 1940, N.S. Vol. XLIX, No. cxciii, p. 48.

B.P.—4

seem to have no bearing on ethics and some are devoted to what may be called Berkeley's idea of an algebra of morals. What is of chief interest are four apparently hedonistic entries:

542. I'd never blame a Man for acting upon Interest. he's a fool that acts on any other Principle. the not understanding these things has been of ill consequence in Morality.

769. Sensual Pleasure is the Summum Bonum. This the Great Principle of Morality. This once rightly understood all the Doctrines even the severest of the Gospels may be cleerly Demonstrated.

773. Sensual Pleasure qua Pleasure is Good and desirable. . . .

787. Mem. to excite men to the pleasures of the Eye & the Ear wch surfeit not, not bring those evils after them as others.

In his notes Luce points out that "sensual" means the pleasure of sense-perception, as suggested by the last of the above entries. Berkeley's meaning would seem to be that such pleasure was not only compatible with moral duty but essential to it—he evidently did not believe in a cold doctrine that made every pleasure wrong. Presumably not only sensual pleasure had to be rightly understood but also moral duty. Nonetheless the entries manifest a certain *joie de vivre*. It did not last, however; he later preached against the decadence of the pleasure-loving times with unrelieved gloom.

(7) Early in Berkeley's life God and Matter assumed a unique relation:

625. Matter once allow'd. I defy any man to prove that God is not matter.

290. The great danger of making extension exist without the mind. in y^t if it does it must be acknowledg'd infinite immutable eternal etc. wch will be to make either God extended (wch I think dangerous) or an eternal, immutable, infinite, increate being beside God.

298. Locke, More, Raphson etc seem to make God extended. 'tis nevertheless of great use to religion to take extension out of our idea of God & put a power in its place, it seems dangerous to suppose extension wch is manifestly inert in God.

310. The danger of Expounding the H: Trinity by extension.

Apart from these entries, we have a consistent picture of a young philosophical dictator, confident, independent, scornful of mathematicians, sceptical of traditional philosophy, refreshing in the field of moral thought. What, then, is the significance of the relation between God and Matter? It provides the key to the subjectivism, even the panpsychism, of (4) and (5). The general meaning of the entries is that if Matter is once allowed, God would be degraded to its level. Evidently Matter and God were possible candidates for the chief place in the system of truth and they could not both be accepted. The question then arises: was Matter banished, and thus room made for God, by his subjectivism; or was there first of all a repudiation of Matter, which led both to subjectivism and to acceptance of God; or was the acceptance of God primary, leading to denial of Matter and hence to subjectivism? It is difficult to believe that the subjectivism could have been the primary factor of the three; it could have arisen only for a purpose, and this purpose could only be the denial of Matter. This rules out the first alternative. Now Berkeley was not content to admit God at the price of having him on the level of Matter; hence God was not the primary factor, and this rules out the third alternative. I think, therefore, that repudiation of Matter was fundamental. Upon it would be built up the belief in God and the subjectivism. But would subjectivism not have been sufficient to banish Matter? For Hume it would have been, but evidently not for Berkeley; he was a freethinker only in the sense of thinking for himself but not in the sense of being a deist or an atheist; he did not accept the Humean logical conclusion of his subjectivism. Evidently, therefore, God was needed as an additional factor to master Matter; God and Matter were, as it were, opposite poles one of which had to be accepted if the other were denied in a passive way and one of which if accepted ousted the other in an active way. It would seem that these conceptions underlay all Berkeley's other philosophical thoughts. It is not, of course, clear from the *Philosophical Commentaries* how God was to reinforce the subjectivism to produce the desired result; the point was developed soon after in his *Principles*, but even there the solution has to be carefully studied to be discerned.

Had Berkeley taken the logical step of basing his philosophy upon subjectivism alone, there is no doubt that he would have been the ablest deist of his day.[1] But that is not the chief point of interest here. The philosophical importance of the *Commentaries*, apart from the light it throws on his mind, character, and the development of his thought, is that, in addition to presenting part of the fundamental principle of empiricism and scientific procedure, it conveys, without however really stating it, what has been traditionally known as Berkeley's philosophy: it is the implied scepticism of the *Commentaries* that has given Berkeley his justly earned place in the history of philosophy and has made him a living force in philosophical discussion to the present day; whether one approves of it or not, it is on this that his importance in part rests.

[1] *Cf.* G. A. Johnston, *The Development of Berkeley's Philosophy*, London, 1923, p. 336.

Chapter 4

THE TRADITIONAL INTERPRETATION
OF BERKELEY'S PHILOSOPHY

IN order to expound this traditional view of Berkeley's philosophy it will not be necessary to state the entire philosophy, since certain sections from his considered system may be taken without alteration as part of it.

(I) The preamble concerns not Malebranche but Locke. It then begins, as does the *Principles*, with (1), which argues that *esse* is *percepi*. The concluding remark of (1), that perceiving is shown only to be an indispensable condition but not a sufficient one, was not made by Berkeley, and it is implicitly denied or at least its possibility is not entertained on the traditional view.

(II) Matter is refuted exactly as in (3).

(III) It is concluded that natural objects depend solely on being perceived by the philosopher conducting the exposition while he is conducting it. Thus if red, sweet, and so on depend upon my perceptions here and now, and if an apple consists of such qualities only, then it too depends upon being perceived by me here and now. In other words, if sensory-ideas are wholly private, so are thing-ideas.

(IV) There is therefore no escape, the argument would proceed, from the circle of my own ideas: I cannot infer the existence of any other person, far less of God, or the stability (persistence and unity) of the natural world. (Thus (4) and (5) are denied.)

(V) It is impossible to assert that there is, as (6) would have us believe, any discoverable principle of causation of divine origin, though regular uniformities in my circle of ideas may occur.

(VI) The problem of identity cannot be solved, or rather no source of identity can be found.

(VII) As (2) asserts, I do not make my sensory- or thing-ideas.

(VIII) Because of the predicament arising from (VI) and (VII), and in spite of (V), Berkeley made a transcendental jump, forming the hypothesis that God and other persons exist. But to do this is merely to invoke a *deus ex machina*; and God and other persons are easily seen to be conceptions on the same level as Matter, unknown and unknowable, devoid of all properties, to be in fact abstract general ideas and meaningless.

(IX) Likewise there could have been no creation of natural objects before the first human being was born.

And the entire philosophy is one of the furthest removed from common sense.

At this point it may be useful to summarise the two interpretations of Berkeley's metaphysic.

His considered philosophy was as follows:— Sensory ideas do not exist unless perceived; perception is a necessary condition of their existence; their *esse* is at least in part *percipi*. A human percipient can create ideas of the imagination but not those of natural objects. Hence the existence of natural objects does not depend solely upon being perceived by a human percipient. Since they cannot be caused in this way, there must be something else that causes them. This cannot be Matter. The only possibility left is God. Independent proofs are offered for his existence as a causal agent. Hence God is the additional factor required. The conclusion is that sensory-ideas exist if and only if they are perceived and the perception is caused by God, or a sensory-idea is a theistically caused perception. Next, a thing-idea is a set of possibilities of perception, any one of which to become actual has to be caused by God to be perceived by a human percipient. Regularity in the presentation of perceptions of a thing-idea is guaranteed by God, as is also the regularity in the relationship between one thing-idea and another. Identity consists in the regularity and continuity with which God causes perceptions. God is thus conceived both as necessitated by the existence of and relationship between sensory-ideas and also as the ultimate causal power producing the two kinds of regularity. This requires him to be quasi-observable and a power; and the synthesis of these seemingly incompatible properties is provided by Berkeley's interpretation that God as a quasi-observable is 'read' in the 'book of nature', and what is read there is a power ordering nature.

The solipsistic interpretation is as follows: The principle of

Esse percipi applies to sensory- and thing-ideas; all objects in the
natural world depend for their existence wholly upon the mind
of the person perceiving them. Thus nothing exists apart from
the circle of ideas he has while he is having them. This is established by the arguments with which Berkeley refuted the existence of Matter. The same sort of arguments would refute the
existence of other minds and of God. An important consequence
is that no source can be found for the identity of things. Since
a percipient does not cause all his sensory-ideas, a cause of these
and a source of identity must be postulated. Berkeley's arguments for the existence of God constitute the postulation of a
deus ex machina who shall endow things with identity, create
things the percipient does not, and guarantee regularity in the
relations between them. In short the position is Solipsism
evaded by an unsubstantiated postulate.

This is the philosophy that no one has believed and that no
one could refute. It is known by a variety of names: Idealism,
Subjective Idealism, Subjectivism, Mentalism, Panpsychism,
Solipsism, and possibly others. The first three are hardly strong
enough; Mentalism suggests that the world is made of mental
stuff; Panpsychism would be appropriate for a system, such as
McTaggart's, maintaining that only minds exist; Solipsism,
which means that I alone exist, is the most satisfactory and will
be used below.

The disparity of length between this chapter and the previous
one must not be taken to mean that the traditional interpretation is no longer important; a moment's reflection will show that
their lengths would have been reversed, more or less, had this
chapter been placed first.

This solipsistic interpretation is important historically, be-
cause it was this that influenced Hume and many later thinkers.
And it is important biographically, because it has its origin in
Berkeley himself.

Chapter 5

HAD BERKELEY AN EARLY AND A LATE PHILOSOPHY?

THIS chapter is concerned with a controversy over the interpretation of Berkeley's early and late works. A summary is given at the end.

We have noted that it had long been customary to interpret Berkeley, the young author of the *Principles of Human Knowledge* and the *Three Dialogues*, as an inconsistent solipsist, who tried to avoid this position by means of a hypothesis about the existence of God; Hume has been regarded as Berkeley made consistent. When during the present century he became perhaps the most widely studied philosopher, it was soon noticed that in *Siris*, his last philosophical work, published when he was fifty-nine, Immaterialism did not loom large, that the emphasis was now theocentric, and that he had moved nearer to Plato.* For this he has been credited with improving on his early system by remedying its one-sidedness. He was therefore credited with two philosophies: the Solipsism of the *Principles* and the Platonic Panentheism of *Siris*. The argument has a variant: he was supposed to have rectified his mistakes—at all events to have made an attempt in this direction—in the second edition of the *Principles*, which appeared in 1734, twenty-four years after the first edition and ten years before *Siris*. Other pointers to the same effect have also been fastened on.

The position that he held at the beginning of his enquiry, says Hicks, he was compelled to modify in a very radical way.

He came soon to recognise that the *esse* of a sensible thing must imply more than its merely being perceived by an individual percipient.[1]

Hicks makes this more explicit:

* This was first suggested by Fraser (*Works*, ed. Fraser, Oxford, 1901, Vol. III, p. 118).
[1] G. Dawes Hicks, *Berkeley*, London, 1932, p. 113.

44

The doctrine of immaterialism underwent no small amount of development during the interval between the appearance of the first and second editions of the *Principles*.[1]

For a long time prior to 1744 there had been, as we have seen, two trends of thought struggling in his mind for mastery—on the one hand, that which comprised the main principles of the empirical theory of knowledge; and, on the other hand, the more metaphysical conception of mind.[2]

In fact, so far as a theory of knowledge is concerned, the whole drift of Berkeley's later reflexion was towards a dislodgment of sense-perception from the place it occupied in the empirical theory.[3]

There is abundant evidence that Hicks was interpreting Berkeley as an incomplete Kant,[4] but, whatever value this may or may not have as an academic exercise, it is beside the point—more, it means that all Hicks' interpretations are open to doubt. Moreover, Hicks supported his view on the grounds that the term "notion" appeared in the second edition of the *Principles* though not in the first, thus bringing in a significant change of doctrine. Jessop, who has made a careful study of the two editions and the manuscript, has knocked this argument firmly on the head; for he found that the manuscript-draft of the first edition contained this term; the presumption is that in the second edition Berkeley did no more than restore what he had originally intended, and that it was the term only and not the doctrine that was omitted from the first edition—and Jessop goes on to point out that the doctrine of notions is present even in the *Commentaries*.[5]*

[1] *Id.*, p. 206.   [2] *Id.*, p. 209.   [3] *Id.*, p. 210; *cf.* also p. 140.
[4] *Id.*, pp. 128, 210, 269, 272, 276–7.
[5] George Berkeley, *The Principles of Human Knowledge*, ed. by T. E. Jessop, London, 1937, pp. v–vi.
* Another faulty argument, which displays considerable negligence, may be noted.
In the third edition of the *Alciphron*, Berkeley withdrew from Dialogue VII three complete sections, which dealt with abstract general ideas; out of this has arisen a body of opinion that he retracted his early doctrine of abstraction. For this Fraser is responsible (*Works*, ed. Fraser, Oxford, 1901, Vol. I, p. 219; Vol. II, p. 323n). Luce has, however, thoroughly disposed of this view (A. A. Luce, *Berkeley and Malebranche*, Oxford 1934, pp. 168–71). The withdrawal occurred in 1752, just before Berkeley's death. It is perhaps unlikely that he would have given up a

G. A. Johnston also takes the view that Berkeley had two theories or changed his mind:

Berkeley is thus forced to distinguish two kinds of existence, a permanent potential existence in the mind of God, and an actual intermittent existence only when things are being actually perceived by finite beings. This intermittent existence owes what unity it has to the fact that its potential permanence is guaranteed by God.[1]

It is fairly clear that in the course of his argument Berkeley has been forced to change completely the meaning of his fundamental principle. At the beginning of his psychological enquiry, *"esse is percipi"* means that presence in my experience, so long as it lasts, is a sufficient account of the existence of a thing. . . . It must now be interpreted to mean that a thing exists really and completely only as a presentation in God's experience.[2]

If the pre-Siris point of view be represented by *esse* is *percipi*, that of *Siris* is *esse* is *concipi*.[3]

It is to be observed that Johnston, though of the same opinion as Hicks, is milder in his expression of it; he makes mention of what Berkeley preserved throughout and the continuity of his thought.

That the philosophy of the *Principles* was Solipsism and that of *Siris* Platonism was the view Luce set out to refute. There were, however, some notable commentators who did not attribute Solipsism to the *Principles*.

In Metz's able exposition of Berkeley the theistic component of Immaterialism was strongly stressed, even as regards the first edition of the *Principles*; he did not hold that Berkeley developed from some form of subjectivism to one of theism:

Der Spiritualismus bildet den Unterbau auch für die idealistischen Konsequenzen, obwohl ihn Berkeley selbst als Konsequenz seines Idealismus entwickelt.[4]

doctrine he had held all his life; in any case, those who argue for a general change of view maintain that this occurred much earlier. But he also republished the *De Motu* in the same year, which is largely devoted to attacking abstract general ideas, and the matter is easily clinched, for the rest of the dialogue *also* attacks them. The reason for the omission is not far to seek: the sections were technical and abstract and therefore out of keeping with the rest of the dialogue.

[1] G. A. Johnston, *The Development of Berkeley's Philosophy*, London, 1923, p. 50; *cf.* also p. 53.   [2] *Id.*, pp. 190–1.   [3] *Id.*, p. 253; *cf.* also p. 248.

[4] Rudolf Metz, *George Berkeley*, Stuttgart, 1925, S. 97–8; *cf.* S. 218.

ƒ

Moreover, he stresses that Berkeley never broke with his early views.[1]

Metz even touched on the corner stone, later established by Luce, that

Das Urphänomen des Geistes als des aktiven, wollenden, wirkenden und denkenden Prinzips, in dem alles lebt, webt und ist, in dem alles Uebrige besteht, von dem es abhängig ist und ohne das es nichts ist, lag sicherlich am Grunde des Berkeleyschen Denkens.[2]

He was concerned also to establish a fundamental link with Malebranche:

Der göttliche Geist jedoch ist der "Ort der Ideen", der Schoss, in dem sie sicher und geborgen ruhen, so könnten wir mit Variierung einer Redeweise *Malebranches* etwa sagen.[3]

His general discussion of the relation between Berkeley and Malebranche is exceptionally clear.[4] He read Berkeleism, not incorrectly, as a blend of Immanence and Panentheism:

Das Dasien der Welt wird einerseits durch Gott verbürgt, andererseits wird Gott durch die Welt bewiesen.[5]

His main stress lay on Immanence.[6]

On the other hand, Metz contended that Berkeley's thought evolved from sensationism, though not subjectivism, to a form of intellectualism, by adding rational knowledge of concepts and relations.[7] The case for this rests mainly on Berkeley's introduction of the concept of 'notion' in the second edition of the *Principles*[8]; this is, as we know, mistaken, for the extant draft of the first edition used the same concept. That there was some sort of change in Berkeley's thought is obvious; but Metz misconstrued the nature of it.

Though Metz considered that the final phase was a philosophy of *esse concipi*, he held that there was no break with the past but that Berkeley retained the New Principle[9] (apparently asserting both *esse concipi* and *esse percipi*). Thus Metz was not so radical as Hicks or Johnston, for he did not ascribe Solipsism to the *Principles*. He claimed that there was continuity in Berkeley's thought

[1] *Id.*, S. 220. [2] *Id.*, S. 103. [3] *Id.*, S. 119. [4] *Id.*, S. 134–7.
[5] *Id.*, S. 128. [6] *Id.*, S. 93–6. [7] *Id.*, S. 113, 214–18, 220, 221.
[8] *Id.*, S. 73. [9] *Id.*, S. 220, 232.

and interpreted the system as theocentric. His view is therefore closer to that given in Chapter 2.

Perhaps the best straightforward exposition of Berkeley from the theocentric point of view is that given by Joussain. It is simple and succinct.

Le monde sensible n'est qu'un ensemble de perceptions, mais ces perceptions s'imposent à nous: elles sont involontaires. . . .

Toute cause est active, et nous ne pouvons concevoir une activité différente de notre volonté. . . . Si donc il existe hors de nous une cause productrice de nos perceptions, c'est qu'il existe hors de nous un être qui veut les perceptions en nous.[1]

Dieu a donc en lui les idées de toutes les choses que nous percevons. Seulement ces idées de Dieu diffèrent des nôtres: 1° en ce qu'elles ne s'accompagnent d'aucune affection; 2° en ce qu'elles ne sont pas passivement reçues, mais activement produits.[2]

Ainsi la comparaison des premier ouvrages de Berkeley nous montre que sa doctrine n'a, en somme, jamais varié dans ses traits essentiels.[3]

Si l'inspiration générale de l'ouvrage est semblable à celle des ouvrages antérieurs, la doctrine qui y est exposée ne révèle non plus aucun abandon des idées maîtresses due système. L'immatérialisme y est expressement affirmé.[4]

Then follows a considerable list of Berkeley's most central doctrines which, according to Joussain, he continued to hold. The only change this author noted was the development of mystical tendencies, which gave rise to a change of attitude:

Il n'y [a] pas dans l'oeuvre de Berkeley deux philosophies, mais deux phases: la phase classique et la phase romantique. . . .[5]

His interpretation of archetypes, however, is open to question.[6]

These authors saw Berkeley's philosophy in a certain light and expounded it accordingly; they did not write polemically. Mabbott appears to have been the first to go further than interpretation and produce weighty and convincing argument against attributing Solipsism to the *Principles*. Pointing out that

[1] André Joussain, *Exposé critique de la philosophie de Berkeley*, Paris, 1921, p. 46.
[2] *Id.*, p. 47.   [3] *Id.*, p. 113.   [4] *Id.*, p. 117.
[5] *Id.*, p. 118.   [6] *Id.*, pp. 217–18.

the early Immaterialism was theocentrically grounded, he maintained that the traditional interpretation, according to which God was a *deus ex machina,*

rests on a misunderstanding of his central theory, a misunderstanding which gives God a place both inconsistent with his main premisses and useless in his system.[1]

The most comprehensive treatment of the issue is due to Luce. He wished to establish several different points belonging to the same general setting. His thesis may be put under three headings: (*a*) that Berkeley derived his inspiration as much from Malebranche as from Locke, a fact that on close examination shows the theocentric position to have been primary in the formation of his philosophy; (*b*) that Berkeley's *statements* indicate no knowledge of his supposed change of views from his earliest work to his last; and (*c*) that he did not unconsciously change his mind.

(*a*) This view of Luce's seems beyond dispute.

The theocentric-Malebranchean interpretation might appear to dissociate Berkeley from Locke, but this does not follow. Nor had Luce any such intention, as he explicitly states.[2] Indeed it should be stressed that Berkeley took from Locke as much as from Malebranche.

It might seem that Berkeley is credited with a philosophy already developed by Malebranche, had no real originality, and developed nothing. But he did not take over the whole of Malebranche's philosophy, and whatever he took he absorbed into his system and rewove into a *new whole,* a fact that is undenied and a witness to originality.

How much did Berkeley owe to Malebranche? Malebranche was not an immaterialist; he held that the causal relation between Mind and Matter to be an 'occasional' one, *i.e.* one that was uniformly and consistently occasioned by God; moreover, the finite person perceived in God the representations of material objects. Berkeley agreed that God was the cause of ideas, but denied Malebranche's view that these ideas were also manifestations of Matter:

[1] J. D. Mabbott, "The Place of God in Berkeley's Philosophy", *The Journal of Philosophical Studies*, London, 1931, Vol. VI, No. xxi, p. 18.
[2] A. A. Luce, *Berkeley and Malebranche*, Oxford, 1934, p. 6.

686a   On second thoughts I am, on t'other extream I am certain of that wch Malbranche seems to doubt of. viz the existence of Bodies.*

Since it will serve to bring out the difference between Berkeley and Malebranche, let us consider the passage on which the argument has been suggested that Berkeley did not accept the Malebranchean doctrine of 'seeing all things in God'. It is[1]:

> He [Malebranche] builds on the most abstract general ideas, which I entirely disdain. He asserts an absolute external world, which I deny. He maintains that we are deceived by our senses, and know not the real natures or the true forms and figures of extended beings; of all which I hold the direct contrary. . . . It must be owned that I entirely agree with what the holy Scripture saith, that in God we live and move and have our being. But that we see things in his essence, after the manner above set forth, I am far from believing.

This accurate statement shows many decisive differences. Berkeley was objecting to certain speculative views of Malebranche; but he does not deny that he would accept the dictum in a theocentric sense that did not imply the existence of Matter. It was Malebranche's Occasionalism to which Berkeley could not assent, because it implied the existence of Matter and the denial of immediate knowledge of objects.

These differences are so far reaching that it would be absurd to think of Berkeley as a follower of Malebranche. It was evidently not Luce's intention to interpret him in this way; and the preceding exposition should make it plain that Berkeley's Theocentric Phenomenalism is by no means the same as Malebranche's system, which with more appropriateness than Berkeley's may be called Panentheism.

What, then, had the Irishman in common with the French thinker? For both, God was the centre; for both, knowledge gained by the senses was of non-material entities. For both, God was the sole fundamental cause. But the relation of sensory-ideas

* The very fact of allowing the possibility of Matter, as Malebranche did, must prevent it (since it is not directly knowable) from being more than problematic, which explains Berkeley's remark that he placed more reliance on the senses than did Malebranche.

[1] *Works*, II, *Three Dialogues between Hylas and Philonous*, Dial. II, p. 214; *cf.* *The Principles of Human Knowledge*, § 148.

to God was not the same. With Malebranche, they were represented panentheistically in God by intellectual essences, reminiscent of Plato's Ideas, archtypes which Berkeley was concerned to deny. Berkeley's Panentheism, on the other hand, so far as one can use these rough labels, contained an infusion of Pantheism; for God was immanent in sensory-ideas in that these formed a language by which he was known, just as meaning is immanent in a word.

But, though Berkeley had certain conceptions in common with Malebranche, this does not necessarily mean he owed them to that philosopher. This is not what is shown by Luce's research; what this does prove is the enormous interest Berkeley took in the Frenchman's thought. This I should attribute not to Berkeley's finding there a large part of a philosophy which he adopted and which would not otherwise have occurred to him, but to his finding in it exactly the right stimulus to bring to the forefront of his mind conceptions that were already simmering within him. And this could happen even if the stimulus did not in detail resemble what was stimulated. I envisage Berkeley reading Malebranche with concentrated attention, and feeling, "This author has some excellent conceptions but he has put them together incorrectly and spoilt them by attaching them to others that are not good"; I envisage Berkeley's general scheme coming to him as a whole rather than as a result of logical deduction and weighing of pros and cons. In short, as Luce says, "Locke taught him, but Malebranche inspired him."[1] I should expound his deliberately intended philosophy by saying that he was not a Malebranchean but that he used an integral part of Malebranche's philosophy as a weapon against the Aristotelian-Scholastic-Lockean element in *that* philosophy; that he was not so much Locke made consistent—a commonly held view[2]—but a Malebranche with one side pruned and another cultivated.

The reader will find the philosophical relationship between the two thinkers fully and clearly discussed in a paper by Jessop.[3] This paper is a necessary complement to Luce's work. Luce has

[1] Luce, *Op. cit.*, p. 7.
[2] G. A. Johnston, *The Development of Berkeley's Philosophy*, London, 1923, p. 35.
[3] Jessop, *Op. cit.*

located one general source or stimulus of Berkeley's thought in Malebranche; Jessop has examined the particular philosophical relationship between their two systems of speculation.

(b) When this was mentioned in a previous chapter, no mention was made that Luce had to substantiate his claim by showing that the theocentric position was not merely the system of *Siris* but also of the *Principles* and *Three Dialogues*, *i.e.* Berkeley's chief philosophical works. Luce's book, *Berkeley and Malebranche*, does this to some extent, perhaps by implication though not explicitly; but his chief demonstration is given in subsequent papers. To show that Berkeley did not change his mind *consciously*,[1] he draws attention to many objective facts. Thus he cites the list of Berkeley's works with *all* the editions Berkeley sanctioned in his lifetime; an author like Berkeley would not re-issue, far less touch up in small ways, a work whose basis he repudiated. But Luce's principal argument consists of a list of Berkeley's own references in later works to earlier ones for the further understanding of the important themes, of his expressed recommendations in his letters to correspondents to consult his works when they were in doubt about his views, and of his actual answers to correspondents' questions, late in life, which tally exactly with his early views. All this is objective and conclusive.

(c) To show that there was no *unconscious* change of front,[2] Luce has written down the references to passages in Berkeley that deal with the chief features of his philosophy; these references concern passages from *all* his philosophical works and show that he retracted nothing. This tabulation, as before, so far as it goes, is objective and open to anyone to inspect.

"Ainsi la comparaison des premiers ouvrages de Berkeley nous montre que sa doctrine n'a, en somme, jamais varié dans ses traits essentiels"[3]; he had but one philosophy, "which he never abandoned, never out-grew, and never changed".[4]

---

[1] A. A. Luce, "The Unity of the Berkeleian Philosophy (I)", *Mind*, London, 1937, N.S. Vol. XLVI, No. clxxxi.

[2] Luce, *Op. cit.*, Ch. VIII; "The Unity of the Berkeleian Philosophy (II)", *Mind*, London, 1937, N.S. Vol. XLVI, No. clxxxii.

[3] Joussain, *Op. cit.*, p. 47.

[4] A. A. Luce, "The Unity of the Berkeleian Philosophy (I)", *Mind*, London, 1937, N.S. Vol. XLVI, No. clxxxi.

The commentators whose views were mentioned above wrote before Luce's work was carried out. Subsequently the theocentric interpretation has been followed by Baladi,[1] but Luce's conclusion has been challenged by Wild. He contends: (i) that it is simply false, because "the simple psychological subjectivism of his [Berkeley's] works is abandoned"[2]; (ii) that in certain details Luce's comparison of early and late passages does not hold; (iii) that Berkeley's republication of his early works is perfectly compatible with his having changed his philosophy; and (iv) that Luce's view leaves no room for development.

(i) This misses Luce's main point, which is his real contribution to the subject, that the considered philosophy of the *Principles* was *not* subjectivism or Solipsism. (ii) The supposed discrepancy of views in the early and late works rests chiefly on passages in *Siris* that disparage sense-knowledge.[3] One has only to read them, however, to see that Berkeley was not contradicting his early view but was focusing more attention upon divine reality, which would seem to have counted more deeply in his personal life in later days. (iii) Wild's opinion about the republication has been answered with care by Jessop, who after some detailed discussion remarks:

His [Wild's] theory can only be made intelligible on the assumption that a thinker means what he says the first time he says it but not when he repeats it after further years of reflection.[4]

(iv) The question of development is more subtle: Wild seems to have made an important point here. Luce would not agree[5]: he gives the impression of holding that there was no development in Berkeley, no change of attitude, and no change of

---

[1] Naguib Baladi, *La pensée religieuse de Berkeley et l'unité de sa philosophie*, Le Caire, 1945.

[2] John Wild, "The Unity of the Berkeleian Philosophy", *Mind*, London, 1937, N.S. Vol. XLVI, No. clxxxiv, p. 457.

[3] *Works*, III, *Siris*, §§ 253, 254, 289, 293, 294, 303-5, 355.

[4] T. E. Jessop, "*George Berkeley: A study of his Life and Philosophy*. By John Wild." *Mind*, London, 1937, N.S. Vol. XLVI, No. clxxxii, pp. 234-5.

[5] A. A. Luce, "The Alleged Development of Berkeley's Philosophy", *Mind*, London, 1943, N.S. Vol. LII, No. ccvi.

emphasis placed on the various aspects of the philosophy, but that Berkeley clung to his views as to dogma.*

Wild, on the other hand, considers that

It is not so much that new doctrines are substituted for old, as that old truths or partial truths are seen in a new light.[1]

There is nothing incompatible, however, in agreeing with Luce that Berkeley maintained one considered philosophy unchanged, which is all the evidence shows, and holding with Wild that there was some development, for there was in Berkeley undoubtedly a change of attitude and tone, and a change in the aspects of his philosophy to receive emphasis. This change is in fact mentioned by Luce's co-editor, Jessop.† I venture to think that this controversy can be resolved in one statement:— In the days of *Siris* Berkeley retained intellectual acceptance of his early Immaterialism without the emotions that brought it to birth; Immaterialism, which had been a living faith to him and entered the very "fabric of his mind",[2] was now but a dogma.

It would be well to conclude by stressing certain findings. There were not two philosophies, one early and one late, but only one. Berkeley's last writing was not Platonist, nor were his early writings solipsistic. His one philosophy was an Immaterialism that was fundamentally theocentric.

Summary

Berkeley's early philosophy was traditionally regarded as subjectivist or solipsist. During this century the belief grew that his last work, *Siris*, was Platonist, theocentric, and objectivist—*Esse percipi* seemed to be discounted. Examination reveals (1) that the arguments to show that he retracted his early views are groundless; (2) that the late work, though theocentric, did not

---

* Luce, moreover, gives the impression that this was to Berkeley's credit; but surely Berkeley would have been still greater if he had it in him to change his mind?

[1] Wild, *Op. cit.*, p. 461.

† Jessop writes: "*Siris* undoubtedly represents a big change of mood, interest, and emphasis" (though he adds, "neither Professor Luce nor I can see in it any change of basic doctrine"), *Works*, II, p. 7.

[2] Luce, "The Unity of the Berkeleian Philosophy (I)", as cited, p. 49; *cf.* "The Unity of the Berkeleian Philosophy (II)", as cited, p. 181.

retract *Esse percipi*, and was therefore not Platonist; and (3) that the early work was not solipsistic, but theocentric.

His 'considered' view was thus one and unchanging. But there was great change of attitude, mood, tone, and interest. He continued to believe *Esse percipi*; but it was no longer the driving force of his metaphysic.

Chapter 6

HAD BERKELEY TWO SIMULTANEOUS PHILOSOPHIES?

IT was important to establish what views Berkeley intended to expound at different times in his life. I would submit nevertheless that the controversy about the unity of his philosophy should have focused on another issue as well, one that is no less important. I would suggest that there are two philosophies in the *Principles* (and *Three Dialogues*): the considered philosophy of Theocentric Phenomenalism and the traditionally attributed Solipsism.

By this it is not meant that Berkeley consciously held both; if he had been a solipsist he would hardly have written down his thoughts for publication if there was no one to read them. We cannot therefore expect to find an unambiguous statement of this standpoint, and in fact, after careful consideration, I have come to the conclusion that there is no single statement in the *Principles* that when properly understood implies the position. There are certainly large numbers that seem to: those that ask what we perceive besides our own ideas or sensations *suggest* that the philosopher cannot penetrate outside the circle of his immediate sensory-impressions. Those that argue that the apple or the cherry consist only of sensory-ideas carry the same suggestion. Nonetheless the account given in Chaper 2 makes it plain that the privacy of sensory-ideas does not imply Solipsism, so long as *percipi* is an *indispensable* but not a *sufficient* condition of such ideas. Two passages from the *Principles* may be noticed that suggest the position more strongly than most:

§ 45 . . . it will be objected that from the foregoing principles it follows, things are every moment annihilated and created anew . . . [I desire the reader] he will consider whether he means any thing, by the actual existence of an idea, distinct from its being perceived.

§ 46 It is thought strangely absurd that upon closing my eyelids, all the visible objects round me should be reduced to nothing; and yet is not this what philosophers commonly acknowledge, when they agree on all hands, that light and colours, which alone are the proper and immediate objects of sight, are mere sensations that exist no longer than they are perceived? Again, it may to some perhaps seem very incredible, that things should be every moment creating, yet this very notion is commonly taught in the Schools.

It is worth while pointing out that these statements are perfectly consistent with Phenomenalism, for the *esse* is annihilated and created anew, *i.e.* in the fundamental sense of "*esse*", and it is simply in the secondary sense of "*posse*" that thing-ideas persist.

Before proceeding to the grounds that seem to indicate Solipsism in the *Principles* and *Three Dialogues*, we must consider the conception of archtype and ectype.

Berkeley allowed, albeit grudgingly, that our ideas are ectypes of archtypes that are in the mind of God:

The former was created in time; the latter existed from everlasting in the mind of God.[1]

When his American correspondent, Johnson, wrote to him about this, he replied:

I have no objection against calling the ideas in the mind of God archetypes of ours. But I object against those archetypes by philosophers supposed to be real things, and to have an absolute rational existence distinct from their being perceived by any mind whatsoever.[2]

The distinction between 'archetype' and 'ectype' could be used to describe the relation in Plato's philosophy between the eternal ideas and natural objects as one of archetype to ectype or copy. Now as is clearly shown from the quotations, Berkeley meant nothing of this kind. But it was not unnatural to interpret the archetype of a thing-idea in the divine mind and the ectype perceived by a human being as separate entities; and in fact this was the gist of Johnson's letters.* That this is untrue to

---

[1] *Works*, II, *Three Dialogues between Hylas and Philonous*, Dial. III, p. 254.

[2] *Id.*, Berkeley to Johnson, p. 292.

* Johnson's perplexity is to be respected. He undoubtedly made a mistake, but a very natural one, as Berkeley had given grounds for misunderstanding, and he expressed his point of view exceedingly well. The student of Berkeley should certainly read the relevant passages, especially in Johnson's second letter.

Berkeley's intention is beyond doubt; it is also untrue to his philosophy on either interpretation, provided ideas are *causari* and not *percipi* by God. Berkeley agreed with Johnson that the terminology could be used—provided it were not abused. What he opposed was the conception that there were, say, *two* reds, an archetype-red in the mind of God and an ectype-red depending on finite perception; what he would grant was that there was *one* red, which was an archetype in the sense that it was sustained by the divine mind, *i.e.* was a possibility of being caused to be an ectype in the sense of *percipi* by human beings. Clearly the terminology either changes his philosophy if abused or adds nothing new if rightly used; and as a means of solving the problem of identity it only restates the problem in a new form. I would agree with Luce that though Berkeley sanctioned the terminology he did not like it; doubtless he saw that it contributed little or nothing and was likely to mislead.

If, however, the correct interpretation of Berkeley is that ideas are *causari* and not *percipi* by God, then the concept of archetype was wholly superfluous. Why, then, did he introduce it? There appear to be two reasons. In one argument to establish divine existence, he stated that ideas are *perceived* by God, and this would render archetypes in some sense relevant*; here we can see how an unsatisfactory argument may lead to further difficulties. But his main reason for introducing the archetype is probably to be found in his reference to it at the end of his discussion of sameness, where he remarked that it served "all the ends of identity".[1]

Grounds for attributing Solipsism to the early philosophy may now be put forward:—

(1) Theocentric Phenomenalism, according to which thing-ideas display a sensory-idea caused by God in appropriate circumstances, or the *percipi posse* part of it, certainly means that, in the basic sense in which a sensory-idea 'exists', nothing 'exists' when no human observer perceives it (a thing-idea 'exists' only in the derivative sense that sensory-ideas can become existents

---

* Thus the introduction of 'archetype' might be held to support the view that ideas are *perceived* by God.

[1] *Works*, II, *Three Dialogues between Hylas and Philonous*, Dial. III, p. 248.

in the basic sense); in other words, in this basic sense of "exist", there is intermittent existence of sensory-ideas. The appropriate regularity of their becoming existent is caused by God. No archetype is relevant, and it would be bizarre to speak either of *percipi posse* or of divine action in causing ideas as archetypal.

In line with this, and from Berkeley's own statements, we must take his considered opinion to be that the terminology of "archetype" and "ectype" merely said, though not so well, what he had said in other ways. Now the proper course would have been to state what the terminology ordinarily meant, to point out that it had never been used in a sense appropriate to his philosophy, and therefore to deny the existence of archetypes. But Berkeley did not take this course: he simply allowed the terminology, entering a *caveat* against interpretations of a rationalistic or Platonic kind, which was a queer procedure in view of its inappropriateness, not to mention the difficulty of finding a suitable interpretation for the conception.

This suggests that Berkeley had doubts about the doctrine of divine causation, which renders the conception of archetypes superfluous. It is difficult to escape the presumption that he relapsed into the plain man's feeling that permanence had gone from things. His 'considered' view was that thing-ideas were preserved in God, in the sense that God would cause appropriate sensory-ideas to appear; but it looks as though Berkeley felt a need to have thing-ideas literally preserved in God. And this is borne out by one of his proofs of divine existence, according to which ideas are necessarily perceived by God. And the need to give thing-ideas a literal permanence would arise because without it he might well have felt that there would be only intermittent existents, *i.e.* a purely solipsistic world.

(2) The doctrine of archetypes arose in part in connexion with one of the proofs of divine existence. There is a strong presumption that he was uneasy about this proof, which made the doctrine of archetypes unavoidable. In fact the proof is bizarre. The short central statement in it, that ideas are necessarily perceived by God, is presented as a tautology; now most tautologies are either intuitively recognisable as such or (with sufficient skill) demonstrable, but this statement is not recognisably a tautology and it remains undemonstrated. Thus the presump-

tion is that Berkeley, with his acute logical sense, was uneasy about its validity. But it was felt to be a key-point in his philosophy and without it his metaphysic is near to Solipsism.

(3) Commentators have usually held that Berkeley's treatment of identity was the weakest link in his system. This link could have been made strong, but, as Berkeley left it, it was undeniably weak. Moreover, he sheared off the subject in his correspondence with Johnson. Thus he had his doubts about it. Now failure to establish it would render the philosophy solipsistic. Thus his uneasiness about this link indicates a doubt in his mind about whether he had avoided Solipsism.

(4) Berkeley failed to bring out adequately the distinction between *percipi* and *percipi posse*; the relation between the two conditions for existence, namely *percipi* and *causari*; and the distinction between necessary and sufficient conditions of a sensory-idea. Is this simply because of the style of the time or does it point to confusion? Passages discussing annihilation and creation would not give the impression of Solipsism if he had directed the reader's attention to his implied distinction between *esse* and *posse*; his failure to do so suggests that at the moment he had forgotten about the *posse* or else was prepared to let the reader forget about it, and thus portrayed Solipsism.

He could also have dealt with the point by means of the causation of God, but his handling of it *suggests* that the percipient causes the annihilation and creation, and, though he cannot have deliberately meant this, he took little trouble to guard against conveying this impression. The doctrine of causation occurs somewhat late in his exposition; he failed to relate it to initial discussion of perception where it would have been particularly relevant. There he only used phrases like "in the mind" or "known" or "subsists", which without the distinction between *percipi* and *causari* naturally leads to the distinction between archetype and ectype and thence to Solipsism.

Failure to distinguish carefully between necessary and sufficient conditions naturally leads to the tacit assumption that ideas depend upon the human percipient and upon nothing else. It is virtually made in § 26, but Berkeley did not bring out the vital significance of it. Moreover, this allusion occurs somewhat late in his exposition; a totally different impression of his thesis would have been given if he had brought it in early, before the attack on Matter. For this reason the opening sections, which are concerned with *Esse percipi*, strongly convey the impression that an *esse* depends wholly upon being perceived.* § 26 admits that some further causal factor is required—too late to undo the previous impression conveyed. Put another way, it was fatal for Berkeley in the early sections to expound his doctrine as *Esse percipi* because in fact it was not this at all but the doctrine that an *esse* is a human perception caused by God. He leaves the reader under the impression that perceiving suffices for existence, which is Solipsism, and the presumption is that this displays an unrecognised attitude of his own.

Broadly speaking, then, in this context it was not what Berkeley said but what he failed to say and the arrangement of his material that suggests Solipsism.

(5) Apart from some striking exceptions, most philosophers have interpreted the *Principles* as Solipsism. Is this to be attributed to stupidity and lack of care, or was there not some excuse for it, if not in what was expressed by Berkeley, in the tone, tenor, and arrangement of the writing and the absence of certain key distinctions? It took Luce immense pains and long research to establish the considered philosophy as representing what Berkeley intended to express; would he have discovered this had he not noticed the extraordinary way in which he found Berkeley's views, illustrations, and phrases turning up in Malebranche? It is easy for us, now that Luce's work has been done, to see Theocentric Phenomenalism in the *Principles*—it is easy to be wise after the event; but was it possible to see this before the link with Malebranche was established? A few did so; but it is significant that Mabbot felt he had to argue very hard for the interpretation. I submit that commentators, who have been blind to the considered philosophy, have correctly interpreted the underlying spirit of what they read.

It may be added that the solipsistic outlook was not foreign to Berkeley, for it is overt in the *Philosophical Commentaries*.

---

* *Cf.* Metz's remark, "Wenn die Gleichung esse = percipi richtig ist, so werden die Dinge bei jeden Wahrnehmung gleichsam aus dem Nichts neu erschaffen und sinken mit dem Aufhören der Wahrnehmung in das Nichts zurück" (Rudolf Metz, *George Berkeley*, Stuttgart, 1925, S. 116.)

If this contention is correct it becomes easy to understand why students of Berkeley usually find him bewildering; for the solipsistic outlook seeps through continually all the more powerful and perplexing because unsanctioned by its author.

The result of this chapter may be put briefly thus: Berkeley strove to expound a philosophy of Theocentric Phenomenalism, though with only partial success, while he succeeded at the same time in portraying a philosophy of Solipsism.

Chapter 7

THE TAR-WATER PHILOSOPHY

WHEN he was nearing sixty, Berkeley wrote the most remarkable work ever penned by a modern philosopher, a mystical writing called *Siris: A Chain of Philosophical Reflexions and Inquiries concerning the Virtues of Tar-Water*.[1] Its importance lies in the insight it enables us to gain into the author's mind; it is thus complementary to the *Philosophical Commentaries*.

Its poor arrangement does not make it easy to describe; but, if it is usually desirable that a reader should have before him a description of a work that is under discussion, it is more than ever necessary in this instance.

The work is somewhat over one hundred pages in length and is divided into three hundred and sixty-eight numbered paragraphs. Since there are no separate chapters or even section headings, it takes one's breath away to begin with a medical prescription and details for the apothecary and to be led by swift stages through biology, chemistry, and mythology to theosophy. For convenience I will divide the work roughly into parts, though this will not disclose overlapping and repetition.

In §§ 1 to 28, which deal with tar-water and tar, Berkeley begins by laying down with the utmost exactitude the recipe for making the brew:

§ 1 Pour a gallon of cold water on a quart of tar, and stir (work,) and mix them thoroughly (together), with a (wooden) ladle or flat stick, for the space of three or four (five or six) minutes, after which the vessel must stand (close covered and unmoved) eight and forty hours that the tar may have (full) time to subside; when the clear water (having been first carefully skimmed without shaking the vessel) is to be poured off and kept covered (in bottles well stopped) for use, no more being made from the same tar, which may still serve for common purposes.*

[1] *Works*, V, which contains all Berkeley's writings on tar-water.
* The words in brackets are either alterations in or additions to the text of the early editions.

In later editions the mixture recommended is stronger, in "A Letter to Thomas Prior Esq.," more care is given to the prescription,[1] and in "Farther Thoughts on Tar-Water" further directions are given for its preparation.[2] The care he bestowed on every detail is clearly evident from his admonishments to Prior:

It is to be noted, that tar-water is best made in glazed earthen vessels. I would have the foregoing sentence inserted in the English edition, and next Irish edition of the letter, at the end of the section that recites the manner of making tar-water. It is very lately I made this remark, that it is finer and clearer when so made than if in unglazed crocks.[3]

Berkeley believed that tar-water was a panacea for all ills, though he was cautious about saying so. He used it successfully in cases of small-pox,[4] eruptions, ulcers, the "foulest distempers",[5] ulceration of the bowels, consumptive cough, pleurisy, erysipelas,[6] indigestion, and asthma. It was a "a powerful and safe deobstruent", *i.e.* something that opened the pores and allowed waste-products to pass, it was good for gravel in the urine and for dropsy.[7] Thus in *Siris*:

§ 55 Another way wherein tar-water operates is by urine, than which perhaps none is more safe and effectual for cleansing the blood and carrying off its salts. But it seems to produce its principal effect as an alterative, sure and easy, much safer than those vehement, purgative, emetic, and salivating medicines, which do violence to nature.

It was excellent for piles,[8] as an eye-wash, good for gums, and effective as a gargle. And there are many other references scattered throughout his writings on tar-water concerning its wonderful virtues. In the first letter to Prior, it is well-nigh a panacea:

[1] "First Letter to Thomas Prior", § 2.
[2] "Farther Thoughts on Tar-Water", p. 207.
[3] In correspondence with Prior: Fraser, *Life and Letters of George Berkeley*, Oxford, 1871, p. 300.
[4] *Siris*, § 2.   [5] *Id.*, § 4.   [6] *Id.*, § 5.   [7] *Id.*, § 6.
[8] "A Second Letter to Thomas Prior", § 15.

§ 11 Now, to speak out, and give this objection or question a direct answer, I freely own that I suspect tar-water is a panacea. I may be mistaken, but it is worth trial: for the chance of so great and general benefit, I am willing to stand the ridicule of proposing it. And as the old philosopher cried aloud from the house-tops to his fellow-citizens, "Educate your children", so, I confess, if I had a situation high enough, and a voice loud enough, I would cry out to all the valetudinarians upon earth, Drink tar-water.

§ 12 Having thus frankly owned the charge, I must explain to you that by a panacea is not meant a medicine which cures all individuals (this consists not with mortality), but a medicine that cures or relieves all the different species of distempers.

§ 20 Howbeit, those theories, as I said, enlarged my views of this medicine, led me to a greater variety of trials, and thereby engendered and nourished my suspicion that it is a panacea.

It is only later that Berkeley makes the slightest admission that tar-water can fail to function in the smallest degree. When a patient took too much and was wrought violently, according to the second letter to Prior, it still did its work:

§ 2 which shews that errors and excesses in tar-water are not so dangerous as in other medicines.

§ 5 Tar-water seldom fails to cure, or relieve, when rightly made of good tar, and duly taken.

Usually it is an excellent aperient. Since, however,

§ 20 tar-water worketh much by perspiration, the body may chance to be bound. But such symptom, though it should be attended with a little more than ordinary warmth, need not be dreaded by the patient, it being only a sign that his cure is carried on by driving the peccant matter through the skin, which is one of the ways whereby tar-water worketh its effect.

Again it has a marvellous power of varying its working, provided it is not interrupted by other medicines.[1]

A patient who drinks tar-water must not be alarmed at pustules or eruptions in the skin; these are good symptoms, and shew the impurities of the blood to be cast out.

[1] "A [Third] Letter to Thomas Prior", p. 194.

A person who had been in a bad state of health above twenty years, upon a course of tar-water was thrown into a most extraordinary fit of an ague, and from that time recovered a good state of health.[1]

Thus there was scarcely the shadow of a doubt about the merit of tar-water at the back of Berkeley's mind; on the few occasions when it was not perfectly successful, the reason was either that it was improperly made, or that its action was interfered with, and so on; when the brew failed it was not really tar-water.

We learn incidentally that in Egypt there was a practice of embalming dead bodies with tar[2]: thus it possessed the important power of being a preservative.

In the rest of this part of *Siris* Berkeley cites many authorities, both Greek and modern, on the places and trees in which tar is to be found.

§ 16 Some modern writers inform us that tar flows from the trunks of pines and firs, when they are very old, through incisions made in the bark near the root; that pitch is tar inspissated [thickened]; and both are the oil of the tree grown thick and ripened with age and sun. The trees, like old men, being unable to perspire, and their secretory ducts obstructed, they are, as one may say, choked and stuffed with their own juice.

He passes in §§ 29–41 to questions of biology, such as how sap and juices circulate in plants and trees, and thence in §§ 40–6 to the spirit of the balsam.

§ 40 And as from Sir Isaac Newton's experiment it appears that all colours are virtually in the white light of the sun, and shew themselves when the rays are separated by the attracting and repelling powers of objects, even so the specific qualities of the elaborate juices of plants seem to be virtually or eminently in the solar light, and are actually exhibited upon the separation of the rays, by the peculiar powers of the capillary organs in vegetables, attracting and imbibing certain rays, which produce certain flavours and qualities, in like manner as certain rays, being reflected, produce certain colours.[3]

Thus light is the basis of organic variety; some of this smacks of mysticism in a scientific dress.

[1] "Farther Thoughts on Tar-Water", p. 215.
[2] *Siris*, § 15.   [3] *Cf.* § 165.

§ 42 The balsam or essential oil of vegetables contains a spirit, wherein consist the specific qualities, the smell and taste, of the plant. Boerhaave holds the native presiding spirit to be neither oil, salt, earth, or water; but somewhat too fine and subtle to be caught alone and rendered visible to the eye. This, when suffered to fly off, for instance from the oil of rosemary, leaves it destitute of all flavour. This spark of life, this spirit or soul, if we may so say, of the vegetable departs without any sensible diminution of the oil or water wherein it was lodged.

§ 43 It should seem that the forms, souls, or principles of vegetable life subsist in the light or solar emanation. . . .

§ 44 The luminous spirit which is the form or life of a plant, from whence its differences and properties flow, is somewhat extremely volatile. It is not the oil, but a thing more subtle, whereof oil is the vehicle, which retains it from flying off, and is lodged in several parts of the plant, particularly in the cells of the bark and in the seeds. This oil, purified and exalted by the organical powers of the plant, and agitated by warmth, becomes a proper receptacle of spirit; part of which spirit exhales through the leaves and flowers, and part is arrested by this unctuous humour that detains it in the plant. It is to be noted this essential oil, animated, as one may say, with the flavour of the plant, is very different from any spirit that can be procured from the same plant by fermentation.

Then follows a long part from § 47 to § 120 on the medical virtues of tar-water, wherein it is compared with other remedies to their disadvantage.

Berkeley's Cosmology

He now turns to elaborate in detail the essence of tar-water. This part, §§ 121–230, discusses acids and salts, air, and fire.

§ 121 The distinguishing principle of all vegetables, that whereon their peculiar smell, taste, and specific properties depend—seems to be some extremely fine and subtle spirit, whose immediate vehicle is an exceeding thin volatile oil; which is itself detained in a grosser and more viscid resin or balsam, lodged in proper cells in the bark and seeds, and most abounding in autumn or winter, after the crude juices have been thoroughly concocted, ripened, and impregnated with solar light. The spirit itself is by some supposed to be an oil highly subtilized, so as to mix with water. But such volatile oil is not the spirit, but only its vehicle, since aromatic oils being long exposed to air will lose their specific smell and taste, which fly off with the spirit or vegetable salt, without any sensible diminution of the oil.

§ 122   Those volatile salts that are set free and raised by a gentle heat may justly be supposed essential, and to have pre-existed in the vegetable.

§ 123   The most volatile of all salts, and the most attenuated part of the oil may be supposed the first and readiest to impregnate a cold infusion. And this will assist us to account for the virtues of tar-water. That volatile acid in vegetables which resists putrefaction and is their great preservative is detained in a subtle oil miscible with water, which oil is itself imprisoned in the resin or grosser part of the tar, from which it is easily set free and obtained pure by cold water.

§ 126   Sir Isaac Newton, Boerhaave, and Homberg, are all agreed that the acid is a fine subtle substance, pervading the whole terra-queous globe; which produceth divers kinds of bodies, as it is united to different subjects. This, according to Homberg, is the pure salt, salt the principle, in itself similar and uniform, but never found alone. And although this principle be called the salt of the earth, yet it should seem it may more properly be called the salt of the air, since earth turned up and lying fallow receives it from the air. And it should seem that this is the great principle of vegetation, derived into the earth from all sorts of manures as well as from the air.

Berkeley's thought passes from tar-water to a fine subtle spirit, which is a volatile salt. Again the volatile acid in vegetables is a fine subtle substance, which is salt or a salt principle.

§ 127   It is the doctrine of Sir Isaac Newton and Monsieur Homberg that, as the watery acid is that which renders salt soluble in water, so it is the same which joined to the earthy part makes it a salt. Let it therefore be considered that the organs of plants are tubes, the filling, unfolding, and distending whereof, by liquors doth constitute what is called the vegetation or growth of the plant. But earth itself is not soluble in water, so as to form one vegetable fluid therewith. Therefore the particles of earth must be joined with a watery acid; that is, they must become salts, in order to dissolve in water, that so, in the form of a vegetable juice, they may pass through the strainers and tubes of the root into the body of the plant, swelling and distending its parts and organs, that is, increasing its bulk. Therefore the vegetable matter of the earth is in effect earth changed into salt. And to render earth fertile is to cause many of its particles to assume a saline form.

Having progressed to salt, he attributes its virtues to its fertilising power—an idea amply confirmed in a remarkable essay
by Ernest Jones, in which he traces in folk-lore thoroughly and
conclusively the common superstition about spilling salt to its
unrecognised significance as a fertilising principle.[1] Berkeley's
epithet for the acid spirit or salt, "that mighty instrument in the
hand of nature",[2] well expresses his feelings in the matter. He
develops this in *Siris*:

§ 128 Hence it is observed, there are more salts in the root than
in the bark, more salts in vegetables during the spring than in the
autumn or winter, the crude saline juices being in the summer
months partly evaporated, and partly ripened, by the action and
mixture of light. Hence also it appears why the dividing of earth,
so as to enlarge its surface, whereby it may admit more acid from
the air, is of such use in promoting vegetation; and why ashes, lime,
and burnt clay are found so profitable manures—fire being in reality
the acid, as is proved in the sequel. Marls also and shells are useful,
forasmuch as those alkaline bodies attract the acid, and raise an
effervescence with it, thereby promoting a fermentation in the glebe.
The excrements of animals and putrid vegetables do in like manner
contribute to vegetation, by increasing the salts of the earth. And
where fallows are well broken, and lie long to receive the acid of
the air into all their parts; this alone will be sufficient to change
many terrene particles into salts, and consequently render them
soluble in water, and therefore a fit aliment for vegetables.

Here Berkeley develops the idea in more detail. It is interesting
to note that animal excrement can produce this fertiliser.

His next ideas, which would seem to have no relevance, is
most striking. Noting that it is impossible to find a law deter-
mining the shape of salt crystals,[3] he cites Homberg in *Siris* as
holding that

§ 132 acids are shaped like daggers, and alkalies like sheathes, and
that, moving in the same liquor, the daggers run into the sheaths
fitted to receive them with such violence as to raise that affervescence
observed in the mixture of acids and alkalies.

Thus the acid contains the male principle, and that acid was

---

[1] Ernest Jones, *Essays in Applied Psycho-Analysis*, London, 1951, Vol.
II, "The Symbolic Significance of Salt in Folklore and Superstition".
[2] *Siris*, § 135.   [3] *Id.*, § 131.

identified with salt, so that once again salt is regarded as mascu-
line. But Berkeley does not accept this:

§ 132 it seems very difficult to conceive how or why the mere
configuration of daggers and sheaths floating in the same liquor
should cause the former to rush with such vehemence, and direct
their points so aptly into the latter, any more than a parcel of
spigots and fossets floating together in the same water should rush
one into the other.

He thinks that Newton's explanation of this phenomenon is
better,

§ 133 whereby he supposeth them to rush towards, penetrate,
shake, and divide the most solid bodies, and to ferment the liquid of
vegetables. . . . It is in this attraction that Sir Isaac placeth all their
activity: and indeed it should seem, the figures of salts were not of
such efficacy in producing their effects, as the strong active powers
whereby they are agitated and do agitate other bodies; especially if
it be true (what was before remarked) that lixivious salts are alike
purgative, whatever may be the shape of their angles, whether more
or less acute or obtuse.

Thus what weighs with him is a cleansing principle rather than
a fertilising one.
 Berkeley now comes to the importance of air.

§ 137 These native spirits or vegetable souls are all breathed or
exhaled into the air, which seems the receptacle as well as source of
all sublunary forms.

§ 138 Thus iron and copper are corroded and gather rust in the
air, and bodies of all sorts are dissolved or corrupted, which sheweth
an acid to abound and diffuse itself throughout the air.

§ 141 Virgin earth becomes fertile, crops of new plants ever and
anon shew themselves; all which demonstrates the air to be a common
seminary and receptacle of all vivifying principles.

§ 140 The air therefore is an active mass of numberless different
principles, the general source of corruption and generation; on one
hand dividing, abrading, and carrying off the particles of bodies,
that is, corrupting or dissolving them; on the other, producing new
ones into being; destroying and bestowing forms without inter-
mission.

Thus air, like salt, stands for a generative principle—an idea
also widely found in mythology.

Further

§ 143 it gives and preserves a proper tone to the vessels: this elastic fluid promotes all secretions: its oscillations keep every part in motion.

Thus, like salt, it conduces to health by keeping the bodily functions in order.

Now there is

§ 144 some one quality or ingredient in the air, on which life more immediately and principally depends.

§ 145 Air, the general menstruum and seminary, seemeth to be only an aggregate of the volatile parts of all natural beings, which, variously combined and agitated, produce many various effects. . . . Being pent up in the viscera, vessels, and membranes of the body, by its salts, sulphurs, and elastic power, it engenders cholics, spasms, hysteric disorders, and other maladies.

That is, air contains not only the seeds of health but also of misfortune.

Berkeley cites Heraclitus "that the death of fire was a birth to air"—noting that "this opinion is also maintained by Sir Isaac Newton". He places the essence of air in fire:

§ 147 Upon the whole, it is manifest that air is no distinct element, but a mass or mixture of things the most heterogeneous and even opposite to each other, which become air by acquiring an elasticity and volatility from the attraction of some active subtle substance, whether it be called fire, æther, light, or the vital spirit of the world.

And he concludes:

§ 151 Æther, fire or spirit, being attracted and clogged by heterogeneous particles, becometh less active; and the particles cohering with those of æther become more active than before. Air therefore is a mass of various particles, abraded and sublimated from wet and dry bodies of all sorts, cohering with particles of æther; the whole permeated by pure æther, or light, or fire—for these words are used promiscuously by ancient philosophers.

Thus acid and salt derive their power from the air; air is an alloy of gross and fine parts, the latter being its active principle; and the pure, volatile element is fire:

§ 152 If air be the immediate agent or instrument in natural things, it is the pure invisible fire that is the first natural mover or spring from whence the air derives its power,

Fire receives a long discussion of some twenty-five pages, from § 149 to § 217.

§ 152 This Æther or pure invisible Fire, the most subtle and elastic, of all bodies, seems to pervade and expand itself throughout the whole universe.

§ 158 There is no effect in nature, great, marvellous, or terrible, but proceeds from fire, that diffused and active principle, which, at the same time that it shakes the earth and heavens, will enter, divide, and dissolve the smallest, closest, and most compacted bodies. In remote cavities of the earth it remains quiet, till perhaps an accidental spark, from the collision of one stone against another, kindles an exhalation that gives birth to an earthquake or tempest which splits mountains or overturns cities. This same fire stands unseen in the focus of a burning glass, till subjects for it to act upon come in its way, when it is found to melt, calcine, or vitrify the hardest bodies.

His cosmology is that of Heraclitus. He contends that pure fire is the divinely operated instrument for bringing about all natural change.[1] He cites many authorities among the Greeks, Egyptians, Hebrews, Chinese, and others to this effect.[2] Thus

§ 186 It must be owned there are many passages in the Holy Scripture that would make one think the supreme Being was in a peculiar manner present and manifest in the element of fire. Not to insist that God is more than once said to be a consuming fire, which might be understood in a metaphorical sense; the divine apparitions were by fire, in the bush, at Mount Sinai, on the tabernacle, in the cloven tongues. God is represented in the inspired writings, as descending in fire, as attended by fire, or with fire going before Him.

He mentions that according to the Stoics fire embraced the spermatic forms of all things[3]; he thus confirms that fire, like salt and air, contains the principle of fertilisation.

Berkeley next points out the need for distinguishing

§ 190 a pure elementary invisible fire from the culinary, or that which appears in ignite bodies. This last they will not allow to be pure fire. The pure fire is to be discerned by its effects alone, such as heat, dilation of all solid bodies, and rarefaction of fluids, the segregating heterogeneous bodies, and congregating those that are homogeneous. That therefore which smokes and flames is not pure fire,

[1] *Id.*, § 154. [2] *Id.*, § 180. [3] *Id.*, § 229.

but that which is collected in the focus of a concave mirror or burning glass.

§ 192 Fire, therefore, in the sense of philosophers, is always fire, though not always flame.[1]

The all-pervading quality of ethereal fire he illustrates by the observation that bodies attract light, so that

§ 193 fire without burning is an ingredient in many things, as water without wetting.

In support of this he cites an experiment of Homberg's, "who made gold of mercury by introducing light into its pores."[2] Thus gold contains latent fire. He accepts the conclusion of Ficinus that light is incorporeal, one of the more notable reasons being that "light cannot be defiled by filth of any kind",[3] with which may be compared the statement that

§ 182 the cleansing quality, the light and heat of fire, are natural symbols of purity, knowledge, and power.

Clearly fire and light are more or less identified in this context; further evidence of their identification is to be found in the statement:

§ 229 As the forms of things have their ideal existence in the intellect, so it should seem that seminal principles have their natural existence in the light.

The upshot, so far as his biology is concerned, is that

§ 214 The principles of motion and vegetation in living bodies seem to be delibations from the invisible fire or spirit of the universe, which though present to all things, is not nevertheless one way received by all, but variously imbibed, attracted, and secreted, by the fine capillaries and exquisite strainers in the bodies of plants and animals, whereby it becomes mixed and detained in their juices.

To summarise the position with regard to tar-water: it is the sweat of trees, which contains pure volatile acid or salt; this comes from the air, the pure element of which derives its power from fire—ethereal, elementary fire, not flame (at each stage a division is made between the gross or visible and the pure or

[1] Cf. § 201.　　　[2] Id., § 194.　　　[3] Id., § 206.

invisible): finally this fire is divine. The universal virtue of tar-water is thus accounted for, since it contains a divine infusion. Tar-water, like salt, light, fire, is a purifier, a cleanser, and fertilising principle. He leaves it with the description that it has a nature so mild and benign as "to cheer but not inebriate",[1] the forerunner of Cowper's well-known lines.

This long account of Berkeley's primitive cosmology is needed because it is essential for an understanding of his mind that the reader should see for himself the depth of mystical outlook it contains. Apart from the camouflage of contemporary science with which he presents his theme, this part of *Siris* might have been written two thousand years earlier. The tacit assumption, made throughout, that agreement by different peoples about a myth is evidence that the myth describes a feature of the natural world, is extraordinary; it does not seem to have occurred to him that all the agreement establishes is the fundamental simi-larity among different peoples of human mentality in its deeper layers.

Berkeley next treats of motion, from § 230 to § 272, the thesis being that God, through (it would seem) the instrumentality of elemental fire, is the sole cause of motion, and that natural events form a language wherein one can read of God. This part is ill-arranged and rambling. Its significance is that it re-affirms the thesis of his *De Motu* (1721), and *The Theory of Vision Vindicated and Explained* (1733). Thus *Siris* was not a reversal of the philosophy of his prime; nor is it to be regarded as a product of his dotage, seeing that his grasp of the principles of *De Motu* is unimpaired. *Siris* has to be taken as a seriously written work, which asserts the mystical principle of divine fire, alongside his philosophy, which was written when he was a man of keen in-tellect, very much alive to the affairs of the world.

The final part, from § 273 to § 368, is again mystical, and of importance to our understanding of Berkeley's mind. The first of the two main ideas is the

---

[1] *Id.*, § 217.

§ 274 received notion of the Pythagoreans and Platonics, that there is no chasm in nature, but a Chain or Scale of beings rising by gentle uninterrupted gradations from the lowest to the highest, each nature being informed and perfected by the participation of a higher. As air becomes igneous, so the purest fire becomes animal, and the animal soul becomes intellectual: which is to be understood not of the change of one nature into another, but of the connexion of different natures, each lower nature being, according to those philosophers, as it were a receptacle or subject for the next above it to reside and act in.

This is expressed more fully as follows:

§ 303 The perceptions of sense are gross; but even in the senses there is a difference. Though harmony and proportion are not objects of sense, yet the eye and the ear are organs which offer to the mind such materials by means whereof she may apprehend both the one and the other. By experiments of sense we become acquainted with the lower faculties of the soul; and from them, whether by a gradual evolution or ascent, we arrive at the highest. Sense supplies images to memory. These become subjects for fancy to work upon. Reason considers and judges of the imaginations. And these acts of reason become new objects to the understanding. In this scale, each lower faculty is a step that leads to one above it. And the uppermost naturally leads to the Deity, which is rather the object of intellectual knowledge than even of the discursive faculty, not to mention the sensitive. There runs a chain throughout the whole system of beings. In this chain one link drags another. The meanest things are connected with the highest.

The universe is united by a divine harmony:

§ 279 as life holds together the bodies of animals, the cause whereof is the soul, and as a city is held together by concord, the cause whereof is law, even so the world is held together by harmony, the cause whereof is God. And in this sense the world or universe may be considered either as one animal or one city.

And again,

§ 328 Aristotle declares that the divine force or influence permeates the entire universe, and that what the pilot is in a ship, the driver in a chariot, the precentor in a choir, the law in a city, the general in an army, the same God is in the world.

In addition to the notion of a great chain of being, divinely harmonised by the ultimate cause of all process at the top of the chain, is that of a *world-soul*. This is not, however, an expression of Pantheism, but the reverse, Panentheism, for the soul of the world "doth embrace all its parts",[1] and

§ 285 those who, not content with sensible appearances, would penetrate into the real and true causes (the object of theology, metaphysics, or the *philosophia prima*), will rectify this error, and speak of the world as contained by the soul, and not the soul by the world.

The bulk of this part, of some twenty-five pages, is taken up with long citations of the opinions of the ancients about the existence of God and the unity of existence; its object seems to be to add the weight of philosophical authority to his cosmology.

The significance of this inverted Pantheism is as follows. It is in line with his earlier considered philosophy, inspired by Malebranche. But there is an important psychological difference in the nature of his belief at these two periods: his earlier theocentric philosophy did not animate him with the same deep intensity as his unavowed Solipsism; but the later doctrine of the world soul undoubtedly came straight from his inmost being, undistorted by conscious thought, and therefore occupied the same position in his life as his early Solipsism did years before. Thus psychologically his most personal philosophy passed with the years from Solipsism to inverted Pantheism. It is the significance of this change that requires investigation. Doubtless the clue will be found at the lower end of the chain: world soul, chain of being, divine motion, fire, air, salts, acids, *tar-water*.

As a whole, *Siris* is an ill-ordered work, with repetition in widely separated sections, and long rambling passages the point of which is not clearly enunciated—had it not been written by a man of Berkeley's reputation it would probably not have been published.*

---

[1] *Id.*, § 284.

* Some Berkeley authorities hold a different opinion—*e.g.* A. C. Fraser, *The Works of George Berkeley*, Oxford, 1901, Vol. III, pp. 118, 135.

The rough divisions used above may be summarised here for the reader's convenience:

THE RESPONSE TO *SIRIS*

Siris had a remarkable reception. It went into six editions in the year of its publication, some of these having several issues, and other editions followed shortly after.[1] It was translated into French, German, and Dutch, and perhaps Portuguese and Spanish—though some of these contained only the sections dealing exclusively with tar-water.[2] The vogue was well-nigh universal: an apothecary, who was asked if he sold the remedy, exclaimed, "Why, I sell nothing else!"[3] and the Archbishop of York wrote that "it is impossible to write a letter now, without tincturing the ink with tar-water."[4]

Siris was published but a month when the first of several works appeared on the subject, some attacking the medicine, some defending it. It aroused considerable annoyance among the medical profession, but a number of doctors gave it their ardent support.[5] Among the works that appeared was one by Berkeley's lifelong friend Tom Prior, whose book contains in-

---

[1] T. E. Jessop, *A Bibliography of George Berkeley*, Oxford, 1934, pp. 11–12.

[2] *Id.*, pp. 27–33.

[3] *Letters of Horace Walpole to Sir Horace Mann*, ed. Dover, London, 1833, Vol. I, p. 370, letter cv, May 29, 1744. (For this reference I am indebted to Professor T. E. Jessop.)

[4] Thomas Herring, *Letters . . . to William Duncombe*, London, 1777, p. 70.

[5] Thomas Prior, *An Authentic Narrative of the Success of Tar-Water*, Dublin, 1746.

numerable descriptions of remarkable cures effected by the infusion. We have many of Berkeley's letters to Prior, but we lack those from Prior to Berkeley; it is interesting, therefore, to find him coming out with a soberly written defence of his friend. Berkeley himself published some further letters and thoughts on the subject, and wrote a letter to the Duke of Newcastle, prescribing the remedy,[1] and one to Linden,[2] who translated *Siris* into German, to mention but two instances out of his large correspondence on the topic.[3]

Doubtless this zeal for tar-water was, then as now, a manifestation of the desire of the general public for magical remedies, proof against all ills; but it must be largely credited to Berkeley's reputation, for the use of tar-water had been described in the *Gentleman's Magazine* for January, 1739,[4] without attracting attention.

After Berkeley's death the vogue passed away as quickly as it came. The brew was still to be seen on tables in modest restaurants in Paris towards the end of the last century; and occasionally a pamphlet appears on the subject.[5]

As to its actual value, there is the evidence of the careful Berkeley himself and the long list of cases described by Prior; yet the claim was obviously a wild exaggeration. One is reminded of the vast quantity of evidence there was in favour of witchcraft, a fraction of which, as Lecky remarks, had it been of moment, would put its existence beyond doubt. A modern scientist who has taken the trouble to estimate the value of tarwater, after mentioning a number of obvious factors that would be likely to have misled Berkeley, goes on to estimate such therapeutic value as it has: from its chemical composition it would act "as gastro-intestinal disinfectant, and as an expectorant and deodorant"; he adds that "as an external antiseptic for various lesions, tar is still used in a manner similar to that recom-

[1] A. A. Luce, "More Unpublished Berkeley Letters and New Berkeleiana", *Hermathena*, Dublin, 1933, Vol. XXIII, pp. 51–2.
[2] A. A. Luce, "Some Unpublished Berkeley Letters with some New Berkeleiana", *Proc. Royal Irish Acad.*, Dublin, 1933, Vol. XLI, Sec. C, No. iv, pp. 160–1.
[3] A. C. Fraser, *Life and Letters of George Berkeley*, Oxford, 1871, p. 323.
[4] Jessop, *Op. cit.*, p. 48.
[5] *Id.*, Nos. 234, 235.

mended by Berkeley"; but he finds that its therapeutic properties are too limited to be useful in the majority of diseases mentioned by Berkeley and Prior.[1]

[1] James Bell, "Bishop Berkeley on the Tar-Water", *The Irish Journal of
Medical Science*, Dublin, Nov. 1933, pp. 4–5.

Chapter 8

BERKELEY'S CONTRIBUTIONS
TO SCIENCE AND ITS FOUNDATIONS

BERKELEY is famous chiefly for his solipsistic philosophy; if his intended philosophy had been understood he would probably have been somewhat less famous. But, whatever contributions he made in his philosophical work, he has at least as solid a claim to be remembered on account of his contributions to psychology, philosophy of physics, mathematical rigour, and economics.

As a young man of twenty-four he published a classic on the psychology of vision, masterly in discussion, observation, and arrangement. In his *De Motu*, published when he was thirty-six, he gave an acute discussion of the concepts of Newtonian mechanics, which anticipated the views of distinguished modern scientists and philosophers. These views contributed to Mach's fame, but philosophers have ignored Berkeley's work in this field as they have his mathematics. His views on physical concepts would not be wholly accepted now, but they retain their importance. As an older man, almost fifty, he made a classic contribution to rigorous inference in mathematics. Philosophers have not recognised this, presumably because they felt that a criticism of Newton's mathematics could not possibly be right. But in fact Berkeley's negative criticism went deep: it was clear, accurate, and incisive; and his criticism had its effect upon mathematics for the next century. Perhaps we overlook it now, because the troubles he unearthed have been smoothed out. In yet another sphere he introduced freshness of thought: in economics he was perhaps less original, yet in his Keynesian approach he was more ahead of his time in some ways than even Adam Smith or Hume. Soon after he had dealt with Newton's mathematics, he put his views on economics in the form of pithy questions.

The present book is concerned to understand Berkeley's metaphysics; consequently a full account has been given of it and of the problems of interpretation. For the further examination of it by means of psycho-analysis, Berkeley's other work is of little additional help. Interesting and important, therefore, as some of his other work is, it will not be examined here; a few remarks on content must suffice. His work on psychology has more relevance than the rest of these contributions and therefore its main thesis will be sketched.

THE PSYCHOLOGY OF VISUAL PERCEPTION

It was in 1709, a year before he produced his greatest classic on philosophy, that Berkeley published his *An Essay towards a New Theory of Vision*. He had indeed a philosophical purpose in writing this, namely to support his philosophy of *Esse percipi*; but in this work there is also an undeniable scientific quality, of being interested in a problem for its own sake, and of making a positive contribution to its solution, a quality that is absent from his great negative criticism of Newton's mathematics.

Most of Berkeley's theory, though not the most fundamental part, was foreshadowed by Malebranche.[1] The Frenchmen's exposition was not, however, so precise, cogent, or free from error as Berkeley's; nor was it in the least degree scientific in spirit. Malebranche grasped enough of the nature of vision to realise the mistakes of the current hypotheses, but he did not, as Berkeley did, take the step of defining vision in terms of *touch*.

Apart from a short passage on metaphysical consequences, Berkeley's design is to show that the visual perception of the distance, magnitude, and orientation of natural objects is based upon their tactual perception; and to discuss the relation between sight and touch. He deals with four concrete problems, all of great interest (but they will not be discussed here). In addition he gives a negative criticism of the geometrical aspect of vision, and thus finds indirect support for his thesis.

DISTANCE

(1) Distance is not immediately seen: *i.e.* an observer does not see how far away an object is in the immediate way in which he sees the object itself:

[1] A. A. Luce, *Berkeley and Malebranche*, Oxford, 1934, pp. 40–6; *cf.* G. S. Brett, *A History of Psychology*, London, 1921, Vol. II, p. 266.

§ 2   For distance being a line directed end-wise to the eye, it projects only one point in the fund of the eye, which point remains invariably the same, whether the distance be longer or shorter.

This startlingly simple argument Berkeley owed to several other writers.[1] Berkeley supported it by claiming that colours are agreed to be in the mind and that the visual extent of an object was located by an observer with its colour, so that this, too, was in the mind.[2]

(2) Estimates people make of the distance of *remote* objects are acts of judgment about perceptual data, such as the presence of intervening objects or faintness or smallness in the distant ones.

(3) Mathematicians had explained the binocular perception of distance by means of the optic axes, and monocular perception by the angle subtended at the eye by the object seen. Berkeley denied, however, that such lines were used in judging distance, since they themselves are not perceived and have no real existence in nature.[3]

(4) Berkeley on the other hand explained binocular judgment by the sensations that arise from turning the eyes towards the object: his point was that different distances are associated with different kinaesthetic sensations, which, unlike optic lines and angles, do really exist.[4]

(5) This does not mean, however, that there is a necessary connexion between the sensation and the distance; the connexion is simply an empirical one: certain degrees of sensation are correlated by experience with certain distances.[5]

(6) Further, nearness of object becomes associated with blurring.[6]

(7) Having distinguished the criteria by which distance is judged from a visual appearance, Berkeley comes to the all-important question of the nature of perceptual distance. He points out that visual appearances vary in degree of faintness according to distance. Hence to judge that a faint tree is about

[1] William Molyneux, *Dioptrica Nova*, London, 1692, p. 113; Locke, *An Essay concerning Human Understanding*, II, ix. 8; Malebranche, *Search after Truth*, trans. by Sault, London, 1694, I, viii, 3; & I, ix, 1.
[2] *Works*, I, *New Theory of Vision*, § 43.   [3] *Id.*, §§ 4–6, 12, 14, 19.
[4] *Id.*, §§ 16, 18.   [5] *Id.*, § 17.   [6] *Id.*, §§ 21–3.

a mile away does not mean that what is seen is a mile away, for then it would look the same on approaching it. On the contrary, every step alters the appearance. His account is therefore this:

§ 45   Having of a long time experienced certain ideas, perceivable by touch, as distance, tangible figure, and solidity, to have been connected with certain ideas of sight, I do upon perceiving these ideas of sight forthwith conclude what tangible ideas are, by the wonted ordinary course of Nature like to follow. Looking at an object I perceive a certain visible figure and colour, with some degree of faintness and other circumstances, which from what I have formerly observed, determine me to think that if I advance forward so many paces or miles, I shall be affected with such and such ideas of touch: So that in truth and strictness of speech I neither see distance itself, nor anything that I take to be distance . . . what [an observer] sees only suggests to his understanding that, after having passed a certain distance, to be measured by the motion of his body, which is perceivable by touch, he shall come to perceive such and such tangible ideas, which have been usually connected with such and such visible ideas.[1]

It cannot be too strongly emphasised that what Berkeley is doing is not to admit the existence of visual distance, then correlating appropriate visual distances with tactual ones, but to deny the existence of visual distance altogether, and to assert that certain visual data, which do not include distance, can be used to estimate a tactual distance.

MAGNITUDE

The discussion of magnitude is similar to that of distance. Thus Berkeley opposed the common view that size is judged by means of the angle subtended by the object at the eye either alone or in conjunction with the perception of visual distance.[2] Further

§ 55   The magnitude of the object which exists without the mind, and is at a distance, continues always invariably the same: but the visible object still changing as you approach to, or recede from the tangible object, it hath no fixed and determinate greatness. Whenever, therefore, we speak of the magnitude of any thing, for instance a tree or a house, we must mean the tangible magnitude.

[1] Cf. Works, II, The Principles of Human Knowledge, § 44; Three Dialogues between Hylas and Philonous, Dial. I, p. 202.

[2] Works, I, Theory of Vision, §§ 52-3.

He then goes on to consider the ways of judging tangible size from visual data.[1]

ORIENTATION

The correct orientation of an object, which Berkeley calls "situation", means that its visual appearance enables us to perceive its tactual shape: that is to say, we shall not be led, when we stretch out our hands, to find on the right or at the top what we expected to find on the left or at the bottom. His view is the same as for distance and magnitude: that associations and correlations are formed between visual appearance and touch, which are not based on optical theory but are purely contingent and experiential.[2]

THE RELATION BETWEEN SIGHT AND TOUCH

Berkeley denied Locke's view that there was something common to the visual and tactual appearances that are called by the same name.[3] His grounds for his denial are these: (a) If there were anything common, a man born blind would, on gaining his sight, "think the things he saw were of the same nature with the object of touch".[4] (b) Visual appearances are different in kind from tactual ones and cannot be perceived by the sense of touch.[5] And (c) he cites the maxim that "quantities of the same kind may be added together and make one entire sum". Thus lines may be added to lines but not to solids, because lines are disparate from solids. Now tangible lines cannot be added to visual ones; therefore they, too, are heterogeneous.[6] In fact Berkeley is here attacking the abstract general idea of Matter.[7]

Naturally it was incumbent upon Berkeley to explain how, if they are not in some degree homogeneous, visual and tactual appearances could have the same name; his answer is that names of visual orientations take the names of the tactual orientations found by experience to be associated with them.[8]

Berkeley's treatment of vision may be summed up thus:—
Properly speaking, visual appearances are at no distance, have no magnitude, and have no orientation in relation to anything

---

[1] *Id.*, §§ 56–7.   [2] *Id.*, §§ 93–119.   [3] *Id.*, §§ 122, 125.
[4] *Id.*, § 128.   [5] *Id.*, § 129.   [6] *Id.*, § 131.
[7] *Id.*, §§ 123, 125.   [8] *Id.*, § 140.

tactual; they simply enable an observer to judge, by experience of past associations, what tactual and kinaesthetic sensations of distance, magnitude, and orientation he would have in moving so as to touch or in handling some object.

INTERPRETATION OF THE LAWS OF MOTION

Berkeley's little-read *De Motu* (1721)[1] contains one of the earliest modern versions of the descriptive theory of scientific concepts and laws, *i.e.* that they have a summarising or descriptive function useful for computation and that they have no other rôle or meaning, a view afterwards made fashionable by Mach and many others. The *De Motu* is also notable as containing good criticism of absolute space, motion, and rest (strangely enough, however, absolute time is not mentioned).

The thesis of the work may be summarised as follows. Motion is something that can be perceived through the senses; there is no motion apart from sensible motion; we find in our observations of moving bodies no active agency that can explain it; further, there is no gravitation apart from motion; gravitation is known only in the perception of motion; to say there is gravitation is to say no more than that things move; hence gravitation does not explain motion. But, though the concept of gravitation adds nothing to our knowledge, it affords a convenient way of summarising our experience of motion; mechanics is not therefore useless; though it gives no clue to the nature of things, it is valuable for calculation:

§ 17 *Force, gravity, attraction,* and terms of this sort are useful for reasonings and computations about motion and bodies in motion, but not for understanding the simple nature of motion itself or for denoting so many distinct qualities. As for attraction, it was certainly introduced by Newton, not as a true, physical quality, but only as a mathematical hypothesis.

Moreover, motion is not to be thought of as something that happens in a box-like absolute space; if all objects vanished, space would *ipso facto* vanish also; hence space is not absolute but relative; other considerations show that the same holds of motion and rest. Even the phenomena that are commonly supposed to imply absolute motion can be interpreted without it.

[1] *Works,* IV.

Lastly, the phenomenon of 'communication of motion' may be seen not to imply any mysterious abstract motion; motion and communication of motion are caused and explained by God.

To some the more plausible ideas in the *De Motu* may now seem commonplace; it took a very long time, however, before they became so. The main matter for regret is that Berkeley made no attempt to examine the difficulties or inadequacies of his descriptive view.

The significance of this work for the present book is that it not only denies any power to Matter but denies in particular that Matter possesses the power of producing motion. Thus not only did Berkeley regard Matter as a danger but also considered it would be dangerous to attribute this power to Matter.

Influence on the Development of Mathematics

Berkeley's greatest single contribution was perhaps his work of negative criticism of the notion of the infinitesimal that underlay Newton's differential calculus or "method of fluxions" as it was then called. This occurs in *The Analyst*,[1] a tract published in 1734 not long after Berkeley returned from America; it was followed by other tracts both by others and by himself, as the *Analyst* controversy gathered momentum.

Berkeley's aim was not fundamentally to refute the differential calculus or to improve mathematics but to attack materialists or believers in Matter, whom he classed as infidels—the subtitle of his tract is *A Discourse addressed to an Infidel Mathematician*. He almost certainly had in mind Halley, the Astronomer Royal, who was believed not to be a Christian. At that time Berkeley was directing his attacks against Freethinkers, but he claimed the right to be a freethinker about mathematics, and his polemic was designed to show that the foundations of mathematics were as illogical as infidels asserted the foundations of religion to be.

Berkeley found that the conception of an infinitesimal was that of a finite quantity of no size; and that it is contradictory to make the infinitesimal vanish (as the method of fluxions did) while retaining its effects for further use. These effects were

---

[1] *Works*, IV, *The Analyst*. All Berkeley's mathematical writings are contained in this volume.

"ghosts of departed quantities", "neither finite quantities, nor quantities infinitely small, nor yet nothing".[1] Berkeley brought out the contradiction with such clarity and force that it is astonishing that mathematicians were not quicker to recognise the flaw and that philosophers have never realised his achievement.*

A long controversy ensued, and it was not till nearly a hundred years later Cauchy's theory of limits made the differential calculus safe from Berkeley's criticism. Berkeley gained his point: the infinitesimal was removed and the differential calculus was developed without it. And in the course of time mathematicians have paid ample tribute to Berkeley's work.[2] Both Cantor and Cajori allot him an honoured place in their histories of the subject.

Berkeley attempted to explain how it was that the method of fluxions produced correct answers: he supposed there was a compensation of errors in the method—an opinion that was held later by such eminent mathematicians as Lazare Carnot and Lagrange. The explanation does not, however, go to the root of the matter.[3]

Berkeley was logically right in his criticism, but he had hardly any creative ability in mathematics. He failed to appreciate the significant direction of Newton's intuition. He gave no hint that the method of fluxions might possibly be made sound though illogical as it stood. He seemed to have had limited power of thinking out mathematics in a general form (he made a curious error in one place which seems accountable only if he thought out his problem in a particular case).[4]

From the present point of view, the most significant feature of Berkeley's attack on the infinitesimal is that his whole approach is dominated by discreteness rather than continuity. The

[1] *Id.*, § 35.
* The issue has a living interest, for nearly all elementary textbooks written in English make the same mistake as Newton.
[2] J. O. Wisdom, "The *Analyst* Controversy: Berkeley's Influence on the Development of Mathematics", *Hermathena*, Dublin, 1939, No. liv.
[3] J. O. Wisdom, "The Compensation of Errors in the Method of Fluxions", *Hermathena*, Dublin, 1941, No. lvii.
[4] J. O. Wisdom, "The *Analyst* Controversy: Berkeley as a Mathematician", *Hermathena*, Dublin, 1942, No. lix.

quantities he discussed were sharply either something or nothing; but, though in the context this was correct, he failed to realise that this did not prevent fluxions from being rehabilitated. This is an indication that he preferred one thing to be clearly separate from another—as the solipsistic form of *Esse percipi* shows—and that he was in difficulties about continuity.

INSIGHTS IN ECONOMICS

Berkeley had returned from America and been made Bishop of Cloyne. Though broken in health, he was quick to come to grips with the squalor and hardship of the Irish peasants, and he threw himself into the task of framing economic principles with an immediately practical application. About a year and a half after he had settled in the seclusion of Cloyne he produced his first economic pamphlet, *The Querist* (1735). Part II followed in the next year, and Part III in 1737. The three parts were subsequently published as one tract. Leyburn* has contributed an invaluable paper on it.

A remarkable feature of *The Querist* was its literary form: it consisted of a succession of short queries, introduced by the word "Whether", a method that recalls Newton's *Optics* to the end of which he attached famous queries. The pamphlets were soon out of print, from which it is to be inferred that they were widely read.[1] Impressions appeared in London as well as Dublin,[2] which shows that Berkeley wished to put this proposal before the English as well as the Irish. When he revised them for the second edition in 1750, he omitted three hundred and forty-five queries and added forty-five new ones; he made a few slight alterations for the next edition of 1752.[3]

The tract consists of a heterogeneous collection of queries— heterogeneous, that is, because remarks upon one theme are often far separated. But, in addition to the difficulty of classifying the main topics, there is a close connexion between the

* E. D. Leyburn, "Bishop Berkeley: *The Querist*", *Proc. Royal Irish Academy*, Dublin, 1937, Vol. XLIV, Sec. C, No. iii. When quoting I follow Leyburn's method of reference, giving the number from the collected edition and in brackets the numbers from the pamphlets published in parts.

[1] *Id.*, p. 86.   [2] *Id.*, p. 85.   [3] *Id.*, p. 94.

economic proposals and a number of comments upon the social conditions of the population. Some remarks merely dispose of minor objections to his plan; some are satire. There is no worked-out theory of economics; the contribution consists of a number of isolated insights.

The social and economic situation that Berkeley found was grievous. The Irish people were wretched and destitute. Yet they had natural advantages, living on a fertile soil in a temperate climate; though the land was good and there was no shortage of labour, bread had to be imported; it was a case of "starving in the midst of plenty". He attributed this in part to the national character, finding his countrymen readier at finding excuses than remedies; they enjoyed complaining and preferred complaining to removing the sources of grievance; he thought, too, that they had an abnormally high degree of cynical content in dirt and beggary and that they were the most indolent and supine people in Christendom.[1] It has been pointed out by an English historian, however, that Berkeley overlooked one factor; that if a man is not allowed to reap he will not sow but will be lazy and dirty. If Berkeley did not give a political explanation of this kind, neither did he give a religious one: he did not, like many of his contemporaries, put the blame for the Irish character on their religion.[2] The explanation he gave was an economic one and he believed that the evil state of affairs could be remedied by economic action.

Berkeley held that reform could be effected by home production and independently of foreign trade. He suggested a programme of public works.[3] But the strictly economic means lay in the circulation of money, and there is no doubt that he grasped the notion that prosperity depends on it:

22 (I, 22) Whether, therefore, less money, swiftly circulating, be not, in effect, equivalent to more money slowly circulating? Or, whether, if the circulation be reciprocally as the quantity of coin, the nation can be a loser?

[1] Works, VI, The Querist, Qu. 19, 132, 138, 272-4, 317, 357, 446.
[2] Robert Dunlop, "Bishop Berkeley on Ireland", Contemporary Review, London, 1926, Vol. CXXIX, p. 764.
[3] The Querist, Qu. 53, 267, 380-4.

242 (I, 269) Whether money, lying dead in the bank of Amsterdam, would not be as useless as in the mine?

479 (III, 185) Whether the same shilling circulating in a village may not supply one man with bread, another with stockings, a third with a knife, a fourth with paper, a fifth with nails, and so answer many wants which must otherwise have remained unsatisfied?

For this purpose he advocated introducing large quantities of money of small denomination, since much trade was held up for lack of small change.[1] This proposal had indeed already been put forward by Locke—one of his very few enlightened suggestions on money.[2]

As regards the concept of money, Berkeley held the modern view according to which notes are money just as much as coin and are not merely credit for coin. This does not mean that he thought notes required no backing. He saw that there was nothing intrinsically economically valuable about metal and that the value attached to it could equally, with safeguards, be attached to paper. And he realised that balances were a form of money and that they could be transferred from one owner to another by making an entry in a bank-book. Thus he had a wide and correct idea of what the term "money" should cover.[3]

Its value he measured not so much in terms of the amount of precious metal that might be in a coin but in its circulation, for he saw that money is a "ticket or counter".[4] The basis of its value lay in industry:

5 (I, 5) Whether money be not only so far useful as it stirreth up industry, enabling men mutually to participate in the fruits of each other's labour?

35 (I, 37) Whether power to command the industry of others be not real wealth?

38 (I, 40) Whether it were not wrong to suppose land itself to be wealth? And whether the industry of the people is not first to be considered, as that which constitutes wealth . . .?

[1] *Id.*, Qu. 231, 468–70, 474, 483.
[2] John Locke, *Works*, London, 1812, Vol. V, *Further Considerations concerning Raising the Value of Money*, p. 204.
[3] *The Querist*, Qu. 33, 294, 296, 427, 440.
[4] *Id.*, Qu. 23, 441, and (III, 180).

Berkeley was clear that production was the vital factor in preventing the use of notes from leading to a vicious inflation:

250 (I, 283)   Whether . . . the circulating paper, in the late ruinous schemes of France and England, was the true evil, and not rather the circulating thereof without industry?

He had a striking conception of 'supply and demand':

24 (I, 24)   Whether the value or price of things be not a compounded proportion, directly as the demand, and reciprocally as the plenty?

He attached little significance to gold:

26 (I, 26)   Whether the denominations being retained, although the bullion were gone, things might not nevertheless be rated, bought, and sold, industry promoted, and a circulation of commerce maintained?

251 (I, 284)   Whether there are not to be seen in America fair towns, wherein the people are well lodged, fed, and clothed, without a beggar in their streets, although there be not one grain of gold or silver current among them?

He asks further:

557 (III, 277)   Whether it would not be a monstrous folly to import nothing but gold and silver . . .?

which is an interesting query considered in relation to the peculiar international position of gold since the end of World War I, though Berkeley here was attacking Mercantilism. What he was pointing out was that gold was not necessary for internal trade. In international trade he also regarded gold as an arbitrary medium of exchange:

494 (III, 200)   Whether in fact our payments are not made by bills? And whether our foreign credit doth not depend on our domestic industry, and our bills on that credit?

In other words, if domestic industry is active, foreign exchange can be left to look after itself, in the sense that foreign credit depends upon home industry and not upon a reserve of precious metal. Interestingly enough, Berkeley was not at all concerned that exports must balance imports; but he does not explain how this is compatible with his view of international credit.

He was also interested in the question of altering the internal value of the currency. His views on this are not very clear; he seems to have favoured a mild inflation as a means to prosperity; but his main concern even here was probably to ensure that there was enough money of small denomination.

It is surely very striking in Berkeley's economic thought that he believed that wealth would be increased by encouraging a higher standard of living—of encouraging the mass of people to want more. The classical view would have been that this would consume wealth. Thus Berkeley asks:

20 (I, 20) Whether the creating of wants be not the likeliest way to produce industry in a people? And whether, if our peasants were accustomed to eat beef and wear shoes, they would not be more industrious?

59 (I, 64) Whether to provide plentifully for the poor be not feeding the root, the substance whereof will shoot upwards into the branches, and cause the top to flourish?

The irony of this, however, is that this view had already been tersely pronounced by Mandeville (and Berkeley had the bitterest feelings towards all deists).[1]

Berkeley also made his contribution to finance by his proposal for a National Bank, designed to give effect to his economic policy and theory. It would provide credit, small coin, and a standard note-issue; he believed that private credit was not enough and that there should be a system of public credit.

Berkeley's economic proposals seem to have been fundamentally sound; his weakness lay in what he ignored. His omissions did not, however, invalidate his contentions; they simply left his theory incomplete—and, after all, he did not set out to write a systematic treatise.

His basic design was to increase home-production, which was to include a scheme of public works. This required that money should circulate freely and was to be facilitated by augmenting

[1] Bernard de Mandeville, *The Fable of the Bees*, Oxford, 1924, Vol. I, pp. 197–8.

the volume of small change. He had correct ideas about the nature of money, and realised that notes were not tokens for 'real' money, but that notes and precious metals were alike money-tokens cashable for industry or its products. He understood that there were limitations to the usefulness of gold as a medium of exchange, and held for the most part a balanced view about foreign trade. His proposal for a Central Bank was sound and far-reaching. He had some understanding of the phenomenon of inflation, but he failed to connect it with the rate of interest. Strangely enough, he did not discuss this important factor, though as a topic for discussion it was not new. Perhaps the reason is that he would have had to advocate lowering the rate, and this would have been wholly unacceptable to his contemporaries. The enormous importance of Berkeley's proposal for a Central Bank can scarcely be overstressed. In eighteenth-century Ireland, writes Joseph Johnston,

the establishment of a substantially capitalised corporate bank was a matter of special urgency. Even if such a bank had contented itself with the limited functions of the contemporary Bank of Amsterdam it could have brought order out of the monetary chaos, and its paper would have circulated at a premium, in comparison with even legal tender gold coin. If it had taken to itself the rôle of the contemporary Bank of England it would have formed a suitable institution for the expansion of a circulating medium based on credit. In actual fact a responsible national banking institution was not established until 1783.[1]

The few historians and economists who have written about Berkeley's work have rated it very highly.[2] Thus according to Dunlop:

The Querist is not merely a notable addition to our knowledge of the economic condition of Ireland in the earlier half of the eighteenth century, but is, perhaps, the most valuable work on the theory of economics that appeared before the Wealth of Nations[3];

[1] Joseph Johnston, "Berkeley and the Abortive Bank Project of 1720–21", Hermathena, Dublin, 1939–40, Vol. XXIX, No. liv, pp. 110–11.
[2] E.g. W. E. H. Lecky, A History of Ireland in the Eighteenth Century, London, 1906, Vol. I, p. 310; George Boas, "Berkeley", Encyclopedia of the Social Sciences, London, 1930, Vol. II, p. 523; Dunlop, Loc. cit.
[3] Dunlop, Loc. cit., p. 763.

but his chief claim to the attention of economists is his suggestion for the establishment of a National Bank and the arguments he used to support it.[1]

Johnston, in comparing Berkeley's contribution with those of Locke and Hume, points out that Locke held the mercantilist doctrine in its crudest form, namely, that a country should export a high surplus of goods to earn precious metal and thus, according to the doctrine, become wealthy. The whole weight of Berkeley's thesis was directed against this—even in economics he was opposed to Locke. Hume in some respects broke new ground, in some he followed Berkeley, but his other divergences from him were retrograde. Johnston considers that if Adam Smith, who was influenced by Hume, had had Berkeley instead of Hume as a friend, economic thought might have developed more fruitfully.[2]

It would appear that where Berkeley differed from the other early British economists he was nearer to the thought of the present day and also nearer to the truth. His Keynesian approach is most striking.

---

[1] *Id.*, p. 771.
[2] Joseph Johnston, "Locke, Berkeley, and Hume as Monetary Theorists", *Hermathena,*, Dublin, 1940, No. lvi.

PART TWO
LIFE

Chapter 9

AN OUTLINE OF BERKELEY'S LIFE

GEORGE BERKELEY was born in Ireland in the county of Kilkenny on March 12, 1685, probably at Kilcrin*. Little is known about his parents. His father, William Berkeley, was English by immediate descent, and was probably born in England but lived in Ireland, where he held a government post of some repute. Berkeley's mother was almost certainly Irish; she was great aunt to General Wolfe. Swift spoke of Berkeley as a kinsman of Lord Berkeley of Stratton, sometime Lord Lieutenant of Ireland; circumstantial evidence supports this but documentary proof is lacking. George was the eldest of a family of six sons and one daughter, unless there were others that died in infancy. He appears to have had an excellent record at the famous Kilkenny School, where Swift had been not long before; here began his life-long friendship with Thomas Prior, one of the founders of the Dublin Society. Little is known about his schooldays.

At the age of fifteen, at the dawn of the eighteenth century, he entered Trinity College, Dublin, where he graduated, took his Master of Arts, became a Fellow and lecturer, and was ordained in the Church of Ireland. Intellectually the atmosphere was very much alive; the writings of Locke, Molyneux, Descartes, Hobbes, and Newton were all familiar in the College circle. The British movement of deism was started in 1696 by John Toland, an Irishman; on the opposite side, the Provost of Trinity and the Archbishop of Dublin were famous theologians. In addition to reading the works of these men with great care, Berkeley made a close study of Malebranche.

* Three different birthplaces are given by good authorities. Luce has examined the evidence and decided in favour of Kilcrin: A. A. Luce, "The Purpose and Date of Berkeley's *Commonplace Book*; with an Appendix on Berkeley's Birthplace", *Proc. Royal Irish Acad.*, Dublin, 1943, Vol. XLVIII, Sec. C., No. vii, pp. 286–9.

He composed some slight mathematical pieces, probably as a Fellowship thesis—but most important of all he recorded his philosophical thoughts in two notebooks as he formed them, and thus has left us what is now known as the *Philosophical Commentaries*, which shows us the amazing freshness of his mind, his early sceptical trend, and the seeds of his mature philosophy. This vitality was manifested and fostered by a society, which he founded, for the discussion of philosophy.

Within two years of becoming a Fellow, Berkeley produced his first great work, which was on the psychology of visual perception. Though this was a scientific work on its own account, it also served as a prelude to his classic work on philosophy, which appeared the next year in 1710: *The Principles of Human Knowledge*. Three sermons on Passive Obedience, delivered in the College Chapel, seemed likely to injure his career, because through an understandable misinterpretation they led to his being taken to be a Jacobite. To counter this he fused them into a tract, but the publication of it did not entirely dispel the unfortunate rumour. Still, unlike Hume and others, he was never made to suffer for his ideas.

Berkeley then put his philosophy in the form of three dialogues, which are perhaps the most famous dialogues in the English language. He left Dublin for London in January, 1713, a few months before the *Three Dialogues* was published, and there he met many of the illustrious men of letters of the early eighteenth century. He was given an excellent reception. Swift presented him to Lord Berkeley of Stratton, according to report, with the words: "My Lord, here is a young gentleman of your family. I can assure your lordship it is a much greater honour to you to be related to him, than to him to be related to you."[1] He met Dr. Clarke, a metaphysician with whom he regularly discussed questions of philosophy at St. James's Palace for the edification of Princess Caroline, and he seems to have visited some of the clubs frequented by deists and freethinkers, which doubtless furnished him with copy, not only for his *Alciphron* of later years, but also for his essays which were soon to appear in the *Guardian*.

A few months later he set out on his first continental tour, as

[1] A. C. Fraser, *Life and Letters of George Berkeley*, Oxford, 1871, p. 6 n.

chaplain to Lord Peterborough, who was going to Sicily as Ambassador Extraordinary on the coronation of the new king. Ten months abroad showed him a good deal of France and Italy, and seems to have whetted his appetite for more, for after spending two years in London, we find him again in Italy in 1716, this time as travelling tutor to the son of the Bishop of Clogher. It was probably in the intervening period that he composed a treatise on ethics which he lost on his next tour. In the course of his wanderings during the next five years he kept a journal, which is remarkable for the close attention he gave to detail of all kinds. Before returning he wrote his *De Motu* and published it in London in 1721. It supplements in one or two respects the philosophy of the *Principles*, but it is mainly a treatment of physical concepts in their own right. It is a most important contribution, which, like his mathematics, philosophers have either ignored or underrated.* After a year in London Berkeley returned to Dublin and received the degree of Doctor of Divinity.

Berkeley was now much occupied with the task of getting a deanery. As happened more than once in his life, several authorities claimed the power of making an appointment; and now, after being given the Deanery of Dromore by one of these, he found himself engaged in a long and tiresome law-suit to defend his right to it. This affair seems to have faded out, as he was made Dean of Derry two years later in 1724. Meanwhile he came in for a legacy in curious circumstances. Swift's Vanessa left her fortune to Berkeley and another, although she was not personally acquainted with Berkeley. As things turned out, her debts swallowed up most of the legacy, but the prospect of the fortune made it possible for Berkeley to think in good earnest about a project that otherwise might have remained a day-dream. He decided to spend the remainder of his days in Bermuda. His scheme was a brilliant and a tragic one. He planned to found a college for the education and conversion of Americans, and he pursued this with all his might as he had never pursued any-

---

* Elsewhere I have mentioned a long line of thinkers whose view of physical concepts was anticipated by Berkeley. See J. O. Wisdom, "The Descriptive Interpretation of Science", *Proc. Arist. Soc.*, London, 1942–3, Vol. XLIII; *Foundations of Inference in Natural Science*, London, 1952, Ch. IX, pp. 74–7.

thing before—and would never do again. With the details of this we shall be concerned in another chapter. Here it will suffice to say that by sheer force of character he obtained large private subscriptions, a vote from Parliament, a Royal Charter, and the help of willing academic colleagues. Doubtless the influence of the philosophical Princess Caroline proved of value—she liked to have Berkeley attend her philosophical circle. There was a long delay in the payment of the State grant, and Berkeley thought it best to go across the ocean and await the money there.

Just a month before he sailed for America in 1728, at the age of forty-three, he had married Miss Anne Forster, daughter of the Speaker of the Irish House of Commons, reputed to be a religious mystic and to have a taste for books. It has puzzled the Berkeley authorities that so many of his letters from London about this time to his friend Tom Prior should have been about the renting of a house about which he urged the utmost secrecy —why should he have wished to travel to Dublin incognito? Surely Miss Forster supplies the answer: he would not have been willing to spend his time in other company, and possibly he did not wish his attentions to be subject to the public gaze. Be that as it may, we now know from a letter discovered not long ago that he did go to Dublin, and that he was there two months before his marriage took place.[1]

In America Berkeley settled near Newport, Rhode Island, and built himself a house named Whitehall. Here he lived in some seclusion, but he moved about enough to be well known to the residents, and he was much liked both for his charm of character and for his religious tolerance. He made the acquaintance of the American thinker, Samuel Johnson, who came to accept the Berkeleian philosophy almost and perhaps completely without reservation. In these surroundings he wrote *Alciphron*, a long work of dialogues attacking the deists, which was published in London almost immediately on his return to Europe.

He stayed nearly three years in Rhode Island, waiting for the money which never came. The Government did not repudiate

[1] A. A. Luce, "Berkeley's Bermuda Project . . .", *Proc. Royal Irish Acad.*, Dublin, 1934, Vol. XLII, Sec. C, No. vi, p. 99.

the grant, but Walpole let it be known that the money would not be paid, and Berkeley was forced to return home. This disaster had a grave effect upon his health. In addition he had family losses. Some of his children died young, and his wife had miscarriages.

All through Berkeley's life, his great friend Sir John Percival of County Cork, who later became the first Earl of Egmont, spared no pains on his behalf. Percival was a realistic and high-minded man, who pursued practical ideas with energy. His friendship with Berkeley began in 1709 when the philosopher was still at Trinity, and their correspondence continued till Percival's death. The easy dignity of their letters can be savoured only from the letters themselves; fortunately all that are known are published. Percival now did his best to have Berkeley appointed to a position worthy of him, to reinstate his reputation after the American venture. This was no easy matter. Berkeley was maligned as a madman on account of his Bermuda scheme; peers, bishops, archbishops, and even the King and Queen were involved in the wrangle about an appointment for him. Eventually, chiefly owing to the influence of the Queen, he was consecrated as Bishop of Cloyne in 1734.

About this time Berkeley's writings took the form of tracts. He produced a further work on vision. This was written to elucidate and justify his previous views and to reinforce his work against the deists; it is important as a framework for his early psychology, but it contained none of the scientific quality of that great early work. Then he was soon involved in the mathematical controversy about fluxions, in which he was right and many of the mathematicians of the day were wrong; he showed that there was a fundamental flaw in Newton's method. The importance of this great negative achievement has been inadequately recognised.

Settled in his diocese in County Cork, Berkeley was not long in discovering the poverty and sickness around him. The next year, at the age of fifty, he brought out his first economic pamphlet. His proposals are notable for their Keynesian approach and practical nature, but though widely read they were not adopted. He followed with other pamphlets on the same subject.

Several years later Berkeley produced the most extraordinary work ever written by a modern philosopher, *Siris*, an investigation of the medical and divine properties of tar-water. He was in search of a panacea, partly because of the conditions of health in his neighbourhood, but also because certain troubles of his own, which had dogged him for a number of years, had now come to a head. Fantastic though the ideas in this work are, it should not be thought that he had become senile.

In this period he lost his favourite son. And his two oldest and best friends, Prior and Percival, died within a short time of each other. He declined the honour of being considered for the position of Vice-Chancellor of Dublin University. He went to Oxford and took a house in Holywell Street. He was by now very weak and he lived to enjoy the academic seclusion for only a few months. He died peacefully in 1753 when he was almost sixty-eight. He was buried in the chapel of Christ Church. So died scholar, psychologist, philosopher, man of letters, courtier, traveller, educational missionary, Christian apologist, bishop, mathematician, economist, and amateur doctor.

For a full account of the philosopher's life, the reader must turn to the correspondence and Luce's standard biography,[1] which supersedes Fraser's.[2] Prefixed to Rand's[3] edition of the Percival correspondence is an excellent essay on Berkeley's life, but its purpose is restricted to providing the background to the letters. Far and away the best general essay on his life was Balfour's, last printed as an introduction to Sampson's edition of Berkeley's works.[4] Even the earliest of these, Fraser's, is reasonably accurate, though it contains some errors; the newest details exist only in Luce's papers and *Life*.

[1] A. A. Luce, *The Life of George Berkeley*, Edinburgh, 1949.
[2] Fraser, *Op. cit.*
[3] Benjamin Rand, *Berkeley and Percival*, Cambridge, 1914.
[4] A. J. Balfour, "Biographical Introduction", in *Works*, ed. by Sampson, London, 1897, Vol. I.

Chapter 10

GEORGE BERKELEY, THE MAN

THE belief that Berkeley was an unpractical idealist 'up in the clouds' was doubtless based upon the interpretation of him as a subjectivist or solipsist; it presupposes ignorance of almost everything he did. His whole life from his earliest days belies this description of him. As a young man he penned a graphic picture of the extraordinary cave of Dunmore, which still lives as an outstanding piece of descriptive prose. His interest in all kinds of details connected with the cave is very striking, and shows itself just as strongly and to such an extent as to become tedious throughout the long diary he wrote during his travels abroad. Nor later on do his family life and care for the poor of his district lend support to the idea of his becoming lost in himself as the years went by. On the contrary, few philosophers, if any, can claim such wide interests and manifold activities as Berkeley.

If we try to arrange his interests in order of importance, we shall place his first with ease—philosophy. But he was also mathematician, architect, man of letters, psychologist, economist, theologian, preacher, and missionary.

As a mathematician he was extraordinarily gifted; but mathematics was by no means the centre of his life, and except in his early days he pursued it only to reinforce his philosophical attack on Matter. His taste in architecture was mature. Not only was he absorbed by what he saw on his travels, but he even helped to plan houses. In his college days, Dublin was not yet the Georgian city it was to become. The foundation stone of the present library of Trinity College was laid eight months before Berkeley left his academic life for London. Though it was not finished for twelve years, he must have seen it both as it was being built and after the main structure was completed in 1724. But even pre-Georgian Dublin impressed him, for in 1714 he remarked in a letter to Percival, written incidentally from Leghorn after he had seen something of the Continent, that Dublin was "one of the finest cities in the world"[1]—which was perhaps a blend of native pride and objective truth. He grew up on the crest of the new architectural wave, and his natural taste had plenty to focus upon. On reaching America he built himself what appears from its photograph in Rand's *Berkeley and Percival* to be a fine example of Georgian art. Writing to Percival he expressed hopes of having

a part in the contrivance of the house you design to build this winter, for you must know I pretend to an uncommon skill in architecture, as you will easily imagine when I assure your Lordship there is not any one modern building in Rome that pleases me, except the wings of the Capitol built by Michael Angelo and the colonnade of Berninies before St. Peters.[2]

As a man of letters, his early dialogues are known to every student of literature, and his one poem (not counting some quaint verses on tar) has, as Jessop puts it, "attained a niche in the Oxford Book of Eighteenth-Century Verse."[3] According to Gosse he was "perhaps the most exquisite writer of English in his generation"; according to Saintsbury he was "almost the greatest *writer* . . . whom the new style *post* 1660 had yet produced."[4] His early style has an incomparable elegance and rhythm. Later in life his writing seems to me to have been no more than good. But Berkeley was not a writer for the sake of writing; he wrote no 'essays' and composed no 'literature' (save the description of the cave of Dunmore, which he read to a society) in the sense that everything he penned was directed towards a non-literary goal. As an economist, his aim was severely practical and his investigations dictated in part by the needs of the moment—that is to say, had Ireland been prosperous he would probably not have written on economics. His small work on psychology, like mathematics, had an ulterior motive, in this case to pave the way for his philosophy; but it also made a positive contribution. As a theologian he had little to say and did not say it well. As a preacher he was fluent, sincere, in all probability devoid of mannerisms, orthodox, unusually good

[1] Benjamin Rand, *Berkeley and Percival*, Cambridge, 1914, p. 133.
[2] *Id.*, p. 172.
[3] T. E. Jessop, *A Bibliography of George Berkeley*, Oxford, 1934, p. vii.
[4] Cited by Jessop, *Op. cit.*, Nos, 169, 171.

but not pre-eminent. As a missionary and reformer, after over-coming superhuman obstacles, he failed tragically. His motive here was again philosophical; the design was not purely to convert Americans to religion, since what he wished to found was a university, and can we doubt that his discovery of the New Principle in philosophy was to be the corner-stone of the education he hoped to provide?

Thus Berkeley was a man of many parts, with singleness of purpose; from his goal, the philosophy of Theocentric Phenomenalism and denial of Matter, he never swerved; so far from setting out to do good or to be learned or to make an impression on the world, he had simply one fixed purpose in life.

What was Berkeley like to his contemporaries?

There are several portraits which help to build up our impression of him. Those I have seen show a strong face with fleshy cheeks, and, some might say, an ambitious disposition. Colour of personality does not seem to me to come through. He put on a good deal of weight at an early age. In addition to what can be gleaned in this way, we are not without a description of his personal appearance by his first biographer:

As to his person, he was a handsome man, with a countenance full of meaning and benignity, remarkable for great strength of limb, and, till his sedentary life impaired it, of a very robust constitution.[1]

Berkeley was an immediate success in social and literary circles when he took up residence in London. His enthusiasm for his American project had the most remarkable influence—albeit temporary—upon public men. He had lifelong friends, who fortunately valued his letters[2]: one was Tom Prior, man of letters and founder of the Dublin Society, and another Sir John

[1] See *Works*, Vol. I, ed. by Wright, London, 1843, p. 14.
[2] All that are known are contained in the following: Fraser, *Op. cit.*; Rand, *Op. cit.*; A. A. Luce, "Two Sermons by Bishop Berkeley", *Hermathena*, Dublin, 1932, No. xlvii; "More Unpublished Berkeley Letters and New Berkeleiana", same, 1933, Vol. XXIII; "Some Unpublished Berkeley Letters with some New Berkeleiana", Dublin, 1933, *Proc. Royal Irish Acad.*, Vol. XLI, Sec. C, No. iv; and "Berkeley's Bermuda Project and his Benefactions to American Universities, with Unpublished Letters and Extracts from the Egmont Papers", same, 1934, Vol. XLII, Sec. C, No. vi. All the letters will be published in the new edition of the *Works*.

Percival, already mentioned, with both of whom he kept up an unbroken correspondence to the end. Whatever claims he may in his own mind have made for himself as a philosopher, he was in all other respects a man of mature modesty. Of Berkeley's general character, Bishop Atterbury's exclamation is scarcely an exaggeration:

So much understanding, so much knowledge, so much innocence, and such humility, I did not think had been the portion of any but angels till I saw this gentleman.[1]

Percival had the greatest regard for him, as is plain on a number of occasions. Thus, just before his return from America, Berkeley was a candidate for the Deanery of Down, but was not appointed; Percival records his disgust in his journal:

I heard the mortifying news there that Dean Berkeley has missed of the Deanery of Down, by a villainous letter wrote from the Primate of Ireland, that the Dean is a madman and disaffected to the Government. Thus the worthiest, the learnedest, the wisest, and most virtuous Divine of the three kingdoms, is by an unparalleled wickedness made to give way to Dean Daniel, one of the meanest in every respect. There is no respect of persons in this world, when God sends his blessings on the unjust as well as just, but in the other world these things are made up.[2]

He also records that Queen Caroline had said she must provide for him in England.[3] Percival used what influence he could wield and expressed his resentment to the Bishop of Salisbury, brother of the Archbishop of Dublin who had helped to put a spoke in Berkeley's wheel:

I said to the Bishop, yonder is one of the worthiest, most learned, and most unexceptionable men in the three kingdoms, who has met with the wretchedest usage that ever was heard of. Who is that, said the Bishop? Dean Berkeley, said I.[4]

The argument that followed was hardly cordial. Next Percival visited the Bishop of London, who dealt sympathetically with Berkeley's difficulties. They went carefully into the possibility of

[1] Fraser, *Op. cit.*, p. 59, first recorded in 1773, according to Jessop, *Op. cit.*, No. 116.

[2] Rand, *Op. cit.*, p. 280.   [3] *Id.*, p. 281.   [4] *Id.*, pp. 281–2.

getting Berkeley a position equivalent to the Deanery he had failed to get, but the Bishop was not sanguine about succeeding. Anxious to clear Berkeley's reputation, after the American failure and the consequent malicious stories that had been circulated, Percival said:

That for myself, I had known him twenty-five years and could say many things in justification of his zeal for the Government. . . . I would engage that if that kingdom [Ireland] had been polled, ninety-nine in a hundred would have testified for him, and that if it were practicable every grand jury there would do the same.[1]

The matter was settled by the Queen, who made Berkeley an Irish Bishop. Another entry, which shows the close relationship between the two men, mentions that Berkeley conducted the marriage ceremony of Percival's daughter, Katherine.[2]

It has to be borne in mind that our records of Berkeley come from his friends. What would Collins, and the other deists, have thought about him; would they have found him smug, over-sure of his ground? That seems very likely. Smug he was not; but he was a dogmatist who would not have discussed fundamental subjects dispassionately.

Again, it must be remembered, his friends were highly cultured—from the flower of eighteenth-century literary circles to Percival and even Queen Caroline. Unassuming and far from being an intellectual snob, save in the field of deism, intellectuals other than deists would have found him without cynicism and full of conversation flowing with unforced sparkle like stories from an Irish bard. But what would the man of good conventional education and no particular culture have made of him? One can imagine him on a journey interesting such individuals by his sense of humour, charm, ease, and gifts of conversation; but he might well have left them with the impression of being an odd fellow, interesting to meet but not to have in the same circle. Though Berkeley was obviously a good 'mixer' up to a point, he would probably not have cared for gossip about horses, sport, and the like; he would not have made the kind of squire who can join the yokels over a glass of ale. Thus his circle was exclusively a cultural one. Knocking about in a

[1] *Id.*, p. 286.   [2] *Id.*, p. 288.

rough and tumble kind of way would have been distressing to him. Thus he wrote to Percival how one day he was accosted in a coffee-house by a drunkard—he was then twenty-five—and was apparently obliged to drink Dr. Sacheverell's health; the drunkard then

swore that all the coffee-house round should drink the same health, and upon a gentleman's refusing it drew his sword, whereupon I made what haste I could out of the house.[1]

Nonetheless after the rebellion of '45, he armed the neighbour-hood of Cloyne as best he could, and wrote two letters to the Press, urging the virtues of military excellence together with a concrete proposal for forming a militia.[2] Of these Luce, drawing on experience of World War I, remarks

they are characteristic effusions of the mind of the war-fevered amateur, who has an abstract idea of war, without concrete know-ledge of the real thing.[3]

But wars change in strange ways; what was amateurish in that of 1914–18 became professional in 1940, and Berkeley's ideas bear a striking resemblance to some of the chief functions of the Home Guard in Britain and the Local Security Force in Ireland. Thus

the modern discipline delighteth much in parade. This is a clog upon our levies and recruits, depriving the public of the service of many a stout active fellow, who falls short of the present standard. And yet such a one hath his advantages. At a distance he is a less mark, and in close fight less embarrassed, more nimble either to avoid or give a blow, he is fitter for dispatch in marches and pursuits, in passing through bad roads, in clambering over rocks and mountains, and scaling of walls, he is a less burthen on a horse or carriage.[4]

Did England ever make a greater figure than it has done in former times by its militia? In our own times have not the militia of Sweden shewn themselves an overmatch for a disciplined army of Danes? . . . It is not the name, the apparel, or the ornaments that make a

---

[1] *Id.*, p. 85.
[2] Luce, "More Unpublished Berkeley Letters . . .", as cited, pp. 45–8.
[3] *Id.*, p. 49.   [4] *Id.*, p. 46.

soldier, but the familiar use of arms, a body hardened by toil, an intrepid heart and resolute mind; talents to be found in labouring peasants, miners or tradesmen, if duly trained and exercised.[1]

In connexion with physical violence several stray remarks in his letters to Percival are of note. After the rebellion of '15, he writes of a report that in a neighbouring town

the Dissenters, who guarded the meeting-house with firearms, got one of the Tory mob, and upon his refusing to curse Dr. Sacheverel they slit his mouth from ear to ear, and gave him other wounds of which he died. . . .[2]

Later he writes of a man that "stabbed himself with a penknife in three places".[3] From Turin he writes in a bloodthirsty vein:

I must not omit another adventure in Dauphine. A huge dark coloured Alpine wolf ran across an open plain when our chaise was passing, when he came near as he turned about and made a stand with a very fierce and daring look, I instantly drew my sword and Mr. Ashe fired his pistol. I did the same too, upon which the beast very calmly retired looking back ever and anon. We were much mortified that he did not attack us and give us an opportunity of killing him.[4]

Later on the tour one letter contains the following:

As riches and honours have no footing here, the people are unacquainted with the vices that attend them, but in lieu thereof they have got an ugly habit of murdering one another for trifles. The second night after our coming to the Island a youth of 18 years was shot dead by our door; but we have had several instances of the like since that in several parts of the Island. Last year thirty six murders were compounded for by the Governor; the life of man being rated at ten ducats.[5]

A few years later he ends a letter

in a prodigious hurry, the Lady being to be buried in a little more than an hour's time. Her funeral is under the direction of the King at arms, where I am to act I know not what part, which puts an end to this hasty scrawl.[6]

---

[1] *Id.*, pp. 47–8. [2] Rand, *Op. cit.*, p. 141. [3] *Id.*, p. 150.
[4] *Id.*, pp. 160–1. [5] *Id.*, p. 169. [6] *Id.*, pp. 208–9.

He could take such things light-heartedly.

Connected with this theme is a curious saying of Berkeley's, recorded by Percival:

I know not what it is to fear, but I have a delicate sense of danger.[1]

Such a supreme sublimation is attained by few; and in Berkeley's case it is more probable that anxiety and dread were diverted into some unusual direction than that he was free of them. However, we note that he claimed to have "a delicate sense of danger". Now this phrase, as Luce observes, occurs in *Alciphron*, and the theme of the context is *duelling*. The Churchman in the dialogue draws a distinction between two kinds of bully: the fighting and the tame. The one tries to foist physical attacks upon the laity; the other vents emotional aggressiveness upon the clergy—and deists are placed in this category.

The qualities constituent of this tame bully are natural rudeness joined with *a delicate sense of danger*.[2]

Thus in this context it is the *deist* that has this sense. That so striking and unusual a phrase should be used by Berkeley both of himself and of his arch-enemies, that the attribute should pass undisguised from one to the other, helps to confirm the conclusion suggested by his *Philosophical Commentaries* that there was still a layer of Berkeley's mind that was at one with deism, though it had for many years disappeared from his deliberated thought.

Doubtless such a strange psychological feature would have some deep connexion with his early days at home; but unfortunately nothing is known about his home life. A strange silence enshrouds it. Though his parents lived to see him a bishop,[3] there is no record of his writing to them or even going to visit them; yet he must have been near Kilkenny often in the course of his life. Not a reference to them occurs in his letters.*

---

[1] Luce, *Loc. cit.*, p. 28.

[2] *Works*, III, *Alciphron*, Dial. V, § 13. My italics.

[3] A. A. Luce, *The Life of George Berkeley*, Edinburgh, 1949, p. 22.

* Luce attaches no significance to this: "Who does preserve family correspondence or records visits home?" (*Id.*, p. 24). Many do. The point is not, however, the absence of letters from Berkeley to his parents but the absence of any reference to them in his other correspondence.

One mention only has been found, in two manuscript drafts
of the description of the Cave of Dunmore, and in both it is
deeply scored out—so heavily that Luce, who made the discovery, could read the originals only with considerable difficulty.[1] Talking of the quantities of bones found in the cave, and
speculating about how they came to be there, Berkeley writes
in the altered drafts and in the third and complete manuscript:
"I remember to have heard *one* tell . . ."; whereas the two drafts
originally read: "I remember to have heard *my father* tell . . ."
Why should he have wished to delete all reference to his
father?[*] Even if we accept Luce's suggestion in the more
specific form that Berkeley did not wish to implicate his father
in the guess that in the rebellion of '41 the Irish massacred some
Protestants there, this does not account for the heavy erasure
of "my father" from the drafts that contained no reference to
the massacre.

Likewise of Berkeley's own brothers and sister little is known.
Some of his brothers distinguished themselves in a modest way.
One, Thomas, however, was infamous: he was guilty of bigamy
and condemned to death in 1726.[2] Some money of Berkeley's
was used without his knowledge for Thomas' defence, but Berkeley when he heard this said:

[1] A. A. Luce, "Berkeley's *Description of the Cave of Dunmore*", *Hermathena*, Dublin, 1931, Vol. XXI, p. 151.

[*] Luce suggests that, as the dead men's bones may have been the
skeletons of Protestants massacred in 1641, Berkeley feared to implicate
his father in 'the troubles'. This is not borne out by the immediate context: " 'Tis true I remember to have heard one tell how an old Irish
man who served for a guide into the cave solved him this problem by
saying that in days of yore a certain carnivorous monster dwelling there
was wont furiously to lay about him and whoever were unhappy enough
to come in his way hurry them for food into that his dreadful den"
(*Works*, IV, "A Description of the Cave of Dunmore", p. 261); for
Berkeley accords this legendary solution the dignity of a reasoned refutation, which shows at least that there was no commonly accepted explanation and that the bones were not commonly regarded as relics of the
massacres. So far, it is hard to see how Berkeley could have implicated
his father. In the third draft only (*Works*, ed. by Fraser, Oxford, 1901,
Vol. IV, p. 80) did Berkeley mention 'the troubles': "There are who
guess that, during the Irish rebellion in '41, some Protestants, having
sought refuge in this place, were there massacred by the Irish."

[2] A. A. Luce, *The Life of George Berkeley*, Edinburgh, 1949, p. 27.

I wou'd not have disbursed half the sum to have saved that villain from the gallows.[1]

It would seem that the sentence was not carried out; for, according to Berkeley's daughter-in-law, Eliza, a reasonably reliable authority,[2] a brother had seduced a lady and refused to marry her; when later he visited Cloyne after he had become "what the world calls a worthy man" Berkeley gave him hospitality but refused to see him and dined alone in the library, saying,

He is a genuine scoundrel. I trust God will forgive him upon his repentance; but I will never see him whilst I breathe.[3]

If Eliza's story is true, this could be no other brother than Thomas.

Of Berkeley's family life a great deal more is known. He married at the age of forty-three when about to sail for America. If the Bermuda project was to be the climax of his career, in which he would attain full maturity philosophically, it would coincide with his reaching maturity of manhood. Of his marriage it is sufficient to say that it was one of the few among the marriages of the great philosophers to be successful. Little is known of his wife, beyond her taste for mysticism, but she seems to have been a consort worthy of a man of great qualities. A good deal about her character may, however, be learnt from a letter of hers to her son:

in childhood you were instructed by your father—he, though old and sickly, performed the constant, tedious task himself, and would not trust it to another's care. You were his business and his pleasure. Short-sighted people see no danger from common vulgar errors of education. He knew that fundamental errors were never cured, and that the first seasoning of the cask gives the flavor, and therefore he chose rather to prevent than cure . . . and when he spoke directly of religion (which was seldom) he did it in so masterly a manner, that it made a deep and lasting impression. You never heard him give his tongue the liberty of speaking evil. Never did he reveal the fault or

[1] Luce, "Some Unpublished Berkeley Letters . . .", as cited, p. 144.
[2] A. A. Luce, *The Life of George Berkeley*, Edinburgh, 1949, pp. 9–12.
[3] Eliza Berkeley, *Poems by the Late George Monck Berkeley: With a Preface by the Editor*, London, 1797, p. ccv.

secret of a friend . . . as he saw no one his superior, or perhaps his
equal, how could he envy any one? . . . He was also pure in heart
and speech; no wit could season any kind of dirt to him, not even
Swift's.[1]

Here is no conventional lip-worship; Mrs. Berkeley knew what
she felt, knew what she admired, and what she wrote expressed
her inner feeling. The Berkeleys had several children, some of
whom died young; and to her husband's strain and suspense in
Rhode Island while awaiting the Government grant must be
added anxiety about her miscarriages.

In some of his letters Berkeley expressed his views on marriage
and his appreciation of family joy. His letter of congratulation
to Percival on his marriage deserves to be noticed in full.

Suffer me to interrupt your joys by a short congratulation. I am
heartily glad to find you are married to a lady who, by all the ac-
counts I can hear, is just such a one as (had it been at my choice) I
should have chosen to be your wife. The first lines of your letter to
your brother persuade me that I cannot make you a more agreeable
wish than that you and my Lady Percival may spend together a long
life in pleasure equal to that you have enjoyed this week past, that
as the fury of love abates, the sweetness and tenderness of conjugal
affection may increase, together with that unknown delight which
springs up in the soul of a parent from the thought of a happy and
well educated offspring.[2]

Berkeley was then twenty-five. And three years later:

The description you favoured me with of your little offspring was
very entertaining, and though slightly amiable has, I am persuaded,
nothing of a father's fondness in it.[3]

Thus before he had a family of his own he was quite clear about
the feelings he would have for his children. Several years after
his marriage, in 1741, he wrote several times on the subject
(fragments of letters have been discovered). With graceful simplicity he congratulated an old friend, Richard Dalton, on his
third marriage.[4] In three other fragments he refers to this:

[1] A. C. Fraser, *Life and Letters of George Berkeley*, Oxford, 1871, pp.
357–8.
[2] Rand, *Op. cit.*, p. 77.   [3] *Id.*, p. 126.   [4] Fraser, *Op. cit.*, p. 266.

Our friend Mr. Dalton is, I hear, married the third time, which shews him to be a prudent man as well as a laudable patriot. . . . Though you are far from being an old man, I will take the freedom to say you are bordering on what we call an old bachelor, a character not the most useful to the public, not the most agreeable to him that wears it. . . . Health and affluence may bear you up for some years, but when age and infirmities come on, you will feel and bewail the want of a family of your own, and the comforts of domestic life. A wife and children are blessings invaluable, which, as a man cannot purchase for money, so he would sell them for no price. . . . I wish I had twenty like George. I assure you I would rather have them than twenty thousand pounds a year.[1]

Mr. Dalton, who I expected was abroad with you, is, it seems, made happy the third time (O terque quaterque beatus); I wish you would once . . . dare to do what he does so often. Without that expedient you will lose the comforts of domestic life, that natural refuge from solitude and years which is to be found in wife and children. Mine are to me a great joy . . . and alone capable of making a life tolerable —so much embittered by sickness as mine has been for several years.[2]

I cannot wish better to all my good unmarried friends than that they should follow his example who is a delicate connoisseur as to the ease and comforts of life. . . . Besides Mr. Dalton . . . can tell you marriage lessens and divides care. I will only say to you that my greatest want is children. I have but three boys and a daughter.[3]

Berkeley's eldest son, Henry, was born in Rhode Island. As he writes to Tom Prior:

Among my delays and disappointments, I thank God I have two domestic comforts that are very agreeable, my wife and my little son; both which exceed my expectations, and fully answer all my wishes.[4]

Our little son is great joy to us. We are such fools as to think him the most perfect thing we ever saw in its kind.[5]

His daughter Berkeley refers to as "so bright a little gem"[6] and "of star-like beauty"[7]; and a couple of years later alludes in glowing terms to his wife's accomplishments:

---

[1] *Id.*, pp. 267–8.　　　　　[2] *Id.*, p. 268.
[3] Luce, "More Unpublished Berkeley Letters . . .", as cited, p. 45.
[4] Fraser, *Op. cit.*, p. 173.　　　　[5] *Id.*, pp. 184–5.
[6] *Id.*, p. 267.　　　　[7] *Id.*, p. 268.

No nightingale could have sung a more pleasing song, not even my wife, who, I am told, is this day inferior to no singer in the kingdom.[1]

She began to draw in last November, and did not stick to it closely, but by way of amusement only at leisure hours. For my part, I think she shows a most uncommon genius; but others may be supposed to judge more impartially than I.[2]

Of his family losses one struck particularly deep: his son, William, died in 1751 and he used afterwards to say to his son George, "I see William incessantly before my eyes."[3] How real the loss was is only too evident from a letter to Bishop Benson*:

I was a man retired from the amusement of politics, visits, and what the world calls pleasure. I had a little friend, educated always under mine own eye, whose painting delighted me, whose music ravished me, and whose lively, gay spirit was a continual feast. It has pleased God to take him hence. God, I say, in mercy hath deprived me of this pretty, gay plaything. His parts and person, his innocence and piety, his particularly uncommon affection for me, had gained too much upon me. Not content to be fond of him, I was vain of him. I had set my heart too much upon him—more perhaps than I ought to have done upon anything in this world.[4]

To pass from his family-relationships to his national sentiment, there can be no doubt that Berkeley was and felt himself to be Anglo-Irish. It is necessary to explain what this means, however, for, though it may include, it does not primarily mean a person one of whose parents is English and one Irish. It refers to that community whose families have lived in Ireland perhaps for many generations after coming originally from England; these families may or may not have intermarried to a certain extent with the Celtic Irish.† An Anglo-Irishman considers himself Irish but does not regard himself as belonging to the community of Celtic Irish; on the other hand he does not look on himself as English. Thus he thinks of himself as Irish, though not in an unqualified way. On the other hand he accepts numbers of deep-seated aspects of English outlook and tradition (or rather the conservative aspects of that tradition), which are

---

[1] *Id.*, p. 289.   [2] *Id.*, p. 308.   [3] *Id.*, p. 325 n.
* I am indebted to Mr. W. T. McLeod for pointing out an error here.
[4] *Id.*, p. 325.
† The distinction between Celtic and Anglo-Irish is not, of course, an absolute one. The terms "Celtic" and "Anglo-Irish" are not standard.

foreign to the Celtic Irish; and, though he does not think of himself as English, he takes it for granted that he is British, an attitude that is unacceptable to the Celtic Irish. Moreover the Anglo-Irishman is an entity on his own. He does not regard himself as a cross-breed in a depreciatory sense but as an independent type with positive attributes, noted for producing many writers, many generals, and some who have made contributions to knowledge. It was to this community that Berkeley belonged.*

Entries in the *Philosophical Commentaries* showing his Irish sentiment have already been noticed; they are most striking entries; they express approval of the good sense of his country and his own views and hint that his Irish nationality or his mother country made his reasoning secure. Their significance in their context is that they reveal his identification with Ireland in his attack on the English Newton and Locke. His family was well connected, with both English and Irish relations, which would have given him leanings both ways.

We may recall that Ireland holds out an irresistible attraction for some men of different lands, and in particular that the sons of English immigrants often embrace the country as if they had been there for generations (becoming, as has been said, "more 'Irish' than the Irish themselves"); indeed some Englishmen who have adopted Ireland as their home have at the same time embraced the wrongs of the country and felt the same embitterment against England as did the most injured of the dispossessed and subjugated Irish. Berkeley may have had something of this in his composition, though it is not as a rule true of the Anglo-Irish; but compatible with his philosophical detachment and broad outlook he would have possessed it in but small degree. What force it may have had, we may be sure, found its outlet in one battle which absorbed all his aggressiveness—his attack on the English freethinkers, whose philosophy (Locke) and physics (Newton) led (in Berkeley's opinion) to atheism.

* The situation has fundamentally altered in the last forty years. The community was decimated by World War I. After the formation of the Irish Free State (1921–2), some of the Anglo-Irish emigrated, to become absorbed elsewhere in a generation or two. Those who remained have identified themselves more closely with the Celtic Irish and have thus tended to lose those characteristics that were peculiar to the community.

In the first edition of the *Principles* (1710), Berkeley referred to Newton as "a philosopher of a neighbouring nation"; this was changed in the second edition (1734), perhaps because he had lived for many years out of Ireland which would have made "neighbouring" queer.[1]

In his letters to Percival his concern for his native country is given expression.[2] Moreover, Percival wrote to Berkeley from Dublin about the success the *Three Dialogues* had gained in England:

However, we on this side will insist on it that the plant is our own, and owes her sprouting up so quick in England, not so much to the nature of that soil, as to the advantage of being transplanted into fresh ground. So if you come back to us altered in your taste and sense of things, we will still pride ourselves that you are of Irish growth, and any improvement you receive shall be owing only to the new ideas raised in you, which your own native genius has by reflection turned to good use, not in the excellency of things that offer themselves.[3]

On the other hand, in one of the three drafts of his description of the Cave at Dunmore, already mentioned, written when he was about twenty-one, he discusses the possibility that in the rebellion of 1641 some "Protestants" were massacred there by the "Irish"—thus distinguishing between Protestants and Irishmen. Again, when back in Dublin in 1722, Berkeley writes:

Your Lordship knows this barren bleak island too well to expect any news from it worth your notice.[4]

This is echoed from Cloyne twenty years later:

Pardon, my good Lord, this political stuff that I write for want of news. This island is a region of dreams and trifles of so little consequence to the rest of the world, that I am sure you expect no important news from it.[5]

Furthermore, as a young Fellow of Trinity (1709), he had written to Percival consoling him about his loss of statues and medals that he had coming from Italy, but expressed doubt whether they would be appreciated in Cork:

[1] *Works*, II, *The Principles of Human Knowledge*, § 110.
[2] Rand, *Op. cit.*, pp. 97–8.   [3] *Id.*, p. 117.   [4] *Id.*, p. 193.
[5] *Id.*, p. 294.

The finest collection is not worth a groat where there is no one to admire and set a value on it, and our country seems to me the place in the world which is least furnished with virtuosi.[1]

It would seem that, while claiming Ireland as his own country, this referred to the country itself and not to its culture, which he depreciates. This is strange, for Irish culture was at that time to the fore, but its peak had perhaps been passed by the time Berkeley was an undergraduate. His opinion of English culture, after he had seen something of the Continent, he expresses in no uncertain terms:

I have already seen enough to be satisfied, that England has the most learning, the most riches, the best government, the best people, and the best religion in the world.[2]

Just before Berkeley returned from America, Percival recorded in his journal that he had discussed Berkeley's chances of preferment with the Bishop of London, who referred to Berkeley as "totally averse, nay fixt upon not going to Ireland".[3]

Further light on Berkeley's national feeling is given by *The Querist* and the pamphlet entitled "A Word to the Wise", both of which he wrote at Cloyne in the hope of improving economic and social conditions in Ireland. There are numerous references to "my" and "our" country; but here again we find him differentiating between the native Irish and the Anglo-Irish. Thus he asks

whether our old native Irish are not the most indolent and supine people in Christendom?[4]

Both pamphlets are pervaded with exhortation to greater industry—which he even suggests might be encouraged by a tax on dirt.[5]

But, alas! our poor Irish are wedded to dirt upon principle. It is with some of them a maxim that the way to make children thrive is to keep them dirty.[6]

[1] *Id.*, p. 57.   [2] *Id.*, p. 137.   [3] *Id.*, p. 284.
[4] *Works*, VI, *The Querist*, 357 (II, 183); *cf. Loc. cit.*, "A Word to the Wise", p. 240.
[5] *The Querist*, 369 (II, 196).
[6] "A Word to the Wise", p. 242.

With this he was unable to identify himself. On the contrary he asks

Whether the upper part of this people are not truly English by blood, language, religion, manners, inclination, and interest?[1]

By "Englishmen", however, it is clear he meant Anglo-Irish, as is shown by the next query:

Whether we are not as much Englishmen, as the children of old Romans born in Britain, were still Romans?[2]

But, of course, he implies that the Anglo-Irish derive their civilised habits and industriousness from their English heritage. His economic proposals and his social comments, as well as the pamphlet addressed to the Roman Catholic clergy of his diocese, show his earnest desire to help the poor, though he did not feel one of the people (it should perhaps be noticed that he was now living a country life for the first time since he was a boy, and he would not have come across the same sloth and dirt in the town life in Dublin.)* The lack of culture, noted above, had not always prevailed, but he did not entertain much hope of a revival:

Whether it was not an Irish professor who first opened the public schools at Oxford? Whether this island hath not been anciently famous for learning? And whether at this day it hath any better chance for being considerable?[3]

All this makes it plain why he did not relish Irish country life; and in fact he states so openly:

Whether a gentleman who hath seen a little of the world, and observed how men live elsewhere, can contentedly sit down in a cold, damp, sordid habitation, in the midst of a bleak country, inhabited by thieves and beggars?[4]

These queries thus resolve the questions suggested by the re-

[1] *The Querist*, 91 (I, 97).   [2] *Id.*, 92 (I, 98).
* It is interesting to note that Berkeley advocated the revival of the Irish language—though as a means for converting the natives—*Id.*, 260 (I, 307), 261 (I, 308).
[3] *Id.*, 199 (I, 194).   [4] *Id.*, 412 (II, 246).

B.P.—9

marks previously quoted from his letters. He was first and foremost an Irishman, but an Anglo-Irishman, who acknowledged his debt to English culture, and who could not associate himself with certain of the characteristics of his native countrymen. He did not, however, recognise that part of the responsibility for the low condition of the Irish was to be attributed to English rule, for he asks:

Whether England doth not really love us and wish well to us, as bone of her bone, and flesh of her flesh?[1]

which would have astonished the Celt of any period. In short, "Berkeley was a patriot—not a *Pat-riot*, as we are told he used to style his 'bawling' countrymen".[2]

The patriotism of Berkeley was not, like that of Swift, tainted by disappointed ambition; nor was it, like Swift's, confined to a colony of English Protestants.[3]

Of Berkeley's personal ambition in the Church little need be said. He used the emoluments of his Deanery for the American project; at the same time it may be true that he was

offered a bishopric by the Queen, but being . . . absorbed by his famous missionary scheme he declined it.[*]

As Bishop of Cloyne he declined a better bishopric, and refused to allow himself to be considered for the appointment of Vice-Chancellor of Dublin University.

When a young man, it is true, he had to use all his influence to get a post, and was even engaged in a tiresome law-suit over a deanery, which involved a long correspondence with Tom Prior. On returning from America he was concerned to get a better deanery, in order to obtain, as Percival put it,

a mark of his Majesty's good countenance to him, and in a reasonable time repair his private fortune, which by the prosecution of his

---

[1] *Id.*, 323 (II, 155).
[2] *Works*, ed. by Fraser, Vol. IV, p. 560.
[3] Quoted by Fraser, *Loc. cit.*, p. 420.
[*] W. E. H. Lecky, *History of England in the Eighteenth Century*, London, 1920, Vol. II, p. 84. Berkeley authorities do not mention this and I have not been able to check it.

design of settling a college in the Bermudas and the defeat thereof
had suffered. . . . That since the wicked letters writ against him from
Ireland representing him a madman and disaffected to the Government, it was become more necessary for him to insist on some mark
of His Majesty's favour to clear his reputation in those respects.[1]

A good deal has been made of his struggles for deaneries by
G. A. Johnston, who writes:

When he is writing the *Commonplace Book* the *arrière-pensée* of religion
is constantly at the back of his mind. He is careful to see whether his
New Principle is consistent with the dogmas of the Church, *e.g.* the
Creation and the Trinity.[2]

But this would bear only on his becoming a Churchman or a
deist and on a desire not to *wreck* his chances of getting a post;
it would not imply unscrupulous behaviour in obtaining ad-
vancement. But Johnston continues:

He was very eager for ecclesiastical preferment, and lost no chance
of improving his prospects by soliciting the favour of those in power.[3]

This Johnston bases on two letters to Percival[4]; but I cannot
find in these any avarice or desire to promote himself to other
people's detriment. Berkeley was foremost a scholar and he
needed a post without too much routine; self-respect would not
be satisfied with absence of some position; but there is no evidence of exaggeration in these motives. And, as regards money-
matters in general, Berkeley seems to have practised a balanced
realism.

Little is known of his generosity in small matters, but he
certainly gave generously to the people of Cloyne during the
famine. In large matters he is well remembered in America, not
only by the abortive attempt to found a college, or by his broadminded personality, which charmed the people of Rhode Island,
but also by his large gifts of books to Harvard. The private sub-

[1] Rand, *Op. cit.*, pp. 285–6.
[2] G. A. Johnston, *The Development of Berkeley's Philosophy*, London,
1923, p. 333 n.
[3] *Id.*, pp. 333–4 n.
[4] Namely, those in Rand, *Op. cit.*, pp. 178–80, 186.

scription he had collected for his venture he diverted to buying a library for Yale. His farm of ninety-six acres at Whitehall, Rhode Island, he made over to Yale for the encouragement of Greek and Latin scholarship, and many 'Berkeleian Scholars of the House' have gained the fruits of his benefaction.[1] An American, after describing the bitterness of Berkeley's Bermuda failure, dwells lavishly on the posthumous compensations:

What gladness it would have brought to him could he but have had a glimpse into the far future, and could have seen how all along its unfolding centuries that seemingly baffled visit of his was to keep on bearing fruit in the innumerable benign effects it was to have upon civilisation in the New World,—upon the establishment of universities here; upon the cultivation of all liberal studies; upon the improvement of society in morals and in manners; upon the upbuilding of the institutions of religion. He had not, indeed, accomplished the immediate object of his expedition—the founding of an American university in the Bermuda Islands; but, by methods different from those intended by him, and in ways more manifold than even he could have dreamed of, he has since accomplished, and through all coming time, by a thousand ineffaceable influences, he will continue to accomplish, some portion at least of the results—which he had aimed at by the founding of his university.[2]

Was Berkeley a happy man? Only a rough answer to such a question is ever possible. In his College days he was fired by his enthusiasm for the New Principle and all it promised. He enjoyed his travels as a connoisseur. But a certain restlessness may be detected from a letter to Percival, after his return to Dublin at the age of thirty-six. He must have felt he was marking time. He had as yet no position in the Church; more than that, his early philosophy had gained little sympathy and no understanding, and the *De Motu*, just published, attracted no attention. His New Principle, which was to confute freethinking and solve many problems with more ease than by any other method, was not being used. It would not be surprising to find him

[1] A. C. Fraser, *Life and Letters of George Berkeley*, Oxford, 1871, pp. 192–5; Rand, *Op. cit.*, pp. 283–4; Luce, "Berkeley's American Project", as cited, pp. 107–8. The list of books given to Yale are to be found in the *Yale Univ. Library Gazette*, Vol. VIII, 1933.

[2] M. C. Tyler, *Three Men of Letters*, New York and London, 1895, pp. 47–8.

thinking of founding a school of philosophy of his own; and in fact it was about this time, the middle of 1722, that he first formed the idea of the American College. After a period of inactivity, his eager nature was now focused upon this great scheme for the next six years, during which he must have suffered much doubt and disappointment. Then, with his marriage and the change of scene in Rhode Island, life would have regained its hue. But the blackest time in his career was to come, from about a year before he returned home—his College stillborn and the New Principle bereft of scope for ever. This period was relieved by the new-found interest of a growing family, without which he would without doubt have become a completely broken man. As it was, his health was gone.

He was a changed man ever afterwards. With the shattering of that gorgeous and eager dream of his against the rough touch of reality, something of the bloom of being went from him,—something, too, of his old elasticity in hope and joy; and in their place came the sadness of a riper wisdom, and the sweetness of having drunk of a bitter cup.[1]

During his remaining twenty years, his horizon was overcast, but he probably felt resigned, softened by the presence of his family. Still, he managed to write his economic tracts in this period, and take practical steps to deal with armed rebellion. Though his bitterness made slight appearances in the works he wrote immediately on his return from Rhode Island, it did not overshadow his entire life. He preserved his genial nature and sense of humour in his letters, and tried to establish good relations with the Roman Catholics in his diocese.

In short Berkeley faced defeat 'philosophically', bowed to the inevitable, but made the most of what remained to him in life.

This disappointment which long lay heavy upon my spirits I endeavour to make myself easy under, by considering that we even know not what would be eventually good or bad, and that no events are in our power.[2]

[1] *Id.*, p. 38.   [2] Rand, *Op. cit.*, p. 273.

Chapter 11

BERKELEY'S AMERICAN PROJECT

THIS great enterprise should be seen against the background of deism, decadence, and corruption, which Berkeley felt were bedevilling life at home.

He wrote three discourses bearing on the state of the society: "An Essay towards Preventing the Ruin of Great Britain", in 1721; "A Proposal for the Better Supplying of Churches in our Foreign Plantations, and for Converting the Savage Americans to Christianity, by a College to be Erected in the Summer Islands otherwise called the Isles of Bermudas", in 1724; and "A Discourse Addressed to Magistrates and Men in Authority. Occasioned by the Enormous Licence, and Irreligion of the Times", in 1736. The first two were written before he visited America; the third one after. They are all of about twenty pages in length. With them may be compared a letter to Percival, dated March 26, 1742,[1] and certain queries in his economic pamphlets of 1735–7.

The first strikes an extraordinary note of pessimism. He portrays the times as permeated by decadent luxury (comparing "our ladies" with the daughters of Zion), moral degeneracy, and effeteness, due to lack of respect for religion; luxury produces vice and vice breeds national ruin and decay: "we are doomed to be undone"[2];

the present hath brought forth new and portentous villainies, not to be paralleled in our own or any other history. We have been long preparing for some great catastrophe.[3]

And more in equally strong vein.

On the other hand this tract also contains some very practical

[1] A. A. Luce, "Some Unpublished Berkeley Letters with some new Berkeleiana", *Proc. Royal Irish Acad.*, Dublin, 1933, Vol. XLI, Sec. C, No. iv, p. 150.

[2] *Works*, VI, "An Essay towards Preventing the Ruin oi Great Britain", p. 77.

[3] *Id.*, p. 84.

suggestions for improving the economic position and social conditions of the country. These include making better provision for the poor, finding useful work that could be done by the infirm, initiating a programme of public works, and encouraging families by granting some allowance to those with several children. Most interesting, perhaps, is the measure "enacting that the public shall inherit half the unentailed estates of all who die unmarried of either sex."[1] Berkeley did not, however, seem sanguine about their adoption.

The proposal for a College at Bermuda is an eloquent appeal for the college of his dreams, dealing in a realistic way with the practicability of his plan for educating, converting, and invoking spiritual inspiration among the colonists and natives of America.

His reasons for choosing Bermuda were these. On the continent of America there were no inns, conveyances, or bridges. The only means of communicating between settlements was by sea, and Bermuda was mid-way between these, and was also on the route to England. The Bermudans had no special industry and had therefore to become the merchant fleet for other parts; thus they had intercourse with all places, an asset possessed by no other plantation.[2]

The Summer Islands were remarkable for health. They would be safe from pirates. Being without riches there would be less vice there than elsewhere. The inhabitants were religious and frugal.

This was how he saw the state of affairs when he framed his American project.

When he returned from the Continent in 1721, Berkeley was thirty-six. He had a profession but not a career. He may well have felt restless. His philosophy was having no particular effect—and we know the great store he set by it, as the principle for resolving all questions in philosophy and science. Whatever need it was in his nature that made him think it was the open sesame of the intellectual world, if not allayed by fruition of his

---

[1] *Id.*, p. 72.

[2] See a letter to Percival in Benjamin Rand, *Berkeley and Percival*, Cambridge, 1914, pp. 204–5; and "A Proposal for the Better Supplying of Churches in our Foreign Plantations" (ed. by Sampson, Vol. II), pp. 111–13.

new principle, would be likely to induce a certain anxiety. Disappointed thus in the Old World, he turned his hopes to the New. In March, 1723, in one of his best-known letters he wrote to Percival:

It is now about ten months since I have determined with myself to spend the residue of my days in the Island of Bermuda, where I trust in Providence I may be the mean instrument of doing good to mankind.[1]

The idea had therefore been germinating in his mind for some fifteen or sixteen months since his return to England and Ireland.

Once decided, he threw himself into the design with all his energy. He obtained from the King a Charter for the founding of what was to be St. Paul's College in Bermuda. He raised £5,000 by private subscription for the enterprise, to which even Walpole contributed £200. Enthusiasm was widespread; nor was the chance missed of making fun of the project—it even found its way into the broadsheets. The Scriblerus Club met at Lord Bathurst's house to make game of Berkeley, but he was allowed to be heard in his own defence, with the result that those that came to scoff remained to pay; Berkeley

displayed his plan with such an astonishing and animating force of eloquence and enthusiasm that they were struck dumb, and, after some pause, rose up all together with earnestness, exclaiming—"Let us set out with him immediately".[2]

His crowning effort was the successful canvassing of Members of Parliament: the House of Commons voted £20,000, with only two dissentient voices. There was the shadow of a set-back when the King died, for the Charter had been signed but not sealed; however the new King, George II, possibly prompted by Caroline, his Queen, signed and sealed a new Charter within a month. All augured well.

Time passed and the grant was not paid. Eventually Berkeley set forth for Rhode Island without waiting for the money. What happened is well known: it never came. He waited in suspense

[1] Rand, *Op. cit.*, p. 203.
[2] Joseph Warton, *An Essay on the Genius and Writings of Pope*, London, 1782, Vol. II, p. 264 n.

for nearly three years, while his friends at home used their influence on his behalf. When Walpole was pressed for a conclusive answer, he replied:

If you put this question to me as a minister, I must, and can, assure you, that the money shall most undoubtedly be paid, as soon as suits with public convenience; but if you ask me as a friend, whether Dean Berkeley should continue in America, expecting payment of £20,000, I advise him by all means to return home to Europe, and to give up his present expectations.[1]

Little imagination is required to understand the vast patience, foresight, energy, tact, and influence both indirect and personal, that such an enterprise demanded; and then the anti-climax.

This story is to be found in any life of Berkeley. Within recent years, however, Luce has made available numerous fresh details. He has, for instance, published Berkeley's Petition for the College at Bermuda and the Report of the Law Officers upon it (1725), both of which were found by Dr. D. A. Chart among the State Papers relating to Ireland in the Public Record Office.[2] The Petition outlines the purpose of the College and requests a certain constitution and government for it. The Report is by far the more important document. Its favourable examination of the scheme is all the more enhanced by reason of its sober, civil-service mode of expression. It proposed one or two amendments in the statutes of the College; but of the general plan it had no criticism to make. This disposes of the opinion that the scheme was a wild one; as Luce says,

we realise we have here no visionary project by a crack-brained enthusiast.[3]

Berkeley's Proposal was published at the end of 1724, the Petition followed in the following February, and the Report one month later. A year afterwards—May 11, 1726—the House of Commons passed the necessary resolution.[4] What happened

[1] Quoted by A. C. Fraser, *Life and Letters of George Berkeley*, Oxford, 1871, p. 186.

[2] A. A. Luce, "More Unpublished Berkeley Letters and New Berkeleiana", Dublin, 1933, *Hermathena*, Vol. XXIII.

[3] *Id.*, p. 34.

[4] A. A. Luce, "Berkeley's Bermuda Project and his Benefactions to American Universities . . . ", Dublin, 1934, *Proc. Royal Irish Acad.*, Vol. XLII, Sec. C., No. vi, p. 98.

during the next two years and four months? Berkeley made his preparations and waited for the money. As time passed and he still did not get it, he decided to set sail in an unofficial way to allay the doubts of private subscribers,[1] and left others to press the Treasury for the grant. This was to have been paid out of the receipts from the sale of lands at St. Christopher's; but

there was another and much larger charge on the same source, and Berkeley himself recognized that the Treasury could not pay his grant until the total revenue from the St. Christopher lands was ascertained and received. Putting together several passages in the Percival correspondence,[2] we see that the money did not begin to come in to the Treasury till a year or more after Berkeley had sailed, and apparently that Berkeley knew it would be so. Certainly so late as September 20th, 1729, the Queen's Secretary told Percival that none of the money had yet come in. Not till about 1730, then, was the Treasury in a position either to pay or refuse to pay. The delay was not due to red-tape or official obstruction. . . . There was no lack of official goodwill at that time.[3]

Nothing, however, can alter the fact that Parliament voted a grant which was not paid, even when the money from St. Christopher's came in. Two circumstances underlay this: Berkeley's absence from London; and a rumour that the new College was to be built at Rhode Island instead of Bermuda. Rand believes that this rumour was undoubtedly fatal,[4] and Luce concurs.[5] But why had Berkeley chosen Bermuda? His many reasons have been recounted above; the pervading note is one of moral and physical purity—Bermuda was far from vice and good health was assured.

The distance of six hundred miles was a fatal objection. In this connexion, Luce has drawn attention to Henry Newman, Berkeley's London agent; coming from New England, he was well acquainted with American life and did not favour Bermuda. Not long after Berkeley had arrived in Rhode Island, Newman wrote to him:

I believe you are now satisfied that if you had made a short voyage to America before you had published your Proposal you would have

[1] Rand, *Op. cit.*, p. 251.   [2] *Id.*, pp. 242, 248, 250, 256.
[3] Luce, *Op. cit.*, p. 98.   [4] Rand, *Op. cit.*, p. 42.
[5] Luce, *Op. cit.*, p. 102.

very much altered your scheme; but I hope you will have it in your power to rectify your first project in whatever it was amiss, and that your friends here may easily obtain a royal Licence for such alterations as may be recommended by you.[1]

Berkeley recognised the truth of this. In vain he strove to counteract the rumour of his change of plan. If he had received the grant he would have tried to have the Charter altered, but, failing that, he would have been willing to go ahead with the Bermuda scheme.

Berkeley's enterprise, though tragically wrong on that important detail, was, I submit, sound in principle, and he ought to have been allowed to mend his hand.[2]

Is it reasonable to suppose the change of plan, even if he had admitted it, would have been sufficient to justify what appears to be the Government's perfidy? If the Government took a serious view of the rumour, would it not have sought confirmation from Berkeley himself? It did not do so. Is it not more reasonable to suspect that the change was made an excuse not to pay the money? If so, what had made the almost unanimous enthusiasm for the project cool off, especially if the change of situation were for the better? The presumption is inescapable that enthusiasm dwindled, perhaps giving other interests more chance to attract attention, once Berkeley's own personality was withdrawn from London; this was a strategic error of the first order, and it is difficult to believe he would not have obtained the money had he remained. It is true that he would have had difficulties with private subscribers; but he could have managed them, if not with tact, by, for instance, sending a vice-President of the new College in advance, if steadfastness of purpose needed proof.

What could have made the diplomatic Berkeley, after successfully overcoming so many hurdles, blunder over these simple points, his ill-timed voyage and his selection of a site? From his description of Bermuda and from his one poem it appears that there was some fatal fascination for him in the moral purity of this virgin island of the West.

[1] *Id.*, p. 102.   [2] *Id.*, p. 107.

While he was in America Berkeley wrote the lengthy dialogues of *Alciphron*, which is an elegant piece of writing marred by defects of presentation. The speeches are often long; the argument lacks the cogency of his early work.* The book as a whole is a sustained attack on deism. Berkeley has been accused of rancour and every kind of unscrupulousness in his handling of his opponents.[1] In fact there are some half-dozen places where he makes questionable insinuations and propagandist remarks; but he is very far from an accurate understanding of his opponents. Perhaps the most important point to notice is that, whereas in the early work Matter was his target, now it was the believers in Matter.

On his return he wrote his *Theory of Vision Vindicated*—his early philosophy of vision with the difference that the theocentric aspect was now overtly placed at the centre. He rounded on the mathematicians, upholders of Matter, with vehemence. And he wrote the third of his social tracts, containing the same note of gloom as his first two, and preached a sermon in similar vein. The tone of the tract, however, is not that of a reformer but of a sick man:

Deliberate, atheistical blasphemy, is of all crimes most dangerous to the public, inasmuch as it opens the door to all other crimes, and virtually contains them all[2];

Can it then be supposed that impious men shall with impunity invent and publicly utter the most horrid blasphemies, and at the same time the whole constitution not be endangered?[3]

Our prospect is very terrible, and the symptoms grow stronger every day.[4]

The ostensible reason for all this was Berkeley's belief that a society had recently been formed in Dublin consisting of an "execrable fraternity of blasphemers" and calling themselves

---

* Opinions are divided. Jessop, for instance, gives the work immense praise, *Works*, III, p. 2.

[1] J. M. Robertson, *A History of Freethought*, London, 1936, Vol. II, pp. 733–5.

[2] *Works*, VI, "A Discourse Addressed to Magistrates and Men in Authority", p. 219.

[3] *Id.*, p. 220.   [4] *Id.*, p. 221.

"blasters".[1] The Irish House of Lords took him seriously but no one else has done so.[2]

This tract differed from the earlier two in having a slightly altered focus: before Berkeley went to America he treated Britain as beyond the power of men to cure and aimed to start anew in happier climes. Now, after his defeat, he was thrown back on the task of attempting to lessen evil at home. This took the form of a crusade for Christianity against the infidels, but it also included proselytising on behalf of Protestantism.

⟋ The one novel feature of the third tract is the stress laid upon civil law and order. Is it too much to suppose that Berkeley, feeling bitter about his failure in America, was deep down provoked to let fly against the State that let him down, against Walpole, and the materialistic outlook that denied support for the ideal cause? His early ethical doctrine of Passive Obedience or non-resistance* would have been sorely tested, and deep down he may have felt the need to support the rule of law against his smouldering sense of revolt. Similarly he urged a revival of religious belief, which would strengthen his own after the shock it would have received from the failure of the American project. "Blasphemy against God is a great crime against the state"[3] is very strong—was he not sorely tempted to blaspheme?

In all these tracts the *motif* is flight from immorality and decadence. The exhortations to respect religion are coupled with references to the freethinkers, and there can be no doubt that Berkeley regarded deism as the fundamental evil from which all other ill-consequences flowed. We can see from these tracts the intensity of his feeling from them and how great was the evil of Matter and of deism that was the spur to his American project.

[1] *Id.*, p. 218.

[2] A. C. Fraser, *Life and Letters of George Berkeley*, Oxford, 1871, pp. 253–6.

* This he put forward in sermons published in 1712, *Works*, VI.

[3] *Id.*, "A Discourse Addressed to Magistrates and Men in Authority", p. 218.

Chapter 12

BERKELEY'S HEALTH

BERKELEY's own health is a matter of no little importance. We know from Stock, his first biographer, that he developed a 'nervous cholic', due to his sedentary occupation;

it rendered life a burden to him; the more so, as his pains were exasperated by exercise.[1]

These were Berkeley's own words, according to Stock. Again:

He was, however, often troubled with the hypochondria; and latterly, with that nervous cholic mentioned above.[2]

The reference to hypochondria is all the more striking in that it is the only mention throughout Stock's book of any weakness of Berkeley's—physical, mental, or moral. His health and fear of illness may explain the composition of *Siris*: despite the immense care he took over this book, it is his most unsystematic and ill-ordered work:

The Author has been heard to declare, that this work cost him more time and pains than any other he had ever been engaged in.[3]

When did he first show signs of this trouble? Several references to his health are to be found among his letters to Percival and others. A letter written in 1713 from Lyons on his first tour of the Continent shows that he was careful about his health.[4] In 1715 he wrote of a return of his ague.[5] Then from Naples two years later, on his second tour, he sends a warm invitation to Percival, trying to persuade him to bring his family out there. As additional reasons for the visit he urges:

[1] Joseph Stock, *The Life of Bishop Berkeley*, reprinted in *Works*, ed. Wright, London, 1843, Vol. I, p. 13.
[2] *Id.*, p. 14.
[3] *Id.*, p. 13.
[4] Benjamin Rand, *Berkeley and Percival*, Cambridge, 1914, p. 131.
[5] *Id.*, p. 140.

The air of this happy part of the world is soft and delightful beyond
conception, being perfumed with myrtle shrubs and orange groves,
that are everywhere scattered throughout the country; the sky almost constantly serene and blue; the heat tempered to a just warmth
by refreshing breezes from the sea. Nor will this serene and warmth
of the climate have a better effect on the spirits, than the balsamine
particles of sulphur which you breathe with the common air will
have on your blood, correcting those sharp scorbutic humours that
molest the inhabitants of these bleak islands.[1]

The reference to sulphur (fire) and air are particularly noteworthy in the light of their prominence in *Siris*.

Six months later from Testaccio in the Island of Inorine
comes an important remark:

My illness, a flux, after about six weeks continuance, hath now
quite left me.[2]

The flux was one of the complaints he found benefited by tar-
water. He was now thirty-two. About this time his Journal
shows a marked interest in illness and cures. The numbers of
illnesses and cures mentioned[3] remind one of *Siris*. Concern
with the inside of the body is very evident from the following
strange entry:

Seely told me that he had drunk ten young vipers taken out of the
womb, all living, as big as large pins, in one glass of wine. Takes
powder of vipers dried in the shade, a drachm a day during the
months of May and September. Sweetens the blood above all things.[4]

Four years after that, on his return to Dublin, he recommends
a preservative against the plague.[5]

A year and a half later appears from London his famous
Bermuda letter, in which he succinctly outlines his project for
an American College.

[1] *Id.*, pp. 164-5.
[2] *Id.*, p. 168.
[3] A. C. Fraser, *The Life and Letters of George Berkeley*, Oxford, 1871,
pp. 585, 586.
[4] *Id.*, p. 587.
[5] Rand, *Op. cit.*, p. 179.

But above all, that uninterrupted health and alacrity of spirit, which is the result of the finest weather and gentlest climate in the world, and which of all others is the most effectual cure for the cholic.[1]

Thus by 1723 he had suffered from cholic, and the desire to cure himself was one motive reinforcing his American plan. He was thirty-eight all but a few days when he wrote this letter. A few months afterwards he writes from Dublin expressing his concern at Lady Percival's having the cholic and urges her to try the waters of Geronster, as she had not improved at "the Bath".[2]

Eighteen months later a letter from Dublin shows he had a bout:

I am now, bless God, quite at ease from a cruel periodical cholic which seized me after my return from Derry. For several days it was very violent, but the loss of thirty-six ounces of blood with about a dozen purgings and vomitings, reduced both it and me to a very weak state.[3]

A year later comes another reference to the cholic which he discussed at some length.

In the middle of 1730, when Berkeley was in Rhode Island, the sense that his mission was doomed was growing, and he writes:

I must own the disappointments I have met with in this particular have nearly touched me, not without affecting my health and spirits.[4]

On his return to England he had a temporary respite, as he mentioned when writing to Tom Prior early in 1734:

As to myself, by regular living, and rising very early (which I find the best thing in the world), I am very much mended; insomuch, that though I cannot read, yet my thoughts seem as distinct as ever.[5]

But only a month later he informed Tom in a couple of letters of a bad attack of gout.[6] Fraser sums up that "his health was broken before he left London"[7]:

[1] *Id.*, p. 205.   [2] *Id.*, p. 208.   [3] *Id.*, p. 221.   [4] *Id.*, p. 268.
[5] Fraser, *Op.cit.*, p. 210.   [6] *Id.*, pp. 213, 214.   [7] *Id.*, p. 229.

The story of his life, his letters, and even his portraits, show the contrast between what he was before, and what he became after the Bermuda expedition.[1]

The evidence of his letters is that his ill-health became chronic soon after he returned from America.

After some years of residence in Cloyne, the Bishop wrote to Prior at some length of a cure for the bloody flux. He adds: "I believe tar-water might be useful."[2] This was early in 1741, just over three years before the publication of *Siris*. A few months later, in a letter to Dr. Clarke, he refers to his "habituall Cholic",[3] and in a fragment writes:

I had many symptoms of the stone, and for a long time suspected my . . . cholic to be an effect thereof. But of late I am satisfied that it is a scorbutic cholic, and that my original disease is the scurvy.[4]

In the middle of the next year he writes to Percival:

For above three years together I have not gone three miles off, being nailed down to Cloyne by a cholic and pain in my side which is irritated by the motion of a horse or a coach.[5]

It would seem that Berkeley's trouble, whatever it was, began when he was about thirty and that it continued on and off for the rest of his life. He chiefly suffered from cholic, which, according to the *Oxford Dictionary* means 'severe griping pains in belly'; he had also suffered from a serious bloody flux, *i.e.* according to the same source, 'a disease with inflamed mucous membrane and intestinal glands, griping pains, and mucus and bloody evacuations'. These may be symptoms of some kidney or bowel complaint or both; but he certainly had enough strong girdle pains to bring to the forefront of his mind any latent fears he might have had about his health.

[1] *Id.*, p. 347.
[2] *Id.*, p. 263.
[3] A. A. Luce, "More Unpublished Berkeley Letters and New Berkeleiana", *Hermathena*, Dublin, 1933, Vol. XXIII, p. 43.
[4] Fraser, *Op. cit.*, p. 268.
[5] A. A. Luce, "Some Unpublished Berkeley Letters with some New Berkeleiana," *Proc. Royal Irish Acad.*, Dublin, 1933, Vol. XLI, Sec. C, No. iv, p. 151.

Was he in some degree a hypochondriac? He had good reasons for dwelling on matters of health, but were his zealous investigation of tar-water and his exaggerated claims for it signs that his concern was over-strong, *i.e.* stronger than was warranted by his actual condition and intensified by some other cause? Had he been content to study tar-water and claim for it a value approximating to its actual merits, no such suggestions would be justified. But his desire for a panacea seems like a demand for a cure for ill-health far beyond what he endured; the excursion into the mystical fire, which endowed tar-water with its omnipotent power, is strong evidence of such a demand; and finally should be noted his scattered references to health and cures written before he suffered at all intensely. It is therefore reasonable to suppose he had a considerable hypochondriacal strain, and that one of the great motives for his interest in tar-water (without forgetting his altruistic desire to help the poor in his diocese) was to deal, not merely with his own physical pains, but with a dread of illness.

Stock's description of Berkeley as suffering from hypochondria is correct; he was hypochondriacal in the everyday sense of having some degree of morbid anxiety about his health. Thus his symptoms consisted of cholic, flux, and also his hypochondriacal attitude.*

From this survey of Berkeley's health, it is clear that his disorders were of very long duration and that he had troublesome complaints even before his American venture. The difference is, however, that on his return they became much worse: they became sufficiently bad to incapacitate him for long periods and to constitute chronic illness.[1] Before that they were no more than disturbances, under control.

---

* It should be remembered that the word "hypochondria" is not now used in psychiatry as a name for a disease; but it may be usefully retained in the colloquial sense for a symptom.

[1] See below, p. 175.

UNCONSCIOUS
INTERPRETATION

Chapter 13

UNANSWERED QUESTIONS

BERKELEY's early classics, the *Principles* and the *Three Dialogues*, were intended, if the argument in Part I is correct, to present a philosophy of Theocentric Phenomenalism but actually conveyed Solipsism. Is this to be ascribed to inefficiency on Berkeley's part or is it not rather a sign of a solipsistic strain in him? This strain was certainly overt in the *Philosophical Commentaries*. And what does this signify?

His early Solipsism was left behind, Theocentric Phenomenalism was reasonably mature in his middle period when he was in America, and this assumed the more mystical form of Panentheism in his later days. Is this a rational evolution of thought or is it not rather a sign of change of outlook? What would have brought this about?

In this evolution, Matter began by being his main target, became replaced in part by deists, mathematicians, and every kind of profligate, and ultimately ceased actively to be his archenemy. What underlay this change of outlook?

Why did Berkeley give vent to his attack on mathematicians, for which the ammunition was being prepared in the *Philosophical Commentaries* and the little essay "Of Infinites", only after twenty-five years?

Why did his broadminded fairness forsake him in dealing with the deists?

Is *Siris* to be explained as a rational attempt to alleviate disease or is it not rather, with all its quality of myth, a sign of hypochondria?

Why did he choose America—and more especially the obviously unsuitable site of Bermuda—for his new College?

Is his marriage at forty-three to be explained on the

grounds that he had not before met the right partner, or has it not rather an intrinsic connexion with his whole development?

Is his ill-health, which became chronic on his return from America when he was forty-six, to be explained as due to a sedentary life, to middle age, to constitutional weakness, or is it not to be regarded as a functional disorder explicable psychosomatically in terms of psychogenetic trends and environmental circumstances?

These questions concern the development of philosophical views, modifications of temperament, and organic changes. Is there a connexion between these phenomena?

Those who cannot see how they could be connected may nonetheless be invited to reflect upon the strangeness of devoting a great part of one's life to attacking Matter, which necessitated the construction of a metaphysic of *Esse percipi*. It is easy, of course, to overlook the problem by assuming something like the following: are not thoughts the logical outcome of thoughts; was not *Esse percipi* the logical outcome of the unsatisfactory ontology and epistemology left by Locke; is not thinking a logical process that requires no other explanation than that, given the premises, the conclusion must follow? This might be commonsense; it would certainly not be a fact; it is at best a psychological theory—a rudimentary psychological theory about higher mental processes. It has the merit of being simple, but it throws no light whatever on Berkeley's sense of mission on behalf of *Esse percipi* against Matter.

Again, it might seem that no special explanation of *Esse percipi* is needed, because it was 'in the air'; Malebranche,[1] Norris,[2] and Collier* were writing on somewhat similar lines. It was something about Berkeley, however, that led him to accept, not to mention develop, this type of philosophy, which other

[1] Malebranche, *Search after Truth*, London, 1694.

[2] John Norris, *Theory of the Ideal or Intelligible World*, London, 1701–4.

* Arthur Collier, *Clavis Universalis . . . Being a Demonstration of the Non-existence, or Impossibility of an External World*, London, 1713. Collier published after Berkeley, but his book is some evidence that Immaterialism was 'in the air'.

thinkers of the time did not accept. Hence either the logic of the situation was so obvious that any clear thinker, such as Berkeley, would have seen it (and even this would not suffice as an explanation), or else there was a personal element in the adoption of the point of view. But, to look at this topic from a more fundamental angle, there are many explanations of any given phenomenon: 'the' explanation is the appropriate answer to a certain question or the appropriate explanation within a given frame of reference. It is therefore quite correct to say that the explanation of Berkeley's philosophy was the philosophical situation at that time. But this is an answer to a different sort of question from the one being raised here, namely what it was about Berkeley that led *him* in the given historical circumstances to adopt a certain view.

The psychogenetic explanation offered in this Part does not imply that had Berkeley been living in another century he would have produced the philosophy of *Esse percipi*; indeed his philosophy, though it would have had the same personal meaning, would have taken a different form. The point is most easily seen by reference to the causes of dreams: environmental circumstances are believed to touch off a genetic process in such a way that the genetic wish behind the dream is expressed, however distortedly, in the imagery of some selection from the environmental circumstances. Thus a child that has been refused some toy may express a wish to play in a dream of being at a grand party where someone tries ineffectively to spoil the fun. To obviate misunderstanding, it is desirable to add that this does not imply either that other philosophies originate in the same genetic factors as we find in Berkeley or that a follower of Berkeley, if there were one, would necessarily have the same mental structure as he; we find the psychological meaning of Matter from Berkeleian contexts, but another philosopher might deny Matter in a different psychological way; the same dream dreamt by two persons may mean different things, according to their associations to it. Some of the interpretations given below would probably hold for all philosophies of a Berkeley type, but some would probably not.

However ripe the times were for a Berkeleian philosophy, the intellectual atmosphere did not impinge on Berkeley's mind as on a *tabula rasa,* reacting automatically or by a rational process so as to produce an immaterialist philosophy. On the contrary, Berkeley's mind was of a kind that welcomed the stimulus, went at least half way to meet it, and made its own contribution. It is the individuality of his thinking that needs explanation.

Chapter 14

THE RÔLE OF TAR-WATER AND
ESSE PERCIPI

THE RÔLE OF TAR-WATER

IF we wish to explore the inner recesses of Berkeley's mind, we may begin by considering the mystical ideas to be found in *Siris*, his extraordinary work on Tar-water. He probably suffered from disorder in the urinary system and the bowel, his letters show concern about his health even before he suffered acutely, and *Siris* reveals a determined striving after a divine panacea.

Now the rôle of tar-water was to remove impurities of all kinds from the body, in particular to carry off gravel, and to act as a deobstruent, to use Berkeley's archaic word—in short it was to be an aperient to *cleanse* the body. It is clear that the special substance that he felt had to be evacuated was of a poisonous and clogging character. This material was felt to do physical harm to the body, but it required divine mystical powers to counter it. Its malevolent harmful quality can perhaps best be expressed by the word "poison", so far as any single word is adequate.

The spiritual significance of cleanness and uncleanness is easily found in the life of primitive peoples. Lévy-Bruhl, for instance, makes it quite clear that cleanness and uncleanness are fusions of material and spiritual meanings (not necessarily moral); he does not suggest that the two are confused or interchangeable, but that they are different aspects of one whole:

Seen from one aspect, to be 'unclean' is a kind of essentially mystic quality, which makes a person find himself in the power of an evil influence and in imminent danger of disaster. From another aspect, it is a material defilement, a blemish that adheres physically to the unclean person or object, which can be transferred, or communicated through contact, or removed by cleansing, etc.[1]

[1] Lucien Lévy-Bruhl, *Primitives and the Supernatural*, London, 1936, pp. 242–3.

To be unclean is both to be physically ill and also bewitched or under a spell; indeed the latter is the greater disaster:

> To the primitive mind . . . the most serious part of a misfortune is not the misfortune itself, however disastrous it may be. It is what the misfortune reveals—that is, the evil influence which has just been exerted on the victim, which will no doubt be exercised again, and which makes fresh disasters imminent.[1]

Likewise to be clean is to be free of physical ill but mainly of evil influences. Moreover, to cleanse or purify often means to fortify or make vigorous.[2]

Among civilised people psycho-analysts have found similar ideas both in adults and children: thus Stärcke,[3] van Ophuijsen,[4] and Klein[5] have found feelings of being harmed or persecuted by something bad inside the body; and Klein[6] has reported cases where patients have described their ailments in terms of 'feeling poisoned' (where there was nothing organically wrong and no poison present).

Berkeley had a certain hypochondriacal concern about his health, which in itself was mental, though this is not in itself to say that the cause of his actual ill-health was mental. But this presumption arises when we recall the magical powers of tar-water as a deobstruent. One might be tempted to urge in all strictness that the magical element in the cure is to be connected only with the hypochondria and that it is no evidence at all for the existence of a mental factor in the aetiology of his physical symptoms. This is certainly a matter for investigation. But, whatever the truth may turn out to be in this regard, we can be

---

[1] *Id.*, p. 154.

[2] *Id.*, pp. 240–1.

[3] Aug. Stärcke, "The Reversal of the Libido-Sign in Delusions of Persecution", *The International Journal of Psycho-Analysis*, London, 1920, Vol. I, Pt. iii, pp. 231–4.

[4] J. H. W. van Ophuijsen, "On the Origin of the Feeling of Persecution", *The International Journal of Psycho-Analysis*, London, 1920, Vol. I, Pt. iii, pp. 235–9.

[5] Melanie Klein, *The Psycho-Analysis of Children*, London, 1937, pp. 78, 79 n., 190, 312, 319, 320, 329, 351; *Contributions to Psycho-Analysis*, London, 1948, pp. 256, 282, 284, 382.

[6] Melanie Klein, *The Psycho-Analysis of Children*, London, 1937, p. 140 n. (*cf.* 78, 79 n.); *Contributions to Psycho-Analysis*, London, 1948, p. 356.

definite concerning Berkeley's own feelings: we can see from *Siris* that late in life he felt poisoned, bewitched, defiled, or had some bad, harmful, or persecuting stuff inside him, possessed of physical and psychical powers, such as only a divine deobstruent or magical purifier would dispel; he felt no longer fortified for life or full of vigour. How far he realised that this was his pre-occupation is less certain, but one would gain the impression from his correspondence that in his later days he did realise it to a certain extent, though he might not have gone so far as to say that he felt poisoned. Thus far we have:

Interpretation I: Berkeley felt that he had poison inside him, clogging and destroying him.

Tar-water was a physical laxative, but we should also give our attention to its magical potency. Tar comes from pines and firs. The juices of plants have their origin in solar light. They contain a balsam, according to Berkeley, consisting of oil which is the vehicle of a subtle volatile oil, and the oil is contained in tar. The volatile oil is a subtle acid, which is pure salt or a salt-principle (*pace* chemists!). Now salt has been shown by Ernest Jones to be a symbol of semen, to be a fertilising principle; he has collected all manner of customs that confirm the connexion beyond all reasonable doubt, such as the practice of carrying salt in the trouser-pocket on a man's wedding day.[1] Berkeley provides material that is in keeping with this[2]: salt is "that mighty instrument in the hand of nature"; manure fertilises because it contains salt. He cites the opinion that acids are shaped like daggers and alkalies like sheaths, and that the daggers run into the sheaths, which obviously ascribes a phallic significance to salt. But he does not entirely accept this and is more impressed with the cleansing power of the substance. He connects salt with air, because air contains acid; but air would seem to be less pure because it corrodes; and air can cause human pain and various disorders. However, he divides air into pure and impure parts, the pure being fire, *i.e.* invisible fire diffused through all the earth. This he also calls aether. He notes from the scriptures that God is a consuming fire—not, of course,

[1] Ernest Jones, *Essays in Applied Psycho-Analysis*, London, 1951, Vol. II, "The Symbolic Significance of Salt" (1912).

[2] *Works*, V, *Siris*, § 132.

flame. Fire, too, is a fertilising principle. Fire and light are identified; "light cannot be defiled by filth of any kind"[1]; "the cleansing quality, the light and heat of fire, are natural symbols of purity, knowledge, and power."[2] From all these associations it is clear that tar-water is a mystical, divine cleanser which promotes life. It is to be noted, however, that a small residual element of dirt is to be found in tar-water: the divine purifying principle is conveyed by tar-water, as salt is by manure; also, trees become "choked and stuffed with their own juice"[3]. Thus the cure for a clogged condition is a highly purified form of dirty substance, transformed so as to be almost unrecognisable, yet not wholly out of touch with its original state.

THE MEANING OF MATTER AND THE RÔLE OF *ESSE PERCIPI*

Berkeley's early philosophy conveys to us a solipsistic world in which an *esse* of every kind depends upon *percipi* here and now. Such a world differs in no way from a dream.

What is the difference between the world of reality and a dream? Objects in the real world have unity, permanence, and order. In a dream they may not have any of these features. All kinds of transformations are possible that could not occur in the real world; objects can lose their identity in the most 'natural' manner. A dream can be created by the whim of the dreamer; but the external world has a 'solidity' he cannot tamper with. Philosophers, such as Locke, have wondered what it is that cements the world into an orderly, unified, and persisting whole. No doubt Locke would have held that without Matter the real world would be reduced to a dream; for qualities of objects were supposed to inhere in Matter, so that without Matter there would be nothing for qualities to inhere in. Thus in the world of reality sensible appearances are somehow *bound together*, so as to produce unity, permanence, and order, which cannot as such be subject to change by human beings; and the chaotic array of sensible appearances of a dream are unbound, lack unity, permanence, and order, and can be modified without limit by the dreamer. The contrast is between something that binds with control so as to produce coherence and the absence of anything

[1] *Id.*, § 206.   [2] *Id.*, § 182.   [3] *Id.*, § 16.

to bind, the absence of control, and the lack of coherence. What, then, is this substance that cements images into reality?

Berkeley denied Matter this function and conveyed the impression that the world is a dream. What is the nature of this Matter, whose function was to bind, control, and give coherence, which the principle of *Esse percipi* was designed to negate?

We may attempt to answer this by making use of what we now know from *Siris*. In *Siris* days Berkeley felt clogged with poison and unable to free himself of the evil stuff. This does not appear to have been so in his youth; but, if we draw on the postulate, well supported by clinical analysis, that psychical trends persist, *i.e.* as regards their roots, though they may assume different forms, we may suppose that the root of the tar-water philosophy was closely connected or identical with the root of the early Solipsism, and hence that he was concerned about poison, though in a different form, when he published the *Principles* in 1710 as a young man of about twenty-five. Thus the mortar that he attacked, the Lockean substratum, when he gave us a picture of a dream-world, may be identified with the poison that he felt to be within him in later years; so that this poisonous stuff constituted the principle that binds the external world together. We are thus in a position to understand Matter:

Interpretation II: Matter symbolised poison in the external world.

The situation, then, was that in the early years Matter (external poison) was eliminated by *Esse percipi* and later in life bad health (internal poison) was controlled by Tar-water— but it was the same poison in both stages. Thus *Esse percipi* and Tar-water were equivalent forms of a purification-principle. But there is a transformation or evolution from one to the other, which from a clinical point of view would be related genetically:

(Genetic) Interpretation III: Tar-water in later years cleansed internal poison, a situation parallel to and also developing from the situation in which Esse percipi *in earlier years cleansed Matter.*

In *Siris*, which Berkeley published in 1744 as a man of fifty-nine, he did not stress the philosophy of *Esse percipi*, which indicates that the problem, the form in which the fear of poison showed, had altered. He retained his considered philosophical views unchanged to the end, as Luce has shown, at most admitting that his earlier mode of expressing them might not have been wholly satisfactory.[1] The correct reading of this would seem to be that he retained an intellectual belief in what he had to say (Immaterialism) but no longer concentrated his emotional life upon the *esse-percipi* approach to this. In short, *Esse percipi* was retained but made to occupy a relatively subordinate position in his Panentheism so that it lost its special prominence. This must be taken to mean that Berkeley was no longer anxious about the poisonous elements of the external world, for the fear had moved its ground; he became hypochondriacal instead. Thus the change of emphasis in his published work falls in with the genetic interpretation—if there were no change at all that interpretation would be wrong.

This is a suitable place to mention one of our fundamental questions which arises naturally at this point: What brought about the change from a conflict about external poison to one about internal poison? This question, though not discussed in the next few chapters, forms a focal point on which they are designed to bear.

[1] *Works*, II, a letter to Samuel Johnson, p. 282.

Chapter 15

THE RELATION BETWEEN GOD
AND MATTER

IMMATERIALISM was not only the denial of the philosophical conception of Matter, nor the mere assertion of a commonsense theory of perception; it was a positive speculative position that spirits are the only causal agents and that the being of God necessitates the denial of Matter. Some active cause was required. This could not be found in ideas, which Berkeley regarded as passive and inert and dependent for their existence upon an active cause. Nor could it be found in Matter, which according to Berkeley's argument has no properties, least of all that of being a causal agent. Thus Berkeley placed active agency in spirit, in human spirits to some degree, but primarily in God.

But this in itself, we may say, does not prevent Matter from existing; yet Berkeley regarded God and Matter as incompatible. He did not put this forward as an overt assertion in his published writings. Nonetheless he believed it, at least for a time and probably always, for in the *Philosophical Commentaries* occurs (though with the marginal sign "+" against it) the following remarkable entry.

625. Matter once allow'd. I defy any man to prove that God is not matter.

It is not generally realised how like one another God and Matter were in Berkeley's philosophy. Matter, as the conception was handed down, was infinite, eternal, uncreated, indestructible, and the foundation of nature. Its relation to nature was twofold: it was a substance in which all sensory qualities inhered; and it was a power, both the power that produced in our perceptual experience an orderly arrangement of percepts and the power that regulated motion. In Berkeley's system, God differed only in not being something in which sensory-qualities inhered; all the other features mentioned were held in common.

145

There is in fact no way of distinguishing them, except to say that Berkeley discussed omnipotent power under two headings, one of which he regarded as good and called "God" and the other of which he regarded as bad and called "Matter".

The tone of Berkeley's entry is emphatic. Moreover it has support:

298.   Locke, More, Raphson etc seem to make God extended. 'tis nevertheless of great use to religion to take extension out of our idea of God and put a power in its place. It seems dangerous to suppose extension wch is manifestly inert in God.

A parallel to this is to be found in Berkeley's attack on mathematicians because of their belief in Matter and denial of God. Again,

290.   The great danger of making extension exist without the mind, in y^t if it does it must be acknowledg'd infinite immutable eternal etc. wch will be to make either God extended (wch I think dangerous) or an eternal, immutable, infinite, increate being beside God.

To this there is a parallel in his *De Motu*:

§ 54   For many, so far from regarding absolute space as nothing, regard it as the only thing (God excepted) which cannot be annihilated; and they lay down that it necessarily exists of its own nature, that it is eternal and uncreate, and is actually a participant in the divine attributes.

That is to say, it is dangerous to put extension, *i.e.* Matter, in God; the assertion of Matter by mathematicians (including physicists) leads them to deny God; Matter if it existed would be indestructible, and possess a divine attribute—if Matter existed, God, if allowed in any sense, must be equal or reduced to Matter. If Matter existed, its divine power would therefore leave no room for God as a separate being; or, being indestructible, it would not be subject to the power of God and therefore limit his omnipotence. That is to say, God would be no longer omnipotent, which would contradict the notion of God, or he would be equated or reduced to Matter.

Thus there was no room in Berkeley's philosophy for both

God and Matter.* And Matter was dangerous and God was needed.

Let us consider this in the light of preceding results. It is part of the panentheistic view expressed in *Siris* that the world is part of God and not *vice versa*[1]; but, if Matter existed, God would contain Matter within himself, an idea that could not be entertained, since God, the source of tar-water, the only being perfectly pure and clean, could not contain such stuff within himself. There is a contrast, therefore, between the *Philosophical Commentaries* and *Siris*: In *Siris* God must not be sullied with Matter *inside* himself, and in the *Commentaries* God must not be subject to the limitation of his power that would arise from the existence of Matter *outside* himself.

This very striking fear of reducing God to Matter has the obvious significance:

Interpretation IV: Berkeley feared turning God into poison.

Poison would overpower God or make him cease to be.

Following a vast amount of clinical experience we should seek behind this *fear* of debasing God the *wish* to do so. Was not Hylas, who represented Locke and argued for Matter in the *Three Dialogues*, a projection of Berkeley's attitudes, desiring the existence of poisonous Matter? For substantiation we need go no further than to recall the sceptical trend to be found in the *Philosophical Commentaries*, which attracted Berkeley to such a degree that it was touch and go whether he became an overt sceptic and a philosophical materialist.[2] He thus experienced at some time in his life a fascination for scepticism, and at that time poison held out some attraction to him. Hence we reach—

Interpretation V: Berkeley did not realise that he wanted to turn God into poison.

To this picture there is a complementary side. On Berkeley's principles he could distinguish between the real world and images conjured up at will by a percipient on the basis of God's active power: God imparts steadiness to the ideas existing in the external world, which human beings cannot effect.

---

* One is reminded of the incompatibility of serving God and Mammon —Mammon and Matter having a common intestinal origin.

[1] *Works*, V, *Siris*, §§ 270, 276, 279, 284, 285, 287, 295.

[2] See above, Ch. 3 (5).

Thus God supplies the binding tissue that makes the external world unified, persistent, and orderly; evidently God possessed some pure form of binding material, of eternal value. Here we have a purified form of Matter, in the main possessed only by God, though to some extent human beings share in his nature, his activity, and consequently his possessions. Thus Berkeley not merely feared turning God into poison, but portrayed him as an architect who produced a pure form of material for building the external world.

Thus the rôle of *Esse percipi* in purging the world of poison has to be supplemented by God's unsullied mortar to sustain the world—*Esse est a Deo Causari*. Here we find the poison driven out by the New Principle make its return in another guise, albeit a purified one. In short we have—

Interpretation VI: Berkeley's conception of God was that of an omnipotent architect, giving unity, persistence, and order to our ideas by means of a pure binding material.

Moreover,

*Interpretation VII: The poison had to be kept apart from the pure cement for fear of rendering it poisonous also.**

In all analysis there is great complexity, which arises from the multiplicity of determinants of any given state. In this analysis of Berkeley I deal mainly with one—the one that is displayed most prominently in his life and work, the one for which there is the most evidence, and the one that is most probably of dominant importance. But we shall later[1] have occasion to interpret another relation between God and Matter. Here we may introduce a further interpretation of poison.

All through his adult days by far the strongest need in Berkeley was to eliminate poison. This he did first by *Esse percipi* and at the end by taking tar-water. He could not tolerate the recognition of poison in himself. This becomes more intelligible

* This may be a suitable place to refer to a difficulty some readers may experience with regard to different levels of analysis. On the one hand Matter did not exist; on the other it was overcome by means of *Esse percipi*. Psychologically what this contradiction means is that for conscious thinking Matter was denied, but, on the level of Berkeley's attitudes as a whole, Matter existed but had to be subject to constraint.

[1] Below, Ch. 20 (*d*).

if we interpret it as being due to a guilt-fraught desire, for we have seen that for some reason or other poison exercised a fascination over him:

(Guilt) Interpretation VIII: Berkeley possessed unrecognised guilt at wanting to have something intimately connected with poison.

This does not seem intelligible—why should we want to have anything even remotely connected with poison? "Poison", it must be remembered, is the most natural description of what he felt he had inside him in the tar-water days, threatening his insides; but we must now go beyond this description to a precursor of all such poison, namely faeces:

Interpretation IX: For Berkeley in adult life faeces were poison.

This link between poison and faeces in explicitly noted in the works of Stärcke, van Ophuijsen, and Klein already cited. Whether in his adult life Berkeley would have realised that he regarded his faeces in this way is uncertain. It is the sort of identification that would be recognised by some but not by others. Probably he recognised it to some extent when he took to tar-water as a deobstruent. The point is not important— what is important and what it is certain he did not realise was the connexion between his attitude that faeces were poison and his unrecognised desires and philosophical principles.

Now Berkeley's adult attitude to faeces would not reflect the whole of his attitude to them as a child. To a child they can be bad and they can also be good; or a child may divide them into two kinds, good and bad. This makes it intelligible that he should have wanted faeces or something intimately connected with them—namely the faeces that as a child he regarded as good. We can now see also the root of the pure cement that Berkeley sought; and we can see that he feared that the good faeces would be destroyed by the bad or reduced to its level. This will be amplified in Chapter 20.

Chapter 16

THE EVOLUTION OF BERKELEY'S CONFLICT (I)

WE have seen evidence of an ambivalent attitude in Berkeley, and in the next chapter we shall see this directed towards mathematicians and deists. It was also displayed in other forms.

In some of the entries in the *Philosophical Commentaries* where he attacked mathematicians, with caustic comment on their absurdity, he added that no Irishman could attain such 'truths'. Here he reveals his identification with Ireland in his attack on the English Newton, "a philosopher of a neighbouring nation".[1] Berkeley was Anglo-Irish,* and would not have identified himself with the Celtic Irish to the extent of feeling politically and personally wronged by England. Such antagonism as he possessed found its outlet in his attack on the English freethinkers, whose philosophy (Locke) and mathematics and physics (Newton) led in his opinion to atheism. At the same time he was an intimate of the most select intellectual and social circles in London, and there is not the slightest indication that he failed to appreciate this; on the contrary, he expressed his admiration for England in no uncertain terms.[2] We therefore add the following:

Interpretation X: Berkeley was somewhat ambivalent towards the English.

This is of interest because it was an Englishman, Walpole, who acting as Prime Minister on behalf of the English Government,† unscrupulously wrecked the great enterprise of Berkeley's life. In the foregoing interpretation the word "somewhat" has been

---

[1] *Works*, II, *The Principles of Human Knowledge*, § 110 (reading of first edition).

* See above, pp. 113–18.

[2] See above, p. 116.

† I speak here of the 'English' Government (rather than the British or United Kingdom Government) which was the psychological reality whatever the constitutional position; for to Ireland the enemy was always the English—never the Scots or Welsh.

inserted because there is no evidence of any very strong ambivalence or of any very pronounced animosity to the English;
his attitude, as it is displayed in his life, letters, and works seems
to preclude it, and if it had been present it would probably have
shown itself. The degree to which he had some ambivalence in
this regard is just worth drawing attention to; but the significance of the rôle that Walpole played is to be found most
probably, not in his being English, but in his being associated
with a society that Berkeley thought corrupt.

The great project in Berkeley's career loomed up when he
was about thirty-seven, when this enterprising man—or unpractical idealist as some have conceived him—decided to found
a College in Bermuda. Our present concern, however, is not
with his plans and expedition but with the President of the
College himself and his motives for forming it; it is obvious that
some powerful driving force impelled him to enter upon such a
project, unwavering amid all impediments and delays. A great
part of the explanation is to be found in his desire to preach the
gospel of *Esse percipi*, the New Principle. But why did he wish to
carry out such a missionary ideal in the New World instead of
in the Old?

Doubtless he was attracted by virgin soil. In a new college, in
a new unspoiled country he could play the rôle of a leader; his
would be the supreme opinion, he would be the sole authority
in all matters pertaining to philosophy and religion. We must
remember that Berkeley did not write in a scientific or academic
vein, inviting discussion in the hope of elucidation or making
further discoveries; he wrote with a note of finality as one who
had already discovered "amazing truth"—he looked upon the
New Principle as a potent weapon with which to discover knowledge and simplify what was already known.[1] We may take it
that he designed to teach as dogma the philosophy of Theocentric Phenomenalism and that he alone should be the authority on any issue that might arise out of it. He was to be god of
the culture of the New World, where Bermuda was to be the
'Athens of the World'[2]; thus the feeling of omnipotence was

---

[1] *Works*, I, *Philosophical Commentaries*, 383; *The Principles of Human
Knowledge*, § 85 f.

[2] Benjamin Rand, *Berkeley and Percival*, Cambridge, 1914, p. 225.

growing in his mind. By all this, however, is not meant any kind of censure; there is no suggestion that this was contemplated solely or even mainly for reasons of self-importance; he was not a self-important man; these things had other motives, to do with what he felt was required of him in this world and with certain inner personal needs to which we shall come.

Nor should it be forgotten that Berkeley married on the eve of his departure for America, for a bachelor of forty-three does not marry if the tenor of his life remains unchanged. He evidently felt his manhood maturing within him.

Moreover, the new college was to be called, not "Trinity" after his own *alma mater*, but "St. Paul's", which revels the dominance in his mind of the good God, "in whom we live and move and have our being"—the note was to be explicitly theocentric. His relation to God was thus different from what it had been in early days when God to him was less a person than a power, a power to constrain external poisonous Matter. Here he was becoming godlike, building a pure new culture, himself dispelling Matter, and thus identifying himself with God. He could not identify himself overtly with the mathematician or the Englishman, who made it impossible for him to direct his energies towards influencing philosophy in England.

Moreover, he despaired of England, as we have seen in his social tracts; society, he felt, was rotten at the core; in fact Matter had corrupted and poisoned life and thought at home.

Confirmation of most of this is to be found in Berkeley's poem, written in 1726 about two years and a half before he set sail for America. It was later called "Verses on the Prospect of Planting Arts and Learning in America"[1] and reads as follows:

> The Muse, disgusted at an Age and Clime,
>   Barren of every glorious Theme,
> In distant Lands now waits a better Time,
>   Producing subjects worthy Fame:
>
> In happy Climes, where from the genial Sun
>   And virgin Earth such Scenes ensue,
> The Force of Art by Nature seems outdone,
>   And fancied Beauties by the true:

[1] A. A. Luce, *The Life of George Berkeley*, Edinburgh, 1949, p. 96.

In happy Climes the Seat of Innocence,
    Where Nature guides and Virtue rules,
Where Men shall not impose for Truth and Sense,
    The Pedantry of Courts and Schools:

There shall be sung another golden Age,
    The rise of Empire and of Arts,
The Good and Great inspiring epic Rage,
    The wisest Heads and noblest Hearts.

Not such as *Europe* breeds in her decay;
    Such as she bred when fresh and young,
When heav'nly Flame did animate her Clay,
    By future Poets shall be sung.

Westward the Course of Empire takes its Way;
    The four first Acts already past,
A fifth shall close the Drama with the Day;.
    Time's noblest Offspring is the last.

He hoped to escape academic pedantry, to leave decadent England behind in disgust, to find absolute purity and innocence, virtue and nobility. But perhaps the most significant idea is the West, where the final stage in the drama will be enacted on pure virgin soil.

Bermuda is an island. It is an island in the West. Ireland, too, is an island in the West. Now we can understand why Berkeley chose this unsuitable site for his university, 600 miles from the main land.

Interpretation XI: Bermuda was a substitute for Ireland.

Berkeley was making a new home in a substitute for his old home, and this connects with the virginity of the soil: for Ernest Jones has pointed out that the conception of an island is associated with virginity, and also that this is connected with home and with the belief that mothers are virgins.[1] Though reaching maturity and aiming at omnipotence, Berkeley was also seeking to return to the virginity associated with his island home. We may make explicit:

---

[1] Ernest Jones, *Essays in Applied Psycho-Analysis*, London 1951, Vol. I, "The Island of Ireland: A Psycho-Analytical Contribution to Political Psychology" (1922).

Interpretation XII: Berkeley was identifying himself more closely with God.

Interpretation XIII: Through this identification he attained a maturity of potency and married.

Interpretation XIV: He valued virginity as being pure, unwittingly regarding his wife and Bermuda as his virginal island mother.

The identification with God calls for further comment. Berkeley was entering the Pauline phase more explicitly. It is true that in early days he believed in God "in whom we live and move and have our being", but in that philosophy God was external to Berkeley. Now the relation was changed. Apart from the clue given by the name chosen for the College, he soon re-expounded his philosophy with a theocentric stress in the *Theory of Vision Vindicated*, published in 1733 after he had returned from America. This work not only argued on behalf of his early theory of vision but also alters the structure of his original argument; for he now begins his exposition with the theocentric relation between God and the ideas he causes in us which constitute a language of nature.[1] Thus the solipsistic interpretation is impossible, and in this work, unlike the *Principles*, what Berkeley conveys is the same as what he wishes to assert. And the Pauline dictum is on the title page.

Now if all things are in God, human beings are no exception; indeed the quotation is definite—that we live in God. This is not now a figure of speech but a specific form of the identification: Berkeley was now identifying himself not by incorporating God into himself, but by enclosing himself in God:

Interpretation XV: Berkeley at this time was projecting himself into God.

Why was the identification needed? In an absolutely pure *esse-percipi* philosophy, pure Solipsism, Berkeley would have had to create the whole world himself as percipient spirit; but he could not do this. He needed God to produce the pure building material in proportion as he felt a danger present of poison reappearing. Now his tendency in the American venture was to identify himself with God to a high degree. Although this led to a short spell of satisfactory life, we must regard the increased

---

[1] *Works*, I, *The Theory of Vision Vindicated and Explained*, § 38 f.

identification as reinforcement of his defences against the appearance of poison. The heightened danger from this source dated probably from about the time of the *De Motu* (1721) when Berkeley was thirty-six, just seven years before he set sail for America; but it had not as yet led to a crisis; this is supported by the external evidence that it was in 1722 that he determined to spend the remainder of his days in Bermuda. But the internal evidence from the nature of the *De Motu* paints the same picture. It was then for the first time that he gave his full attention to the philosophy of theocentric causality, according to which God was the central cause of all change and existence. It is true that this conception was in the *Principles* (1710), but it was then but one doctrine among many and was not dominant in the solipsistic philosophy conveyed, whereas in the *De Motu* it was the overt living background of the whole thesis. Thus in that work pure omnipotent power began to be the dominating conception of his mind.

This does not, of course, explain *why* there was increased danger from poison; the intention here is only to make the interpretation that this was in fact the tendency. Given the tendency, however, we can understand the need for identification with God. But why should he have projected himself into God for this purpose rather than introject God into himself? This question will be discussed in Chapter 19. Here we must be content with the following:

Interpretation XVI: In the middle years of his life Berkeley felt the danger from poison to be on the increase.

Then came the downfall of his American project. Walpole broke his promise, and, after three years of waiting in Rhode Island for the money that never came, Berkeley was forced to return home. We can imagine something of what he felt. The full brunt of this disappointment he probably never realised; we might expect that it found its way into the dialogues and the mathematical controversy that he entered upon when he returned to Britain. His health was ruined; the reasons for this must underlie the secret of *Siris* and the change of outlook that distinguishes *Siris* from the *Principles*.

Chapter 17

BERKELEY'S ATTITUDE TO DEISTS, MATHEMATICIANS, AND MATHEMATICS

AMBIVALENCE TOWARDS THE DEISTS

WHEN he wrote his *Philosophical Commentaries* Berkeley had the seeds of deism within him:

266.   I was distrustful at 8 years old and Consequently by nature disposed for these new Doctrines.

He became the most orthodox of churchmen. Is this to be ascribed simply to rational thinking, or is it rather a manifestation of ambivalence, of feeling his sympathy with deism to be dangerous? He made a point of taking special care to correct his language and make it as philosophically nice as possible, to avoid "giving handle", and to use the utmost caution not to offend the Church.[1] This does not in itself mean that he held views that would not be acceptable to the Church. It was Berkeley's pride that he always thought for himself and called no man master; he might have accepted any new doctrine that turned up, when he was a very young man.

If we consider *Alciphron* which was written under a rock at Rhode Island and published in 1732 soon after his return from America, we find, not the venom and spleen with which he has been charged, but intellectual unfairness towards his opponents. It was certainly not beyond Berkeley's intellectual powers to have understood the works and men he criticised in *Alciphron*. The effect of misunderstanding was to make them less reputable and intellectually worthy than they were. The presumption therefore is that to understand would have been to risk seeing the case of his opponents and entertaining a certain sympathy for their point of view.

One reason for this possibility lies in the identification of

[1] Above, Ch. 3 (1).

156

deists with mathematicians as simultaneous objects of attack and as believers in Matter. Since Berkeley's whole difficulty with Matter was that it held out a peculiar fascination for him, he would have an unwelcome core of sympathy for any of its exponents. Further, we shall see that, despite his attack on mathematicians, he envied them. There is in addition one small concrete piece of evidence. We noticed that Berkeley claimed to have "a delicate sense of danger", while in his writing on deism it is to the deist that this sense, expressed in identical words, is ascribed.[1] There is wide clinical experience of identifications displayed in such a manner.

AMBIVALENCE TOWARDS MATHEMATICIANS

Berkeley was largely a self-taught mathematician, and he had an excellent grasp on the most advanced mathematics of his day. He put his finger on a flaw—the flaw—in the method of fluxions invented by the incomparable Newton, and thereby affected permanently the course of pure mathematics. Yet, for all this, the direction of Newton's thought was more significant than Berkeley's. The philosopher showed much enthusiasm for the subject, and he hoped to devise algebras of nature and of morals. He also regarded mathematics as an important discipline for ordering the mind. It is something of a shock, therefore, to find, side by side with his gift for the subject and his interest in it, intense aggressiveness and contempt towards mathematicians. Several quotations from the *Philosophical Commentaries* reveal his feelings in no uncertain way.[2]

All the aggressiveness in Berkeley's nature seemed to be concentrated against mathematicians: they were clever but misdirected their energy; they reached weighty conclusions which turned out to be nothing, and they took immense trouble to prove what he could do at a stroke with his new philosophical principles. In short, mathematicians were pretentious bunglers, ineffective in using a mighty weapon—and no Irishman could behave so. But in his cutting aphorisms there is also an unmistakable flavour of admiration. Though mathematicians have trifling subjects he holds they "reason admirably about them.

[1] Above, p. 108.   [2] Above, Ch. 3 (2).

Certainly their method and arguing are excellent". The comment, "I'll not admire the mathematicians", strongly suggests deliberate suppression of admiration he felt was their due. He clearly displayed an ambivalent attitude towards them: on the one hand he admired them deeply, while on the other he despised them. Now, since in his attacks upon them he regarded them as infidels, it is easy to conclude that he feared them because they might demonstrate atheism and the existence of Matter; for Newton's work was the mathematical and physical counterpart of Locke's, and they had the concept of Matter in common. Hence the danger to be feared in mathematicians was that they would turn God into poison.

The great liking he had for mathematics would suggest that, underneath his animosity and fear, he sided with the mathematicians—which conforms with the presumption that he had a layer of agnosticism in the depths of his composition, and an unrecognised desire to turn God into poison.

This may be presented in the following way:

Interpretation XVII: Berkeley's attack on mathematicians was the outcome of envy, i.e. of an unrealised desire to exercise their power.

Interpretation XVIII: What Berkeley envied in mathematicians was their freedom to handle dangerous ideas and poisonous things, and willingness to turn God into poison.

The foregoing attitudes to mathematicians Berkeley preserved from the time when he wrote the *Philosophical Commentaries* at least to the time when he returned from America and engaged in his mathematical polemic with a number of mathematicians. This was short and sharp with little quarter given. These were the attitudes that he kept pent up for about twenty-five years and only let loose after the failure of his American venture.

CONTINUITY, DISCRETENESS, AND NUMBER

Despite his superb criticism of Newton's methods of fluxions, Berkeley showed a certain lack of insight into what Newton was trying to do, and this was certainly due to his not being able to grasp the notion, the then current crude notion, of a limit approached by a mathematical function. This notion depends psychologically (though not logically) upon continuity—one thinks of a limit as a goal *towards* which a function *moves* and moves *continuously*, though such pictorial representations do not enter into the modern mathematical notion. Indeed all the discussions of it at that time were conducted in terms of movement. Berkeley could not agree that a function could become smaller and smaller indefinitely; any attempt to make it less than a certain minimal size would instantly reduce it to zero; here therefore there was a breach of continuity. In his philosophy also Berkeley denied continuity; for on the solipsistic version there can be no continuity between two ideas of one table because there cannot be such a unified thing as a table. Then there are the strange entries in the *Philosophical Commentaries:*

590. No broken intervals of Death or Annihilation. Those Intervals are nothing.

651. Certainly the mind always and constantly thinks. . . .

83. Men die or are in state of annihilation oft in a day.

Whatever apparent inconsistency there may be here, the important point just now is that Berkeley took extreme measures to preserve continuity in the mind, by denying the existence of time between states of consciousness. He was not prepared to allow discontinuity between ideas in the mind, but the price for this was to make a gap in the temporal sequence of events in the real world.

In a lesser man it would cause no surprise to learn that a concept of the most advanced mathematics then current, a concept that was not yet adequately expounded, had not struck home; but that one so gifted mathematically and of such deep interests and attainments should have had a blind spot for it at least demands scrutiny.

Apparently some notion of flux or motion strained his mind too far; and it was this part of the work that he attacked in no uncertain terms. If we join this to his fear that the evil mathematicians would turn God into bad stuff through the conception of Matter, we may presume that the fundamental notion of a fluxion contained this poison.

Now Berkeley suffered both from a 'bloody flux' and also from what he felt was a clogging poison inside him. Of the two, the former would be the more alarming and the latter would

afford some protection against it. Here we have the conception
of the need to stop a continuous flow by having instead isolated
solids, which are not continuous with one another:

*Interpretation XIX: Berkeley's antagonism to the method of fluxions
and his attempt to replace it by a method involving discrete quantities
were due to his fear that his insides would dissolve into a flux and to his
need to have his insides solid, even though this in its turn would prove
disturbing.**

This would, of course, imply that there was for Berkeley a
faecal element in mathematics itself; otherwise his repudiation
of flux would not have attached itself to the mathematical sphere.
Is there any justification for such an attitude? Let us consider
the basic building materials of mathematics, *i.e.* numbers. Numbers have to do with *quantity* and *order*. The first notion of
quantity experienced in infancy would be derived from milk,
urine, and faeces; the faecal form of it would later develop from
play with dirt, clay, sand, and the like, and later still in connexion with money, well known to be a faecal derivative, where
counting assumes importance. Again, as regards order, faeces
are the first objects the infant has to learn to make orderly; they
must come at intervals in an order and be put in the right place
at the right time; whole numbers likewise have an order, and
are even related to position in space and time on the abacus.
The abstractness of numbers—like the abstractness of Matter—
raises different considerations. Numbers are not rich in properties that distinguish one from another. This is not ultimately
true of faeces, but the strong repressions that occur of faecal
properties tend fairly quickly to make all faeces seem alike,
without much variation in colour or smell and with little variety
of shape (which is suggestive of the formless Matter of the

* Berkeley made a small mathematical mistake (putting *q* equal to
unity) in his thesis about compensating errors in Newton's method. This
I have attributed to his thinking out a problem in a particular case and
wrongly generalising it, instead of thinking out the problem in general
terms. Having to think out the problem in particular terms indicates
that the boundaries between particular cases was fixed and not fluid. In
other words, he suffered from an inhibition about fluidity in his general
thinking. (J. O. Wisdom, "The Compensation of Errors in the Method
of Fluxions", *Hermathena*, Dublin, 1941, No. lvii, p. 60; "The *Analyst*
Controversy: Berkeley as a Mathematician", *Hermathena*, Dublin, 1942,
No. lix, p. 122.)

Scholastics). Thus there would seem to be ground for taking numbers to be replacements through sublimation of faeces. Not that this would be the only root: milk would be equally important, and the relation between milk and faeces discussed in Chapter 20 would be relevant.

With his repugnance to faeces, how was it that Berkeley showed no dislike of mathematics itself? The sublimation involved would be one that takes place extremely early in life, at a time when the feeling that some kinds of faeces are good is still very much alive. To this we might add that the poisonous element became associated with the flux or method of handling mathematical entities but not with those entities themselves.

In this connexion it is worth recalling Berkeley's interest in the question of the infinite divisibility of matter. Numbers can be halved and sub-divided indefinitely; and the same would be true of Matter, for it was devoid of qualities and would be the same at all stages of division. But for Berkeley there was no Matter—only the world of sense. Now this world of Berkeley's could be sub-divided as far as the *minimum visible* (or *minimum tangible*) and no farther. This is in line with his attack on the notion of the infinitesimal. Thus his conception of mathematics banished the notion of flux from very small quantities just as the principles of *Esse percipi* banished Matter. While, however, his conception of mathematics was directly related to repudiation of flux, *Esse percipi* was only indirectly related to it: *Esse percipi* banished the solid poison and, interestingly enough, conveyed the solipsistic picture of a dream-like flux—an example of what Freud has called the "return of the repressed".[1]

We may conclude this chapter by making part of Interpretation XVIII more specific:

Interpretation XX: What Berkeley envied in mathematicians was their freedom to regard some faeces as good and to manipulate derivations from these.

---

[1] Freud, *Collected Papers*, London, 1940, Vol. I, "Further Remarks on the Defence Neuro-Psychoses" (1896), p. 163.

Chapter 18

THE EVOLUTION OF BERKELEY'S CONFLICT (II)

AT the factual level, though we have not yet reached the explanation of it, Berkeley's conflict about poison became transformed after the American *débâcle*, for he now felt the danger to be within him and no longer in the external world. In view of this it would not be surprising if he found it possible to handle certain external faecal derivations with more freedom, indulge his infancy interest in faeces while dosing himself with tar-water.

Throughout his life Berkeley seems to have displayed a balanced realism about money; probably, as with numbers, the conception of money derived from a time before faeces had come to be regarded as poisonous. At the present period in his life, back from America, with his polemical works in print, he turned his attention to questions of money, and he produced in succession his somewhat ill-ordered economic pamphlets. We shall see that his ideas on this subject, though not the conception of money itself, were closely linked with what he feared in poison; yet he did not have to push them out of sight.

The ontogenesis of the interest in money has been admirably reconstructed by Ferenczi.[1] That there is a close connexion between attitudes to money and coprophilia is well known. Thus Freud,[2] Ferenczi, Jones,[3] and many others have found that some infants will not evacuate the bowel because they later gain an additional pleasure from the act, and that the contents thus held back form the first 'savings' of the individual. In describing the development from the one interest to the other, Ferenczi points out that faeces are the child's first toys—their primitive

[1] Sandor Ferenczi, *Contributions to Psycho-Analysis*, Boston, 1916, Ch. XIII.

[2] Freud, *Three Essays on the Theory of Sexuality* (Vienna, 1905), London, 1949, p. 64; *Collected Papers*, London, 1924, Vol. II, "Character and Anal Erotism" (1908).

[3] Ernest Jones, *Papers on Psycho-Analysis*, London, 1948, "Anal-Erotic Character Traits" (1918).

plasticine, to be squeezed by the sphincter muscles or the hands. The first mental change comes about when the smell becomes repugnant. The child then turns its interest to mud, which is distinguished from the original only by the absence of smell. Later this, too, becomes objectionable, because of its stickiness, moisture, and colour; and sand becomes the substitute, as de-odorised and dehydrated faeces. At this stage, however, there is a compensation for what is lost, for the child pours water on the sand; even the infantile liking for the smell does not entirely disappear, but becomes displaced to other bodily excrement, from the feet, nose, and so on. The interest in sand gives way to the collecting of pebbles, attractively coloured. Unpleasant smell and moisture were first replaced by absence of smell and dryness; now softness is replaced by hardness.

After this come artificial products, no longer connected with the earth—marbles and so on, used by children as a medium of exchange. Lastly comes the desire for pure shining money, which begins by being treasured for its lustre, clink, smooth feel, and absence of smell. Money is odourless, dehydrated, hard, shining faeces.

The ontogenesis of Berkeley's conception of money seems to have developed normally. But he had conflicts about the parts of the body associated with the production of it. These might have been expected to have prevented him from handling economic topics; but this was not so.

The most characteristic feature of Berkeley's views on money was the need for *circulating* it: it was to *flow*. Thus some con-ception of continuity managed to creep into his opinion on this, though it was denied in his philosophy and mathematics. The continuity was not unrestricted, for money did not have to flow like a stream, but in discrete quantities, as it changed hands one moment and remained in someone's pocket the next. Though Berkeley retained a turgid conception of mathematical quantities, there was a new emphasis on flow. External faeces were not to be too turgid like those inside him requiring tar-water, nor yet too free, but to pass in steady but distinct move-ments. A distinctive feature of his theory was that there should be plenty of small money—not great constipating lumps that would lie idle and be impossible to move. He was now against *hoarding* or storing vast quantities of precious metal in vaults. He was advocating that there should be motions from the vaults, an idea corresponding to his wish to move the poison from the vault within himself.

Paper notes were to count as money. This was an innovation; they were not to be credit for money but money itself. Paper is not so durable as coin; it was not, according to orthodox opinion, 'the real thing'. The tradition of saving or hoarding precious metal implies that the use of paper would lead to over-spending and also to an unpleasant sense of being in debt, for those to whom one had given notes would have a claim to have them redeemed by 'real' money. But this would cause no anxiety to Berkeley who was eager to spend; and the belief that notes were just as much money as specie might well give him the re-assuring feeling that a good deal was being spent. To stress paper-money, however, was to shift the focus away from coin, away from hard material, so that, though he was now freer in relation to external realities, his repugnance to Matter possibly played a small rôle here.

The Central Bank was the great bowel capable of defecating all the money that was needed; here was a new institution with great power to produce great quantities of good faeces. This bank had, however, the character of a good bowel: it was to function smoothly and produce what was demanded. In this sphere, then, Berkeley was not dealing with Matter, poisonous beyond hope of cleansing; nor yet was it a mystical cleanser like *Esse percipi* or tar-water. Instead a reality-derivation of good faeces was being used to improve conditions in life.

It is of some interest that his monetary policy was not in the short run favourable to landlords; they had become the repre-sentatives, though very mildly, of the social setting involving Walpole and corrupt dealing, and they would not take steps to aid the poor. The Central Bank, on the other hand, was to be an improved form of financial government, which would dis-gorge the money that Walpole denied to him.

Some seven years after the third part of *The Querist* Berkeley published *Siris*. All this time he devoted himself to the interests of his diocese and the poor. The poor, who as *The Querist* tells us wallowed in dirt, therefore constituted another external faecal element with which he had to deal—but in this instance it was dirt or bad faeces, which he wished to eliminate.

It was in this period that Berkeley took active steps to form a militia for defence. His misdirected aggressiveness against Matter, freethinkers, and mathematicians was now being used for reality purposes. The sequence in his changing use of aggression was this: as a young man he directed it all against Matter; on returning from America his long pent-up hostility to mathematicians came out, and in this the deists were included; and lastly, just before he took to tar-water, he was using aggression for normal purposes. Here, as with the question of money, he took appropriate action in the world of reality when his conflict about poison was ceasing to be focused there and was being withdrawn inside himself.

How was it that Berkeley was able, in a way that many economists were not, to make such realistic economic proposals; how was he able to handle the subject at all; and how was he able to deal sensibly with derivatives of Matter in the external world? It would seem that, faced with growing internal disorder, Berkeley was making a special effort to exercise control over the external world, increase the amount of good things in it, and preserve order; for, if the external world became worse, this would add to his despair over his internal disorder—if he made on effort to preserve good faecal derivations externally that would mean that his internal poison was assuming greater power and harming not only himself but also the good outside.

The foregoing material may be presented in the following:

Interpretation XXI: When poison was felt to be internalised as bad faeces, Berkeley dealt realistically with products in the social world (flow of money, hoarding, Central Bank) that were psychogenetic derivations from an original conception of good faeces.

Interpretation XXII: He tried to produce in this social world products with good activities that he was unable to promote inside himself.

(Defence) Interpretation XXIII: The existence of these good activities could serve as a defence, to reassure him that the power of his internal poison had not assumed uncontrollable proportions.

Chapter 19

THE CENTRAL PROBLEM
AND SOLUTION

THE early philosophy of Solipsism, which was practically overt in the *Philosophical Commentaries* and unintentionally displayed in the *Principles* and *Three Dialogues*, disappeared; there was a transformation over a period of about twenty-five years in which the intended philosophy of Theocentric Phenomenalism became fully explicit, the first sign of this development being in the *De Motu* (1721), and the next in *The Theory of Vision Vindicated* (1733). This tendency was thus at its height just before and during Berkeley's stay in America. The Pauline dictum associated with it reveals the panentheistic emphasis in the philosophy even at that time, though explicit Panentheism was not proclaimed before *Siris* (1744). We may also find reason to believe that there was a somewhat different significance attaching to Panentheism at these two periods. This would mean that there were three phases in Berkeley's thinking: Solipsism, a form of Panentheism involving Theocentric Phenomenalism, and another form of Panentheism without much left of the Phenomenalism. However this may be, there were at least two phases, and the development has to be accounted for. There is nothing known about Berkeley's philosophising to suggest that this was a result of deliberate logical refinement or correction (though if there were we should still wish to understand why he felt the need to make such a refinement or correction); it seems to have been the outcome of change of outlook flowing from purely internal personal changes not spurred by logical scrutiny. This has been interpreted above as a psychogenetic evolution of a conflict about external poison controlled by *Esse percipi* into a conflict about internal poison controlled by tar-water. Our problem is not in any way solved by such as interpretation; it is merely replaced by a new one. We have seen what changes took place in Berkeley's life in the intervening years and we understand something of the trend of his mind. But we have now to ask what brought about the transformation of his conflict. And we have to investigate the relation between this and his broken health. Are we to explain his health by the change in his philosophy or the change in his philosophy by his health, or neither?

Are we to say that his health gave way from 'natural causes', that in middle age it is not surprising if a man leading a sedentary life succumbs to ill-health, that he was at an age when 'involutionary' changes set in? This is to open the wholly unsolved problem of the explanation of dysfunction in the organism. Berkeley did not suffer, so far as we know, from any disease traceable to infection or physical trauma or any of the classes of disease explicable in terms of definite factors in the physical environment, which modern medicine has learnt to understand very thoroughly. Vitamin deficiency—of C or one of the B group—is a possibility, but it is unlikely to have been more than a contributory factor. He almost certainly suffered from a functional disorder, the large variety of which may be typified by asthma, peptic ulcer, certain kidney and heart diseases, hardening or silting of the arteries, and so on, which are due to disorders of function in that they are not traceable, so far as is known, to an extraneous causal factor and whose dysfunction is more like the ill-ordered behaviour of a motor-car when run too slowly in top gear than that due to dirt in the carburetter. Such disorders are regarded as 'psychosomatic' by those who believe that they are due in an important measure to mental conflict.

But, even if we knew the origin of Berkeley's disorder in physical terms, we should still have to try to use this to explain in detail how it brought about the internalisation of his conflict, and moreover led to the release of his pent-up hostility to the mathematicians. The spirochaete of syphilis explains the lesions of the brain in general paralysis, but no one who understands what is required of a scientific explanation would assert that this explained the variety and content of the symptoms of insanity that ensue. On the other hand such symptoms are of a kind that are intelligible in terms of psychological concepts.

Moreover, a certain amount is understood about the way in which organic disease originates in mental conflict. The effect of infection, physical trauma, and the like, according to Selye,[1] is to stimulate the pituitary gland to secrete certain hormones. These act upon the adrenal cortex which in its turn secretes other hormones. The hormones thus secreted are not in themselves abnormal or harmful; they are harmful only if produced in abnormal amounts. The picture is rather like that of a country that has to spend too great a proportion of its national income on armament for defence, with the result that its total economy gets out of harmony and control. The hormones thus produced in undue amounts then attack some part of the body, the selection of which does not concern us here. The interesting point is that the initial stage in the process, in which the pituitary gland secretes hormones* as a result, say, of infection, can also be set going by anxiety. The mechanism is not known, but this does not lessen the importance of the fact.

With Berkeley, the psychosomatic approach is the more hopeful: to explain his illness by means of his conflict, or more precisely by seeing how his defences against his conflict were broken down by some current experience. In understanding his conflict the basic step is to understand the internalisation process described above. We have then to use this to answer the other

[1] Hans Selye, "The General Adaptation Syndrome and the Diseases of Adaptation", *The Journal of Clinical Endocrinology*, Springfield, 1946, Vol. VI, No. ii, pp. 117–230; *Textbook of Endocrinology*, Acta Endocrinologica, Montreal, 1947, pp. 837–67; David le Vay, "Hans Selye and a Unitary Conception of Disease", *The British Journal for the Philosophy of Science*, Edinburgh, 1952, Vol. III, No. x, pp. 157–69.

* Still more recent work reveals a stage prior to this. According to Alexander, Long has shown that the hypothalamus stimulates the anterior pituitary by releasing through sympathetic action epinephrine from the adrenal medulla which acts on the pituitary, and others have shown that more direct action of the hypothalamus on the pituitary may also occur. See Franz Alexander, *Psychosomatic Medicine*, London, 1952, pp. 77–8, where the following are cited: C. N. H. Long, "Conditions Associated with Secretion of Adrenal Cortex", *Federation Proceedings*, Baltimore, 1947, Vol. VI, No. ii, pp. 461–71; J. E. Markee, C. H. Sawyer, and W. H. Hollingshead, "Adrenergic Control of the Release of Luteinizing Hormone from the Hypophysis of the Rabbit", *Recent Progress in Hormone Research*, New York, 1948, Vol. II, pp. 117–31; C. H. Sawyer, J. E. Markee, and B. F. Townsend, "Cholinergic and Andrenergic Components in the Neurohumoral Control of the Release of LH in the Rabbit", *Endocrinology*, Wisconsin, 1949, Vol. XLIV, No. i, pp. 18–37.

THE CENTRAL PROBLEM AND SOLUTION

questions. And we shall have to try to understand also what childhood lack of adjustment lay at the root of Berkeley's difficulties and why he failed to make the necessary adaptation at the beginning.

Berkeley's great American venture came to naught. Commonsense will see that a man who has put into a project all his ambition, enterprise, and zeal will not survive its downfall unshaken; and commonsense will not be surprised if health is undermined. It will readily locate the precipitating cause—Walpole. Walpole settled the issue by determined procrastination. That was the end of promulgating on a godlike scale the gospel of *Esse percipi*; the New Principle, whose aim was purification of poison in every form, was rendered impotent. No longer had Berkeley a pure means—by identifying himself with God—of dispelling the poison in the world. Since this originated in himself, he was now defenceless against the poison in his system. The weakened man could only bow to the inevitable and succumb to physical poisoning. From that time forth ill-health must prevail. Thus the bad material that Berkeley in his solipsistic days had succeeded in expelling by *Esse percipi* remained within him in his middle age to sap his vitals. The growing need for a pure outlet, growing till it reached bursting point when he felt himself omnipotent, could only reach an anti-climax at the first strong setback. And out of this came *Siris*. Such an account, however, leaves too much about the processes and connexions involved obscure and unexamined.

To function as a precipitating cause of a mental state an episode must possess a significance for the conflict it arouses. Thus:

(*Precipitation*) *Interpretation XXIV: Walpole = Englishman = mathematics = Newton = Locke = Matter = Poison* (where the sign of equality means 'equals in significance').

The question now arises: on what did this excitation impinge? To answer this requires us to explore further his defences against poison. We have seen (Interpretation II) that Matter was external poison; and we know that he denied Matter. Thus his early defence was one of scotomisation (*i.e.* denial of a projection):

(*Defence*) *Interpretation XXV: External poison had to be denied existence.*

This is incomplete unless we state what he was protecting himself against. There are two possibilities: (i) recognition of internal poison, of which Matter was a projected form; and (ii) danger of incorporating external poison into himself. The first is of a type that is clinically well known: that is to say, a projection occurs because of something unacceptable inside,[1] and then even the projection may become unacceptable.[2] The second is also clinically familiar: that is to say, patients sometimes fear incorporating something despite their dislike of it.[3] The question here is whether there is any evidence of this in Berkeley.

He was a man who zealously sought knowledge. He wished to discover a principle that would simplify existing knowledge and place new knowledge within his grasp. This he believed he found, as is evident from his triumphant entry in the *Philosophical Commentaries*:

279. I wonder not at my sagacity in discovering the obvious tho amazing truth, I rather wonder at my stupid inadvertency in not finding it out before. 'tis no witchcraft to see.

This was almost certainly the famous principle of *Esse percipi*, What, then, underlies the gaining of knowledge?

Reik interprets comprehension as a development of the physical effort to grasp something, the precursor of which is incorporation; he draws attention to some well-known sayings with this signification; and he points out the parallel between the way a primitive sometimes eats other human beings to gain their powers and the saying that knowledge is power.[4] Moreover, knowledge in the Garden of Eden was gained by eating. Strachey has also made such points in his discussion of reading (and reading, after all, is one way of gaining knowledge):

[1] Freud, *Collected Papers*, London, 1934, Vol. IV, "Instincts and their Vicissitudes" (1915), p. 78.

[2] René Laforque et Pichon, *Rêve et Psychonalyse*, Maloine, 1926, cited by Laforque, *Inter. J. of Psycho-Analysis*, London, 1927, Vol. VIII, Pt. iv, p. 473; Freud, *Inhibitions, Symptoms and Anxiety* (1926), London, 1936, p. 146.

[3] Melanie Klein, *The Psycho-Analysis of Children*, London, 1937, pp. 168, 278; *Contributions to Psycho-Analysis*, London, 1948, pp. 282, 299, 330.

[4] Theodor Reik, *Surprise and the Psycho-Analyst*, London, 1936, pp. 186–90.

Reading . . . is actually a method of taking someone else's thoughts inside oneself. It is a way of eating another person's words.[1]

And gives additional evidence enabling him to say:

I will even go further and suggest that a coprophagic tendency lies at the root of all reading. The author excretes his thoughts and embodies them in the printed book; the reader takes them, and, after chewing them over, incorporates them into himself.[2]

Fenichel examined the connexion between scopophilia and incorporation with some thoroughness and adduced clinical evidence for it.[3] Both Strachey and Fenichel find a sadistic component in looking; and an underlying sexual curiosity is recognised by all analysts.*

The question is, however, whether Berkeley showed the main tendency. *Esse percipi*, which was to a large extent a visual principle, is a principle of incorporation, in that it places the world of nature within the mind, and is thus a psychical incorporation. It might be said, however, that on the one hand this only places nature in the mind but not in the body and on the other it expressly excluded Matter from its net. The first point may be met thus: the important idea is not one of incorporating something into a *physical* body which is a sophisticated conception but into the arena of bodily feelings or *phenomenological* body; and incorporating nature in the mind is just this. On the other point, it is true that Berkeley denied that Matter was knowable, and hence it was not part of nature and could not be incorporated by *Esse percipi*. Now this denial of external poison was a scotomisation, denying the existence of a poison he felt to be present; but anything that existed in any sense would be incorporated by *Esse percipi*; hence below the level of the scoto-

---

[1] James Strachey, "Some Unconscious Factors in Reading", *The International Journal of Psycho-Analysis*, London, 1930, Vol. XI, Pt. iii, p. 326.

[2] *Id.*, p. 329.

[3] Otto Fenichel, "The Scopophilic Instinct and Identification", *The International Journal of Psycho-Analysis*, London, 1937, Vol. XVIII, Pt. i, pp. 6–34.

* I have not found evidence of normal sexual curiosity in Berkeley, *i.e.* curiosity on the genital level; it appears to have been concentrated on faeces.

misation it would be incorporated also—which means that scotomisation was developed in order to prevent incorporation.

This part of the discussion arose out of considerations of two possible reasons why Berkeley had to deny external poison existence. We have been examining the second possibility mentioned, that it was to protect him against the danger of incorporating external poison into himself. But, from the examination of this, we see that the other possibility mentioned, that Matter was denied to prevent him from recognising the existence of internal poison, is in fact part of the same defence. We may therefore say that his defence was against two intolerable fears:

(*Defence*) *Interpretation XXVI: External poison was a defensive projection of internal poison, recognition of which would have been intolerable.*

(*Defence*) *Interpretation XXVII: The projection itself had to be scotomised to obviate the intolerable danger of re-introjecting it and of recognising it to be present internally.*

These were the defences used by Berkeley at the time of his early philosophy. But, in his middle life before and during his stay in America, his philosophy became more explicitly panentheistic, for he held with a new emphasis that it was in God that "we live and move and have our being". Here he was projecting all human beings, including himself, into God—the existence of Matter, of course, continued to be denied. We might suppose that an alternative defence was open to him: to incorporate God inside himself. The choice of defence, of projecting himself into God instead of introjecting God, becomes intelligible, however, if we answer another question: why did the change from one defence, namely scotomisation, to another, namely self-projection, become necessary?

The scotomisation defence was conducted in terms of *Esse percipi*: hence if a change in the defence was needed we should suspect that in some way or other *Esse percipi* was proving ineffectual. To investigate whether this was so, we look to the circumstances of Berkeley's life during the period between his early publications and his American visit, to see if anything took place—or failed to take place—that might have undermined his confidence in *Esse percipi*. One disappointment stands out: he failed to convince the learned world of the truth of *Esse percipi*—more, he failed to win for his principle even serious consideration. A disappointment of this kind would not necessarily weaken his faith in it; his reaction might have been to become its defiant champion. One fact would militate against this, however. If *Esse percipi* had the power he attributed to it, it would not only have dispelled Matter but the entire rôle of Matter in the realm of knowledge: it would have modified physics and even mathematics, and converted natural philosophers to religion. Berkeley did not lose his sense of realities; it must have been brought home to him that his hopes were not materialising. In this sense, then, his principle possessed but limited power. It was not simply that he failed to win social support for his ideas and thus lost confidence; it was that the principle failed to produce the effects he strove for.

If contemporary intellectuals would not support his principle, the next step in the strengthening of his defences would naturally be to invoke the help of God:

(*Development*) *Interpretation XXVIII: Failure to convince the learned world of* Esse percipi, *i.e. to purify natural knowledge, revealed a lack of power in the principle; to obtain a new source of power Berkeley had to project himself into God.*

This last operation may be called "the Pauline mechanism".

We can now understand how the theocentric element in his philosophy became explicit. We can understand also that the alternative defence of introjecting God was hardly open to Berkeley; for it would have meant leaning heavily on his capacity to introject when the efficacy of his chief introjective mechanism of *Esse percipi* was waning; moreover, that principle excluded persons from its net.

The new defence would work in a simple way: all things were projected into God, and God was a spirit powerful enough to keep Matter away; pressure on the tendency to incorporate would be relieved. Here Berkeley was, in effect, duplicating himself, for he was placing a double of himself in God. Thus, though in his own self he had his conflict, he was able to divert himself from it by focusing attention on his projected self. Clearly this was a powerful defence, more powerful than the one it replaced.

We are now in a position to consider the effect of Walpole's treachery. It was on the new defence that this would first impinge, and we have to enquire how his action led to the break-down of the defence.

Walpole's action meant that external poison was shown to have power in the world of affairs. It meant the end of St. Paul's College designed to teach the omnipresence of God, the New Principle, and protect students from deism. It meant that the influence of God was limited by the deeds of wicked men and by the Matter they possessed; by rendering God less than omnipotent it meant that Berkeley's Pauline defence was shaken.

He could not fall back successfully on the older defence of *Esse percipi* and scotomisation. This had been weakened by its failure to influence the learned world; and now Walpole's action would sharply bring home its ineffectualness; for that action displayed the living power of Matter.

What underlay the two defences of *Esse percipi* and Pantheism was the same. When the defences failed, the underlying situation which had been shut off from view must come more into the open. Recognition of the intolerable was not to be avoided; and this is what constitutes neurosis (using the word, of course, for an overt disorder and not merely for a latent one):

(*Neurosis*) *Interpretation XXIX: Recognition in high degree of external poison was unavoidable. The existence of internal poison had to be sensed* (though the projective relation between the two would not have been realised); *the danger of introjecting external poison became acute and introjection in large measure inevitable* (though the introjective relation would also not have been realised).

Thus Berkeley was doubly poisoned, by the internal form of poison now active and by the external form now incorporated. Thus we can begin to understand why he became ill: feeling poisoned by Walpole, unable to expel internal poison, unable to avoid contamination by external poison, is there much to be surprised at that he should have become a really sick man?

It would be well at this point to try to fix more exactly the date at which Berkeley's health began to decline. The indispositions we have noted when he was a young man were probably of the same sort as his later illness, but they differed in being isolated attacks. On the other hand, after his return from America his ill-health became chronic. Fraser was right in saving that his health was broken before he left London, but it is not easy to narrow the interval when his chronic disorder became manifest. His letters to Tom Prior contain constant references to ill-health from January 7, 1734, when he was "much mended" but still could not read; he was not well enough to travel for some months, had several attacks of gout, and on March 12, 1736, he wrote of his ill-health "which is now pretty well re-established"—"re-established" would seem to refer to the period in London before he went to take up his episcopal duties at Cloyne in the middle of 1734. He had arrived back from America towards the end of 1731. Hence his health gave way some time in 1732 or 1733 at the latest. But he speaks of periodic indisposition in April, 1729,[1] and of his health "mending" in May, 1733.[2] His ill-health may, therefore, have become chronic very soon after he returned from America and possibly shortly before that.

A sick man, no longer omnipotent, Berkeley returned to his native country, to help the poor, his fellow-sufferers:

whatever article of clothing they could possibly manufacture there, the Bishop would have from no other place; and chose to wear ill clothes, and worse wigs, rather than suffer the poor of the town to remain unemployed.[3]

In the poor of Southern Ireland he perhaps saw others like himself who had suffered at the hands of an Englishman. Soon he was to tolerate in his immediate surroundings not only poor clothes but the squalor of the inhabitants, and to advocate realistic views about money. Not very long afterwards appeared *Siris* with its divine panacea and cleanser, together with the philosophy of Panentheism in a thoroughgoing form.

Here a question awaits us. Why did Berkeley continue to hold Panentheism, even develop it explicitly, once he had become ill and a certain recognition had to be accorded to the internal

[1] A. A. Luce, "More Unpublished Berkeley Letters and New Berkeleiana", *Hermathena*, Dublin, 1933, Vol. XXIII, p. 37.

[2] A. A. Luce, "Berkeley's Bermuda Project . . . with Unpublished Letters . . .", *Proc. of the Royal Irish Academy*, Dublin, 1934, Vol. XLII, Sec. C, No. vi, p. 109.

[3] Joseph Stock. *The Life of Bishop Berkeley*, in *Works*, ed. by Wright, London, 1843, Vol. I, p. 15 n.

counterpart of Matter. In fact he retained both the panentheistic defence and that of *Esse percipi*. The latter no longer loomed large as an active force; the former did not lose force but even seems to have been strengthened. How was this, since if it had been effective Berkeley would not have become ill, and if he became ill the defence would be realised to be ineffective?

A hint of the answer to this comes from the rôle of the Central Bank; but discussion of this may be deferred to Chapter 21, because it would not be fully intelligible without the introduction of an important feature of child psychology.

We have now seen what factors were responsible for producing the change in the defence Berkeley used against Matter from his early philosophy to that of his middle age, and how these defences became undermined with the consequence of ill-health. Within this framework it is not difficult to account for his sudden outburst against the deists and mathematicians, equated in his mind with Walpole and Matter. The 'natural' explanation is that he met defeat with anger—one of the most widely used ways of meeting frustration from the cradle to the grave. But we can go somewhat deeper than this by pointing to his desire to use his internal poison against his enemies:

(Response) Interpretation XXX: Frustrated in his quest for purity by the exponents of Matter, Berkeley wanted to expel the poison that was within him on to these enemies.

To this we may add that this sadistic element, which Strachey and Fenichel mentioned in connexion with perceptual incorporation, here arose after Berkeley's incorporation tendencies had been strongly activated. The relation between his fear of internal poison and his sadistic or destructive tendencies will be considered in the next chapter.[1] Here it suffices to point out that he feared destroying his enemies with his poison.

The investigation into the main problems dealt with in the present chapter concerns a single theme. It remains to ask if there were other determinants as well, acting as reinforcing factors. We can hardly doubt that Walpole provided the main precipitating cause of Berkeley's troubles, but we know that his wife about the same time had miscarriages, after one of which she was very ill. Such an occurrence would not merely have

[1] Below, Ch. 20 (*d*).

been a strain but would have had the same import as Walpole's action, *i.e.* that evil influences were gaining the upper hand:

(*Precipitation*) *Interpretation XXXI: Miscarriages mean poison, either in his wife or in himself, gaining control.*

In this connexion we recall that Berkeley married at the age of forty-three, on the eve of setting sail for America. This was the time in his life that promised most. The grant for his transatlantic project had been voted. For a time, at least, he had a social backing for *Esse percipi* and for his growing Panentheism. The danger from Matter would have been at a minimum. Whatever realisation he had in earlier years that Matter was not securely denied would have faded at this time of growing omnipotence. He would not now feel there was any risk of finding Matter in a wife or in himself or any attendant risk of receiving it from her or giving it to her. But before this hopeful period in his life the risk of Matter was dimly present, and we should expect this to include the risk of finding it in a wife or himself—more probably in her, because it was poison outside himself that concerned him in his early days. Thus the lateness of his marriage is compatible with the foregoing interpretation of the miscarriages provided we add:

(*Inhibition*) *Interpretation XXXII: Disappointment with the* Esse percipi *defence* (up to, say, 1725) *made marriage impossible because of the risk that his wife would contain a poisonous element.*

We turn in the next chapter to questions involving the reconstruction of early childhood: this is partly in order to answer a question about Panentheism, and partly to investigate the question why the danger of poison loomed so large in Berkeley's mind.

Chapter 20

CHILDHOOD RECONSTRUCTIONS

(a) FAECES

ATTENTION was drawn in Interpretations VIII and IX to Berkeley's guilt-fraught desire to have something connected with poison and to his attitude in adult life that faeces were poison. With regard to the latter it might be urged, if Berkeley felt poisoned, that suffices; why assert that the poison was faecal? The reason is that poison is not in itself specific and that clinically it is found that within certain limits unspecific things constitute defences against the realisation of specific things. And the specific things that can be felt to be dirty, bad, or dangerous on or inside a person are nose-pickings, dirt from the toes, and, far-outweighing these, faeces (this is not to say that other things, urine, menstrual blood, and so on may not also be considered in the same light). There is one other thing of the same level of importance as faeces and that is food. Faeces and food constitute the primary and typical bad objects of which others are only derivations. The relation between faeces and food will be discussed below; here we shall consider faeces.

That faeces constitute primary dangerous objects inside a person, as we have seen, has been strongly emphasised by Stärcke, van Ophuijsen, and Klein. The purpose of bringing in this specific interpretation here is that it leads to others of importance. We can see that even the concept of faeces is not psychologically ultimate or primordial: Scott[1] points out that there occurs a time in infancy, before one object is well discriminated from another, when faeces are not discriminated from anything else. At such a time, feelings of badness or poison are not specifically located. Then, as discrimination develops and faeces become recognised, they become associated with feelings of valuation; and the valuation may be positive as well as depreciatory. This leads to a split being made between good

[1] W. Clifford M. Scott, an unpublished communication.

178

faeces and bad faeces, either as two types of faeces or as alternatives or even simultaneous characteristics of one type of faeces. Subsequent development is likely to lead to the denial that any faeces are good or valued.

Quite apart from this reconstructed ontogenesis, all analysts beginning with Freud have recognised the attitude that faeces are among the infant's most cherished objects and have found a number of psychogenetic derivations from them—the conception of money being one of the best known.

In view of all this, it would have been misleading to use the concept of faeces instead of poison for the interpretations given in previous chapters, for we were concerned with Berkeley's adult attitude according to which faeces were regarded as bad only. This has now to be understood against the background of his childhood attitudes:

Interpretation XXXIII: In infancy Berkeley felt some faeces to be extremely good.

It should be remarked at once that, unlike most of the preceding interpretations, there is no direct evidence for this in Berkeley's life and writings—though we have seen evidence that can readily be interpreted to fall in with this one and that could hardly be interpreted in a way that would be incompatible with it, namely the material in Berkeley's economics. This interpretation is asserted here because of its universal application in clinical practice and because of its obvious application to his economics; and its justification and relevance are that it enables us to explain interpretations previously made and to proceed to further explanatory interpretations.

Similarly, in line both with clinical practice and with observation of infants, we have:

Interpretation XXXIV: In infancy Berkeley both felt he was making extremely good faeces and wanted to incorporate good faeces.

This throws light on his fear of incorporating poison. He wanted to incorporate something good; but all incorporation would activate his attitude at that period of his infancy before he had yet discriminated faeces into good and bad forms; and, even after some discriminations had been made, greed would lead to the incorporation of good and bad together; hence there would be a residual anxiety that in incorporating something good he would take in poison at the same time. We can therefore understand not only his defences but also his fears of poison: they owed their acuteness to a strong desire to incorporate good faeces:

Interpretation XXXV: Berkeley's fear of poison was the fear that the intensity of his desire to incorporate good faeces would make him unable to avoid taking in bad faeces as well.

On the other hand, this is paralleled by the need to expel bad faeces. Since Berkeley needed such aids as *Esse percipi* as he grew up, we make the usual clinical presumption of a similar need in infancy:

Interpretation XXXVI: In infancy Berkeley found his bad faeces intolerable and felt without sufficient power to expel them.

Here we may consider a curious point in connexion with Matter. The philosophical conception of Matter was of a power devoid of all qualities. Our first interpretation of it was to equate it with poison—which may also be regarded as a power with unspecified qualities. Later we linked it with bad faeces. Now faeces have qualities. Hence that interpretation (implied by Interpretation IX and others) was approximate. To make it exact we should equate Matter with the *power* in bad faeces. In this equation qualities are put on one side. That is to say, in the psychogenesis of the conception of Matter, a splitting occurred, a separation between bad power on the one hand and qualities on the other. Thus it was the conception of qualitativeless bad faeces, *i.e.* a power alone, that evolved into the conception of Matter. In the scotomisation of Matter, it was the power that was banished—as in *De Motu* it was the power of producing motion that was denied to physical reality. The power was banished because it was felt to be a bad power. Now bad power is destructiveness; hence we may presume that destructiveness was what he felt to be the underlying danger. Thus the badness of faeces lay in their destructive power:

Interpretation XXXVII: Matter = power of external bad faeces = projected destructiveness.

On the other hand, the absence of all qualities in Matter means that the qualities of faeces were not scotomised along with their power. And the principle of *Esse percipi* placed all qualities without exception in the mind. Hence the qualities of faeces were acceptable as were any other qualities. It would seem, therefore, that the distinction between good and bad faeces for Berkeley is this:

Interpretation XXXVIII: The good component of faeces (what has been called "good faeces") *consisted of faecal qualities; the bad component* (what has been called "bad faeces") *consisted of destructive faecal power.**

The reason for the separation between power and qualities would lie in the ambivalent attitude of anxiety in which power was regarded as persecutory and qualities regarded as desirable. If power and qualities were allowed to come together, destructiveness would become manifest in good desired qualities, creating a state of confusion in which good and bad things were incorporated together.

(b) FATHERS, DIVINE AND HUMAN

Clinically it is found that children identify themselves with any adult whose powers they wish to possess—usually, of course, with a parent when the child is very young. Let us therefore make the reconstruction that in infancy Berkeley tried to deal with his difficulty in expelling bad faeces by using good faeces as a cleanser or by identifying himself with his father whose defecatory power would fulfil his need—the difference between these two would not originally have been fully discriminated. Thus:

Interpretation XXXIX: Berkeley wanted, when a baby, to incorporate his father and his father's good faeces.

This has some sort of parallel in the philosophy of *Esse percipi*, in that Berkeley found this principle to be insufficient without God. The rôle of God, on the solipsistic or theocentric view of it, is to give substance to or to create the world, to provide regularity of connexion between cause and effect, and to ensure unity, permanence, and order. Here we have:

Interpretation XL: God cemented the world together or created it by means of pure faeces, acting always with regularity.

This is of course in line with the well-known beliefs of early

* Of course there could be bad qualities and good power as well; in fact good power was located by Berkeley in God; but the more active factors were good qualities and bad power.

childhood that the child has created the world and that it is his (or her) faeces, for up to a certain time in his life he regards his faeces as his main and greatest creation.

Now this progression from self to father to God means that Berkeley's need was not adequately satisfied by his father. This could come about by the physical and social difficulties preventing him from obtaining his father's faeces; and even if he had succeeded he would at last have come to realise that they were totally ineffective; and it could come about also by other conflicts about incorporating his father, because, for instance, of wanting to keep his father in the external world or because he feared destroying his father in the process. The end-result would be the same and would lead to disappointment, indeed repudiation of his father, as not only ineffectual but a bad person whose only aim was to frustrate him. The obvious counterpart to this in later years was when Walpole, opposing Berkeley's good designs and thus upholding Matter, refused good money, *i.e.* good faeces, for the American College. To regard his father as hostile in this way would be to connect him with his bad faeces. Just as there are, then, two conceptions of faeces, so there are two conceptions of a father—a good and a bad one. The bad one throws light on Berkeley's attitude towards mathematicians and deists. They had the hated evil power of Matter. They were thus derivations from his bad father, just as God was a derivation from his good father. And they resembled God in possessing godlike power, for Matter, as we are told by Berkeley, if once admitted would possess divine attributes.

Interpretation XLI: God, as pure creator who commanded unsullied power and possessed a pure cement in the form of good faeces for building the world, is a substitute for the father Berkeley valued; and the mathematicians and deists, creators of Matter and bad faeces, godlike enemies of God, were substitutes for the father Berkeley hated because of withholding from his son his faeces and great power of defecation. There were two separated psychical streams of positive valuation and hate.

Here a further question arises. The foregoing reconstruction is given in terms of incorporation of the father. But we have seen reason to think that in Berkeley's mature philosophy, with its theocentric stress, the mechanism was not one of introjection of

God but of projection of himself into God. As a counterpart we therefore reconstruct:

Interpretation XLII: In addition to trying to incorporate his father, Berkeley also tried to project himself into his father, i.e. the good one.

No evidence can be offered for this interpretation of the Pauline mechanism; its justification must lie in putting it to constructive use. If it is correct, then probably Berkeley followed up his attempt to introject his father by another attempt later in childhood to identify himself by projection.

(c) CHILDHOOD CAUSES IN THE FAECAL SITUATION

If Berkeley's lifelong conflict centres about his need to incorporate good faeces, why should this have been so dominant? There are many possibilities, and it would be purely speculative to fasten on one rather than another in the absence of any pointers. He may have been punished for coprophagia; there may have been insufficient appreciation of his stools; and actual diarrhoea or constipation might have been a contributory factor. There is one possibility, however, for which there are pointers. The rôle of God was to provide regularity of connexion between cause and effect, as well as unity, permanence, and order, all of which were imposed as wholly arbitrary. These requirements characterise solid stool and the apparently arbitrary demands that parents make on children in respect of defecation. They contrast, moreover, with bloody fluxes, fluxions, and continuity, and are in line with Berkeley's objections to these. We may put this together in the following way:

Interpretation XLIII: In the first few years of life Berkeley suffered unduly from soiling by very liquid faeces, which he was taught were bad and which he wished to replace by solids passed regularly in accordance with arbitrary parental rule.

Actual constipation, if it occurred in his childhood—it almost certainly did in the days of *Siris*—would have developed as an over-intense reaction to liquid faeces.

(d) EARLY OBJECT-RELATIONSHIPS

Berkeley's relationship to his parents lies in obscurity; the only mention is the one reference to his father which is heavily scored out of the manuscript. Can any hint bearing on this be gained from his philosophy? His early Solipsism strongly suggests that there were some barriers in his relations to others. And the prototype of other people would be his parents. Moreover, solipsistic denial of the existence of others would carry with it the denial of relations between them; and one of the principal reasons for this would be fear of their having intercourse. Thus:

Interpretation XLIV: Solipsism means that Berkeley scotomised all intercourse between his parents.

This accords with Interpretation XIV, the belief in the virginity of his mother, a belief, as Ernest Jones has pointed out, that is widespread. It would have its origin in Berkeley's strong tendency to incorporate, and probably in his taking intercourse to be a faecal relationship of a sadistic kind—indeed the symbolic relation between acids and alkalis as daggers and sheaths, described in *Siris*,[1] clearly stands for sadistic intercourse. The presumption would therefore be that he could not readily have a living relationship with his parents, and that the erasure of the reference to his father meant blotting out everything to do with his father. The context concerned wild beasts and human massacres, the sadistic nature of which may have evoked this one reference.

Here we may consider a further interpretation of the relationship between God and Matter.* The conception of Matter could have been derived from that of mother. The function of Matter in Locke was to provide unity, persistence, and order in the world, but Berkeley denied that it could do so. This may be connected with his earliest frustrations at his mother's hands in the following way. Resentment when she failed to handle him as he wanted or despair at her absence when he needed her most could make him feel that the world was reduced to chaos—feeling either that she had brought this about or that she had not saved him from disintegrating everything. Thus at times of discord with her, he would have felt that she failed to ensure unity, order, and persistence, and thus felt the great anxiety or rage that goes with chaos. In this way Matter could be an offshoot of a conception of a bad, unhelping, unrestraining mother. Here we recall Berkeley's striking entry in the

---

[1] Quoted above, pp. 69, 70.
* Mr. Roger Money-Kyrle kindly drew my attention to this.

Philosophical Commentaries, already noted, about the danger of allowing Matter, for then God would equal Matter. Since God represents the father Berkeley felt was good, this entry means that his good father would be degraded and be reduced to Matter or to equivalence to his bad mother. He would have had to keep his good father and bad mother apart because he could not have tolerated the idea of his bad father and bad mother coming together. More explicitly, any failure by his good mother would awaken fear of intercourse between two bad parents, which would be conceived sadistically. The impossibility of tolerating this phantasy would lead him to deny the existence of a bad mother and thence of Matter, and also to try in his own mind to keep his parents apart. We may express this in the following:

Interpretation XLV: Matter was a derivative of a conception of a bad mother, who made his father bad also, having sadistic intercourse with him.

Solipsism implies further that Berkeley himself created not only the world but also other persons as well and even himself. And this is another way of saying that he was not created by parental intercourse.

In this context the conception of badness is bound up with sadism and destructiveness. But, whether or not his mother gave him real ground for thinking her bad, the badness he found in her would be a projection of Berkeley's own destructiveness. His explosion against the mathematicians and deists displays pent-up aggression against what he considered most evil; and it is clear that they stood for an aspect of himself that he repudiated. To control his early destructiveness, which he would have felt was turning the world to chaos, he would have needed his mother, so that whenever she failed him at all acutely he would project on to her his destructive feelings. And behind this would lie the feeling that he had made her bad by assaulting her. Thus the ultimate terror, against which all his denials were designed to protect him, was his fear of his own destructiveness directed against her. That is to say:

Interpretation XLVI: Berkeley's attribution of excessive badness issued from his own destructiveness.

And he would have been unable to allow in phantasy his good

mother and good father to come together because of feeling left
out and because of the consequent danger of turning them bad
and wanting to destroy them. In line with all this is Berkeley's
repudiation in his *De Motu* of real force of attraction between
bodies, *i.e.* force capable of producing motion. He displaced
this power to God. In natural objects it would have been bad.
What this means is that a real power to move would promote
sadistic intercourse and goad his own destructive muscles.

We may link these ideas with Berkeley's fear of internal
poison. The chief reason for his fear of bad faeces would be that
he would use these to attack his mother with uncontrollable
violence. Faeces felt to be good are associated in the infant
mind with unity, persistence, and order, or the sense of well-
being of which these are sophisticated descriptions, and also
associated with projection that is pleasurable; faeces felt to be
bad are associated with chaos, destructiveness, and with projecting in pain or rage. Thus:

*Interpretation XLVII: Underlying Berkeley's life-long defences
against bad faeces was his fear of reducing his mother to chaos by means
of them.*

We shall now consider Solipsism more closely in relation to
his mother.

(e) PRESENCE AND ABSENCE

Scott[1] has pointed out that in the early months of life a child's
experiences lack continuity in a certain way and objects are not
yet endowed with persistence through time. The mother leaves
him. After being present she is absent. She returns. Is she the
same mother or a different one? The conception of identity
would not have been developed. Likewise when she left him
there would be no conception of her return. Thus temporal
experience would consist of having the mother present and of
gaps felt as loss unmitigated by hope. In the course of development these gaps are closed, and in two ways: both by attributing
identity through time to the mother and by having the phantasy
of her presence during intervals when she is absent. The former
seems to have been evolved by Berkeley into his notional view
of persons as persisting through time; and the latter into the

[1] W. Clifford M. Scott, an unpublished communication.

permanent presence of God to prevent gaps from occurring in the world when things are not perceived. One would suppose that these situations would be connected in some way with *Esse percipi*. Is this so? The rôle of this principle was to make gaps, by removing the unity, persistence, and order from the world. It would therefore seem that it should have brought to mind the painful absences that Berkeley suffered as an infant. But in fact we know that the principle was felt to be a triumph. We must therefore place its origin not at the time when the gaps between the appearances of his mother were intolerable but at the time when he reacted to this depressing situation by a triumphant adaptation, namely when he had succeeded in creating a stable phantasy of possessing his mother, or initially his mother's breast, inside him:

Interpretation XLVIII: In infancy Berkeley learned to attribute unity, persistence, and order to things by introjecting his mother's breast.

Moreover, *Esse percipi* was a means of internalising the world within the mind and eliminating Matter. Hence the success in introjecting his mother's breast would be the success of introjecting a good breast, keeping a bad frustrating breast outside him. In the natural run of events frustration must occur; and, after sufficient frustration, he would begin to feel that the breast inside him was failing him, for this phantasy breast would not supply real milk. This would lead him to feel that the good breast had turned bad and that he had introjected a bad breast. For clinical knowledge of introjection and projection of breasts, good and bad, we are indebted to the original work by Klein, who gained it partly from the treatment of adult patients but mainly from the analysis of young children[1]; a number of others have followed up her work.

These introjections would have an important bearing on Berkeley's attitude to faeces. In the first place, before objects became well discriminated, he would have begun to discriminate intestinal sensations as a group from others before these sensations would have been further differentiated. The sensations of food taken in through the mouth and those of faeces given out through the anus would have been all part of one un-

---

[1] Melanie Klein, *The Psycho-Analysis of Children*, London, 1937, pp. 248 f.; *Contributions to Psycho-Analysis*, London, 1948, pp. 282 f., 327 f.

differentiated experience, the whole digestive tract being stimulated together. Thus the transition from good milk to valued faeces and from bad milk to poisonous faeces would originate in undifferentiated identities. Hence the need to deny Matter would have come ultimately not from discriminated bad faeces but from an undifferentiated conception of bad faeces-milk. In the second place, after milk and faeces had become differentiated, defecation would be a means—one of the chief means—of getting rid of milk and of a bad introjected breast. Hence bowel training, interrupting the flux of faeces would mean to Berkeley that he had to retain bad milk inside him. Moreover, defecation would be two-edged, for he would be likely to feel that he could not control what was being eliminated and what was being retained—that is to say, he would lose the good with the bad. And this could be remedied only by incorporating milk or faeces once more.

We can thus see that, though faeces constituted a precursor of other objects of value or persecution to Berkeley, their structure and function can be found in prototype form in oral activities. Thus breast situations can throw light on Berkeley's faecal need. But is such a reconstruction satisfactory as an explanation? Berkeley's exposition of *Esse percipi* with the illustration of perceiving an apple and perceiving a cherry, in the *Principles* and *Three Dialogues* respectively, supports by its symbolism the interpretation of an introjected breast. The reconstruction may be made, however, not from what we know about Berkeley, but from what every child is almost certain to undergo, as clinical experience tends to show. This may make the construction fairly certain, but its very generality must prevent it from being an explanation of the variety of later child development. Some children undergo these experiences without developing Berkeley's intense need of faeces into a syndrome and without developing a philosophy of *Esse percipi*. An additional factor must therefore be sought. What this is we do not know. In clinical practice it is largely sought in the day-to-day relations between the infant and the breast—the variations in individual handling and the amount of frustration meted out is enormous. And there is also the possibility that genetic considerations make one infant more hungry than another or more grasping with its mouth. Whichever it was, his aggressiveness, either in reaction to frustration or through his being endowed with unusually active jaws and lips, would have been goaded.

Let us consider another possible mechanism for dealing with absences. The child, finding his introjected mother insufficient, could project himself in his mother whenever she left him—a process that presupposes some development. After discriminating his father from his mother, part of this projection could also go with the father, so that he would in effect accompany her by proxy.

So far as one can separate out different trends in psychoanalysis, one might say that it may be presented on the one hand in patriarchal form, in which the father plays the dominant part in the mental development of the child, and that on the other hand it may also be presented in matriarchal form, in which the mother alone is significant. Undoubtedly, from the point of view of social anthropology, patriarchal society is the kind we know most about and the one that has prevailed for thousands of years. But it was preceded by matriarchal society. Hence we might expect to find the patriarchal structure of the mind stand out at first when we analyse an individual but to find the matriarchal structure underneath it if we continue to search. However, it is certain that both mothers and fathers count in the life of children; and, if we find difficulty in accounting for the rôle of the father when we analyse in terms of the earliest matriarchal influences, then something will have been omitted. I suggest that one of the mechanisms for the transition from the matriarchal to the patriarchal, from dependence on the mother to dependence on the father, is the one just mentioned, namely by the child's projecting himself (or herself) into his father as a method of closing gaps between his mother's presences, and then utilising the father to accompany his mother in phantasy. In Berkeley, such a mechanism would throw light on the more mature form of his philosophy, in which it appears that he projected himself into God:

Interpretation XLIX: Berkeley closed gaps in the world left by Esse percipi *by projecting himself in God, as a psychogenetic development from an earlier attempt to close gaps between his presences by projecting himself into his father and thus accompanying her.*

This would be in accord with what we know of Berkeley's life, in that this phase of his philosophy was achieved about the time when he married, *i.e.* when fear that had once been aroused by parental intercourse would have been quiescent.

Nonetheless Berkeley would have had his difficulties over these projections and introjections. Excessive need for good milk and excessive fear of poisonous milk arising through frustration, the fear of expelling the bad kind and poisoning his mother with it, all these could lead to the fear that she contained Matter; and this once allowed would preclude the existence of God and therefore originally prove fatal to his father. Thus he would have had difficulty in conceiving happy relations between father and mother. In consequence, in his early manhood when the danger of faecal Matter was pressing, maturity of genital relations with a wife would have been checked because of being conceived in faecal terms (and partly in terms of food). In view of this, it is not surprising that he should have removed himself far from the setting of his early conflicts and sought a new virgin island in the West—an idealisation created out of phantasies of good things, unsullied with poison, like his original conception of a good mother—and at the same time found a wife in line with this conception.

(*f*) TIME

Berkeley had metaphysical difficulties about time. In a letter to Johnson he admitted he could not surmount them:

One of my earliest inquiring was about Time, which led me into several paradoxes that I did not think fit or necessary to publish; particularly the notion that the Resurrection follows the next moment to death. We are confounded and perplexed about time. (1) Supposing a succession in God. (2) Conceiving that we have an *abstract idea* of Time. (3) Supposing that the Time in one mind is to be measured by the succession of ideas in another.[1]

These points are to be found also in the *Philosophical Commentaries*; in the *Principles* there is only an insignificant reference to the subject[2]; he did not discuss it in the *De Motu* where it was really relevant. Consider the remark in the *Commentaries*:

[1] *Works*, II, p. 293.
[2] *Id.*, *The Principles of Human Knowledge*, §§ 97–8.

651. Certainly the mind always & constantly thinks & we know this too In sleep and trances the mind exists not there is no time no succession of Ideas.

Plainly Berkeley must have regarded going to sleep and the vanishing of his mother as death, and awakening and the re-appearance of his mother as rebirth. The difficulty of synchron-ising two people's time sequences would arise: since he held each sequence to be determined by the personal succession of perceptions, there would be no ground for supposing that the two time sequences would correspond. Thus his own sequence of perceptions from feed to satisfaction, to contentment, to dis-content, to hunger would not necessarily correspond to his mother's sequence of perceptions from giving him one meal to giving him another. That he never made a workable adjustment to this difficulty—a real one in infancy—finds support in his admitting defeat about the philosophy of time. Put another way, his failure to deal with time in his philosophy means that early difficulties about the timing of feeds were basic, and re-mained without even the vicarious resolution of other aspects of his conflict found in *Esse percipi*.

Interpretation L: In infancy Berkeley failed to find an adjustment to his intolerance of lack of synchronisation between presence of hunger and presence of food.

Chapter 21

THE RÔLE OF PANENTHEISM

In Berkeley's middle phase, lying roughly between the *De Motu* (1721) and *The Theory of Vision Vindicated* (1733), the Pauline note was emphasised: all persons have their being in God. This form of Panentheism was to reinforce the denial of Matter. After that a new tendency becomes apparent, which came to the surface in *Siris* (1744). Here the world-soul in which all things are contained presents a picture of being the womb of the world, where all the most perfect objects from fire to tar are created. Now in the young mind womb, bowel, and belly are not differentiated: there is just one large closed container. As regards contents, we recall the passage cited from § 16 that trees can become constipated by their juice, so that a faecal aspect of tar creeps through—to which we may add that tar would easily symbolise faeces in virtue of colour and plastic texture. The Great Chain of Being, in which the highest is connected with the lowest, would include the chain from food to faeces. There is a psychologically located place, sometimes scotomised, somewhere in the passage down where food becomes faeces[1]; this resembles the transition from fire to resin and thence to clogging juice; thus there is a point where there are good faeces after which they cease to be good. Further, the purpose of tar-water was to rid Berkeley's bowel of poison and make him healthy, which would mean that his faeces would be good. Thus we reach:

Interpretation LI: The Panentheism of Siris *represents a good bowel producing good faeces.*

Prior to *Siris*, Berkeley's work on economics depicts a good bowel in the form of a Central Bank, which would provide plenty of currency in the form of credit and small change and thus promote circulation.

Hence the conception of a good bowel and good faeces, which had not been clearly in evidence, began to manifest themselves

[1] W. Clifford M. Scott, an unpublished communication.

after the downfall of the American plan. According to childhood reconstructions made above, this was no new conception. But why should this 'return of the repressed' have occurred?

We have seen that *Esse percipi* and the explicit theocentric philosophy were undermined as defences. That is to say, the sublimated forms of defence had proved ineffective against the attack of a real person as a protection against ill-health. What further defences were left to Berkeley? He would be thrown back on earlier good objects: the one possibility would be that with the recognition of poison would come also the recognition of its good counterpart. We can now perhaps see more force in Interpretations XXII and XXIII, according to which Berkeley tried to maintain good faeces in the external world because he felt poisoned within, to reassure himself that his inner poison was not getting out of control. And this process, begun in the context of the Central Bank, culminated in the Panentheism of *Siris*.

Berkeley's hostility changed its focus: instead of being wholly directed against Matter, it became partly directed against certain types of men—deists and mathematicians. In infancy persons and things are interchangeable before discrimination takes place, but as they become discriminated their differences become important, so that in later life it is a mark of regression if they exchange rôles. Now the change of objects of aggression from things to persons took place in Berkeley's middle period after he had reached his zenith and married—it was a progression. We may presume therefore that, because his inner fear of parental relations was at that time quiescent, persons could play a more living rôle in his life than previously. This was when affairs of great moment to him were going favourably. After the *débâcle* his conflict was still conducted in terms of persons; and Walpole, the chief environmental factor, was a person, not an inanimate poison. The regression from persons to things took place, however. It was a person who initiated the downfall of his plans; but it was an inanimate poison that he felt to be inside him ruining his health. And there was a parallel regression in the panentheistic defence, for in his middle phase it was persons who lived in God, while at the time of *Siris* it was things that largely formed the furniture of the world-soul

Chapter 22

A THEORY OF PSYCHOSOMATIC DISORDER*

In giving the main features of the solution to the problem of Berkeley's illness, which turned on the undermining of defences against recognition of internal poison, I have offered an explanation of why he became ill when he did. But there was a fundamental point not dealt with, the fundamental psychosomatic question to which no one knows the answer: why does a psychosomatic disorder arise instead of a psychological one? Why did Berkeley not develop anxiety-hysteria with phobias, obsessional neurosis, or schizophrenia; why instead did he develop a disorder of the intestinal tract? As I left the matter in Chapter 19, the solution offered may have had a certain plausibility: if Berkeley felt poisoned by faeces inside him it would be 'natural' to expect him to suffer a physical illness. But we have only to state this to dispel the plausibility; for it could be argued that it would be more 'natural' for the poison to have kept him in a state of continual anxiety while leaving his physical health unimpaired.

In order to answer this question in the next chapter, it is necessary to turn aside to discuss the nature of psychosomatic disorder.

There are at present only two theoretical formulations about psychosomatic disorder that can be said to have the status of theories; they are due respectively to Alexander and Deutsch. In addition, an almost explicit theory is to be found in the inspiring work of Selye. Others to whom theories have been attributed seem to me to have written without the definiteness and the attention to mechanism that are required of a theory.

Alexander begins with the concept of 'conversion', which was introduced by Freud[1] for one particular kind of disorder,

* Communicated in brief, apart from the first two paragraphs, to the Medical Section of the British Psychological Society, June 25, 1952, and reprinted from *The British Journal of Medical Psychology*, London, 1953, Vol. XXVI, Pt. i.

[1] Freud, *Collected Papers*, London, 1940, Vol. I, "The Defence Neuro-Psychoses" (1894), p. 63.

namely 'conversion-hysteria'. This meant that an organic symptom was a symbolic substitute for a psychical conflict. Alexander accepts this account of this particular disorder, but he provides considerable evidence against the view that all psychosomatic disorders are of this kind. On the contrary he holds that the conversion-mechanism is applicable only to frustrated motor behaviour and perception, *i.e.* only to the voluntary neuro-muscular and perceptual systems, but denies that it is applicable to the vegetative system controlled by the autonomic nervous system. Here, he maintains, the somatic symptoms are the normal physiological accompaniments of the conflict, just as the secretion of adrenalin is the accompaniment of rage and not the symbolic substitute for it. Thus a psychosomatic gastric dysfunction, such as sickness without a lesion, is the accompaniment of a conflict about greed. Finally, he holds that there is a group that consists neither of conversion-symptoms nor of physiological accompaniments but of structural consequences of organic dysfunction arising in either of the first two ways. A gastric ulcer would illustrate this.[1]

It should be stressed that this is a *classification* of psychosomatic disorders, and also that it is a hypothesis, though a fairly well attested one. Alexander next considers a question of parallelism: he holds that specific psychosomatic symptoms go with specific overt mental attitudes. For instance, he has given an analysis of gastro-intestinal disturbances in terms of 'directional'[*] attitudes. These are incorporation, retention, and elimination; and he finds that they correlate with distinct psychosomatic disorders, namely gastritis, constipation, and colitis.[2] It should not be assumed, however, that such a directional

---

[1] Franz Alexander, "Fundamental Concepts of Psychosomatic Research: Psychogenesis, Conversion, Specificity", *Psychosomatic Medicine*, Philadelphia, 1943, Vol. V, No. iii, pp. 205–10. (Reprinted in Alexander and French, *Studies in Psychosomatic Medicine*, New York, 1948.)

[*] Alexander used the word "vector", which is regrettable. A vector has a definite magnitude and direction, and is such that two vectors are added in a very special way and are multiplied in two very special ways. Of all these important properties Alexander's concept possesses only one —direction.

[2] Alexander, "The Logic of Emotions and its Dynamic Background", *The International Journal of Psycho-Analysis*, London, 1935, Vol. XVI, Pt. iv, pp. 403 f.

hypothesis would apply to other disorders where nothing crosses the body-boundary; nonetheless personality-attitudes, characterised not by one fairly definite attitude but by a recognisable group of attitudes, do appear sometimes to correlate with psychosomatic disorders.

Deutsch's theory is an aetiology of three different factors that are each necessary and that are together sufficient to produce a psychosomatic disorder. For a certain disorder, such as asthma, to occur, there has firstly to be an appropriate overt personality-attitude, such as dependence. Secondly, there has to be a compliant environmental situation of which the attitude can readily make use, such as a pampering household. Thirdly, there has to have been in early childhood a physical disorder of the organ involved, such as an infection of the respiratory tract, that fostered at the same time a psychical conflict producing the personality-attitude, in this illustration dependence. Given the attitude and the environment, a given disorder is purely organic if the early physical illness did not give rise to a psychical conflict or if such conflict was not touched off before the onset of the disorder; otherwise it would be psychosomatic.[1] Fenichel gives a very similar aetiology.[2]

From his work on endocrinology Selye considers that stress of any kind, such as an infection or an injury, stimulates the anterior pituitary to secrete hormones. Some of these attack an organ directly, and some stimulate the adrenal cortex to secrete further groups of hormones in unbalanced proportions, thus damaging some organ. This is a purely physiological theory. But it becomes a psychosomatic theory when we add that one important form of stress that stimulates the pituitary—though the mechanism is unknown—is anxiety. So far, then, we have a theory in which a psychological factor leads to organic dysfunction and ultimately to lesion. But what determines the

[1] Felix Deutsch, "The Choice of Organ Neuroses", *The International Journal of Psycho-Analysis*, London, 1939, Vol. XX, Pts. iii and iv, pp. 252–62; "The Production of Somatic Disease by Emotional Disturbances", *Proceedings of the Association for Nervous and Mental Diseases*, Baltimore, 1939, pp. 271–92.

[2] Otto Fenichel, "Nature and Classification of the So-called Psychosomatic Phenomena", *The Psychoanalytic Quarterly*, New York, 1945, Vol. XIV, No. iii, pp. 300–1.

location of this consequence, that is to say, what determines the selection of a 'target-organ'? Selye's answer is that there is no simple answer: the target-organ is determined by a large variety of factors, such as inherent weakness, previous injury, and so on.[1]

What are the problems being dealt with by these theories? To answer this we may first distinguish several psychosomatic problems of a very general nature. Selye will be mentioned only in connexion with (5).

(1) Is the aetiology always of the same kind? Deutsch holds that it is, Alexander that it is not.

(2) What is the relationship between personality and types of disorder? Can every type of personality develop some form of psychosomatic trouble? This has not been raised. Will certain personality-types fall ill only of correlated disorders? Alexander and Deutsch to a certain extent hold this; and it is one of the principal questions Alexander has set himself to investigate.

(3) Are all psychosomatic disorders or an important group of them preceded by a purely organic disorder in childhood? Deutsch believes this is true of all; Alexander with hesitation thinks this possible.[2]

(4) Must the environment play into the hands of this disorder? Deutsch insists on this, Alexander denies it,[3] but holds that all disorders are a defeat at the hands of the environment.[4]

(5) What determines the choice of organ? Deutsch's theory offers an explanation of this in terms of previous organic affection and personality-attitude. For Alexander the answer would

[1] Hans Selye, "The General Adaptation Syndrome and the Diseases of Adaptation", *The Journal of Clinical Endocrinology*, Springfield, 1946, Vol. VI, No. ii, pp. 117–230, esp. p. 190; *Textbook of Endocrinology*, Acta Endocrinologica, Montreal, 1947, pp. 837–67, esp. p. 865 (*cf.* pp. 17–18); David le Vay, "Hans Selye and a Unitary Conception of Disease", *The British Journal for the Philosophy of Science*, Edinburgh, 1952, Vol. III, No. x, pp. 157–69.

[2] Alexander, "The Influence of Psychologic Factors upon Gastro-Intestinal Disturbances", *The Psychoanalytic Quarterly*, New York, 1934, Vol. III, No. iv, p. 522. (Reprinted in Alexander and French, *Op. cit.*)

[3] *Id.*, p. 506.

[4] Alexander, Addenda to "The Medical Value of Psycho-analysis", *The Psychoanalytic Quarterly*, New York, 1936, Vol. V, No. iv, p. 556.

depend on which group of disorders is involved. A conversion disorder would affect an organ that could be a symbolic substitute for a conflict; but this would not determine the organ uniquely, and a previous trauma, probably physical, Alexander tentatively suggests, would fix the choice. Wilson[1] has given clinical material largely supporting this, and Seitz[2] has given confirmation from experiments in hypnosis. Kardiner's view that a psychosomatic disorder is the result of frustrated action would presumably fall under this heading.[3] French[4] on the other hand considers that the target-organ is one that is particularly under stress in a living situation (his work contains a significant contribution that will be discussed below). Selye's theory that the target-organ is selected in a wide variety of ways does not preclude determinants such as the foregoing.

The group of psychosomatic disorders, in which the organic dysfunction is a normal physiological accompaniment of a conflict, such as a distressingly fast heartbeat in a person who thinks he has been found out, offers no problem here. Nor does the third group, if it exists, in which the structural change is a consequence of either of the two preceding types of organic dysfunction. Saul[5] substantiates Alexander's work with regard to this type.

It is thus clear that Alexander tends to accept Deutsch's theory almost completely so far as conversions are concerned (with a reservation about the compliance of the environment), and that he largely rejects it for other groups of disorder.

(6) Another general question is this: Why do some people

[1] G. W. Wilson, "The Transition from Organ Neurosis to Conversion Hysteria", *The International Journal of Psycho-Analysis*, London, 1938, Vol. XIX, Pt. i, pp. 23–40. (Reprinted in Alexander and French, *Op. cit.*)

[2] P. F. D. Seitz, "Symbolism and Organ Choice in Conversion Reactions", *Psychosomatic Medicine*, Philadelphia, 1951, Vol. XIII, No. iv, pp. 254–9.

[3] A. Kardiner, *The Traumatic Neuroses of War*, Psychosomatic Medicine Monographs, Wisconsin, 1941, Vol. I, Nos. ii and iii, pp. 169–71.

[4] Thomas French, "Physiology of Behaviour and Choice of Neurosis", *The Psychoanalytic Quarterly*, New York, 1941, Vol. X, No. iv, pp. 561–72. (Reprinted in Alexander and French, *Op. cit.*)

[5] L. J. Saul, "A Note on the Psychogenesis of Organic Symptoms", *The Psychoanalytic Quarterly*, New York, 1935, Vol. IV, No. iii, pp. 476–83. (Reprinted in Alexander and French, *Op. cit.*)

develop, say, a gastric ulcer, while others develop gastric pain only, without an ulcer?

(7) The most general question concerning choice of organ, however, is not why one organ succumbs rather than another, but the following: what determines whether a person shall fall ill of a psychomatic disorder rather than one that is purely psychological? This does not appear to have been explicitly discussed, but we can see Deutsch's answer—the existence or otherwise of a previous purely organic complaint. Alexander would probably concur. This is a claim that is particularly difficult to establish, and the work by Wilson and by Seitz already referred to throws doubt upon it. The effort should therefore be made to see whether this hypothesis could be dispensed with. Besides, the most general problem of all is worthy of explicit discussion. The theory to be put forward has very different roots from the foregoing and it begins at the phenomenological level.

I wish to put forward a set of hypotheses to do with mechanism; at best, however, they are likely to be an over-simplification.

Let us begin with imagining and images. We shall not be concerned with the phenomena of double images or after-images but with the kind of images that occur in dreams and day-dreams. The theory to be developed hinges on the difference between imagining that is conducted in terms of visual or auditory images on the one hand and tactile and kinaesthetic imagining on the other (the intermediate cases of smell and taste may be omitted for simplicity). The difference may be brought out by a little experiment of the kind proposed by Scott.[1] On asking some members of an audience to describe what happened when imagining an egg, some answers showed that the imagining was visual. But one lady said she had no visual image but felt that she could draw an egg—and as she was saying this she was making movements with her hand as

[1] W. Clifford M. Scott, "Some Embryological Neurological, Psychiatric and Psycho-Analytic Implications of the Body Scheme", *The International Journal of Psycho-Analysis*, London, 1948, Vol. XXIX, Pt. iii, p. 153, col. 2.

one might when drawing. She evidently had a kinaesthetic imagination. The movements of her hand may also have been attempts to feel the egg, so that her imagination probably worked in tactual as well as kinaesthetic terms.

Now there is one striking difference between imagining something visually or auditorily on the one hand and kinaesthetically or tactually on the other. A visual or auditory image is generally located at a place away from the surface of the body, usually outside it, while whatever is kinaesthetically or tactually imagined, apart from certain exceptions, is located on or in the body. This difference may be described by saying that the visual and auditory images are 'projected'. This description is not strictly accurate, as we shall see, because of some borderline phenomena; but it seems better to use a brief expression that is fairly appropriate and approximately correct rather than a cumbrous circumlocution. I wish to show that certain fundamental relations hold between projective images and what is kinaesthetically or tactually imagined.

We may initiate the discussion with a nodal point made by Sartre,[1] which is concerned with the function of magic. He holds that fainting is a magical escape, fear is magical removal of a dangerous object, anger is magical vengeance, joy is magical fulfilment of what is longed for, when this is delayed—a magical anticipation. In general something is magically fulfilled.

The second nodal point in Sartre concerns the mechanism of magic. He considers a person struck with horror at a face seen outside the window-pane. The face is supposed to be able to enter and be close and menacing, without interference from the glass and without opening the window. The magical idea is that the realistic concepts of the window as an object that has to be broken or opened and of the intervening distance that takes time to traverse are set aside—annihilated, according to Sartre.

This account closely resembles certain anthropological findings, e.g. that given by Lévy-Bruhl[2], in which he depicts a 'pre-rational' type of primitive mentality, and the interpretation of

[1] Jean-Paul Sartre, *The Emotions: Outline of a Theory*, New York, 1948, Ch. III.

[2] Lucien Lévy-Bruhl, *How Natives Think*, London, 1926.

magic given by Frazer[1]. In 'pre-rational' mentality, 'influences' (spiritual, magical) are the only agents by which anything comes about, and they do not operate according to the laws of nature accepted by civilised mentality.* Magic by contact and resemblance may be illustrated thus. If a chief finds the hair or nails of an enemy, he believes he has only to destroy them in order to encompass the enemy's death; if he kills an effigy of his enemy, the same result is believed to follow. In both mechanisms, there may be said to be magical denial of ordinary laws of nature and of the reality of distance and duration.

Psycho-analysts meet with this mechanism in disorders of every kind, but particularly explicitly in obsessional neurosis. This 'omnipotence of thoughts', as Freud[2] called it, is exemplified in the compulsive need some women have to make sure that the hall-door is bolted, knowing full well that it is; if they do not check the matter, the thought that the door is not bolted is felt to be powerful enough to open the door and admit a burglar.

The whole approach, whether of Sartre, anthropologists, or psycho-analysts, may be expressed as follows: an object, dangerous or enticing, is magically or by omnipotent means transported across space and time, without regard to ordinary laws of nature. I would add, in modification of Sartre, as a result of Scott's work on time,[3] that the omnipotence should be regarded as a power to *manipulate* but not necessarily *annihilate* places and dates with complete disregard for realities.

We are now in a position to understand one stage in the process when a person imagines something. There is an imaginary enactment of a drama in the sense that an object, dangerous or winsome, is magically or omnipotently brought towards the

[1] J. G. Frazer, *The Golden Bough*, London, 1932, Vol. I (*The Magic Art*, Vol. I), Ch. III.

* We may agree about the value of this feature of Lévy-Bruhl's work without accepting his sharp distinction between primitives and civilised men. 'Pre-rational' mentality occurs in both, though to us it is of course much more in evidence in primitives.

[2] Freud, *Collected Papers*, London, 1925, Vol. III, "Notes upon a Case of Obsessional Neurosis" (1909). *Cf.* Sandor Ferenczi, *Contributions to Psycho-Analysis*, Boston, 1916, Ch. VIII.

[3] W. Clifford M. Scott, "Some Psycho-Dynamic Aspects of Disturbed Perception of Time" (1935), *The British Journal of Medical Psychology*, London, 1948, Vol. XXI, Pt. ii, pp. 111–20.

person, despite the actualities of place and date (we are not concerned just yet with instances in which the object is imagined to recede). According to Sartre, it is the imagined approach of the object by magical power that arouses the sense of horror.

This is as far as Sartre takes us. His account is correct, I believe, so far as it goes, but there is another nodal point to be made. Let us raise a further question: we believe in the horrible object and suppose it magically approaches—but why does it somehow not quite arrive? When people are chased in dreams they usually awaken just before their pursuer reaches them. Horrifying day-dreams usually stop short of the final act. Why?

I suggest there is a very simple reason for this: what is imagined is better kept at a safe distance. The person undergoing the experience can tolerate—though only just—an increase of horror as the face approaches, but he cannot tolerate this beyond a certain point. In other words, the image, in this instance visual, is kept projected because otherwise something far worse than horror would be experienced.*

A film on children's sleep, which portrays bad objects approaching or receding, and thus evoking anxiety or tranquillity, would seem to bear the same construction.[1]

We proceed next to the tactual field. We are not concerned here with distinctions of warmth, hardness, resistance, texture, and sharpness. We are concerned with pleasure and pain, which may be either kinaesthetic or tactile. Tactile and kinaesthetic experience may vary from being mildly pleasant to being intensely erotic and from being mildly unpleasant to being agonal, with all degrees in between. We now come to the question of the degree to which they can be imagined. It will be sufficient for present purposes and make for simplicity of terminology to omit reference to tactile and kinaesthetic images and to confine ourselves to tactile and kinaesthetic *sensations*; we may then con-

---

* Since this was written, Wellisch has published an interesting paper with relevant clinical material (E. Wellisch, "Dreamy States in Children with Apparent Recession and Approach of Objects", *The British Journal of Medical Psychology*, Cambridge, 1952, Vol. XXV, Pt. ii, pp. 135–47).

[1] *Your Children's Sleep*, Central Office of Information film produced by the Realist Film Unit for the Ministry of Health and the Central Council for Health Education, written and produced by Brian Smith, 1948. Distributed by the Central Film Library.

fine the name "images" to those that are projected; thus the contrast lies between images, which are visual or auditory, and sensations, which are kinaesthetic or tactile. (Thus we do not speak here of 'visual sensations'; a loud noise or bright light may produce an unpleasant sensation, but in the present usage neither is itself a sensation.) Moreover, "sensations" is not being used here for something with a physical cause and "image" for something without a physical cause. On the present usage either may be produced by a physical cause or produced without one. The point of this distinction between sensations and images is to contrast images as projected with sensations as unprojected. This makes it necessary to draw attention to a neurological sense in which all sensations are 'projections' from the brain; but this sense is not connected with 'projection' as used above. The reason for speaking of 'projection' at all comes from the hypotheses that are to be made. A further point about the use of 'sensation' is this: there is no intention of suggesting that a 'pure sensation' can exist by itself without referring beyond itself to other sensations and even images and objects. We shall be concerned with the difference between the sensation of, say, one's leg being bitten by a dog and the image of this; but it is not suggested that one can have such a sensation or idea in abstraction from the context involving the dog.

The whole discussion that ensues may convey to the reader that images and sensations exist for conscious perception alone; it is therefore important to make it clear that this is not true. There is little difficulty, however, in showing that one can have images and sensations without being aware of having them. One does not notice the clock ticking but one notices when it stops—one realises that one heard it without noticing it. One does not notice the posture of one's leg, but if it goes numb one realises that one had some sense of its posture. In fact our main concern is with images and sensations that occur unrecognised.

Relevant to the question of imagining a sensation is a nodal point made by Scott. He suggests that an infant dreaming or having a hallucination of a breast, if it also began to dream or hallucinate sucking, would have to annihilate the sensation of sucking, else it would be frustrated by the absence of milk and awaken. And the same would hold for imagined sucking. That is, the imagined sensation would be *self-defeating*, *i.e.* the absence of the sensation would defeat the imagining. This account has to be supplemented, I think, by consideration of what happens in connexion with less basic kinds of sensation.

We might say that any wish whose satisfaction is an end in itself cannot give rise to an imagined sensation, tactile or kinaesthetic, if the sensation is dependent upon some absent factor, such as milk in the example given. But wishes that lead to other satisfactions could. Thus a hallucinated sensation of erotic foreplay, and not simply a visual dream, must be assumed in order to explain seminal emission during sleep; here the sensation is not self-defeating because it can lead to a further sensation that can in fact be experienced.

We may express the foregoing discussion in the following:

Hypothesis I: If what is imagined is dangerous or if it promises a pleasure that cannot be fulfilled, it is less disturbing if kept at a safe distance as a projected image.

And to explain the non-arrival of images, as illustrated by the grinning face outside the window-pane or the milk that is not obtainable, I put forward the following:

Hypothesis II: The approach of an image, whether it is frightening or stimulates a wish for pleasure that cannot be fulfilled, arouses apprehension that some painful tactile or kinaesthetic sensation will arise.

In general such a sensation would be self-defeating. However it should be possible in some circumstances to imagine a tactile sensation of being hurt (burnt, frozen, torn, squeezed), though the difficulty of tolerating it would make it rare. It should be possible to imagine a mild sensation of this kind to alleviate some deep apprehension; thus one might imagine the tactile sensation of a cyst being cut out or burnt to prevent it from becoming a cancer, or a septic wound being cauterised to prevent it from poisoning the system, or a tooth being drilled to remove a constant gnawing pain. Again it should be possible to imagine a hurt if this foreshadows pleasure; thus a tactile sensation of defloration could usher in tactile and kinaesthetic erotic sensations. But one would suppose that it would be a rare occurrence to imagine tactile or kinaesthetic sensations of great pain, for some defence or other would nearly always be possible. Nonetheless the hallucination of great pain is not unknown. One would expect to find that some pains of this kind occurred to prevent the occurrence of a still greater pain; but it would be necessary to investigate individual cases to find out whether or not this is so. Support for the possibility may be found in one instance given by Daniels where his patient did have one set of unwelcome kinaesthetic sensations to avoid having others.[1]

In addition, however, there is reason to believe that it is possible to have a hallucinated pain that is not a defence against something worse. Thus, when a psychotic (the phenomenon can also occur in neurotics) reaches the final stages of giving up hallucinating, *i.e.* when he has dispensed with all his defences against it, what was a hallucination involving pain becomes a memory, he remembers the hallucinatory experience both as failing to match reality and also as being in the past, and he no longer has the pain.[2] This suggests that hallucinated tactile and kinaesthetic pain constitutes the ultimate distress in relation to which other forms of distress are used as defences.

We can now see that an image, though brought close to the person who has it, is kept projected and can only rarely be brought right up to him, because it would be replaced by an imagined tactile or kinaesthetic sensation, which is a rare occurrence because every possible kind of defence would be mobilised against it. We may go further:

Hypothesis III: A basic function of projective images is to enable imagining to occur without arousing imagining in terms of sensation.

Hypothesis IV: Anything tending to arouse an unwelcome sensation could be mastered by substituting a projective image for the sensation.

This gives the most fundamental point on which to build, namely that projective imagining is defensive, *i.e.* has the rôle of protecting a person from unwelcome sensations. A modification of these two hypotheses should be noted, however. Visual and auditory images are not always projected outwards. They may be projected inwards and located inside the body. In an extreme case they could even be conceived as introjected to a place within. But these alternatives do not constitute exceptions to the protective rôle of images.

[1] G. E. Daniels, "Analysis of a Case of Neurosis with Diabetes Mellitus", *The Psychoanalytic Quarterly*, New York, 1936, Vol. V, No. iv, p. 534.

[2] W. Clifford M. Scott, personal communication.

Wilbur also has pointed out this rôle in the context of vision, but he has utilised it for other purposes than those under discussion.* French has drawn particular attention to it. He gives an analysis of a dream which represents "vigorous muscular activity" on the part of the dreamer's mother and represents the dreamer himself "as being beaten upon an anvil"[1]; he considers that there is a projection away from the site of excitation "to the visual apparatus"[2]; this he regards as an attempt on the part of the dreamer to content himself with a visual picture and "to inhibit muscular discharge"[3]; he reports another dream the latent content of which, castration, was projected and denied "by the substitution of a visual image"[4];

In each of the two dreams cited we note that the implied activity has been completely 'frozen'.[5]

I would mention also a striking feature of many dreams in which the dreamer is doing something: he *sees* himself doing it, *sees* his hand grasping something, but is not aware of the tactile or kinaesthetic sensations that ought to occur.

We are now in a position to consider a hypothesis differentiating psychosomatic disorders from others:

Hypothesis V: A purely psychological disorder is one in which the imagination conducts basic conflicts in terms of projective images; a psychosomatic disorder is one in which the imagination conducts basic conflicts in terms of tactile or kinaesthetic sensations.

* G. B. Wilbur, "Some Problems Presented by Freud's Life-Death Instinct Theory", *The American Imago*, Boston, 1941, Vol. II, No. ii, p. 191: "By vision we can maintain the utmost distance between ourselves and our objects. If the tactile and haptic sensations form the lowest pole of our psychic existence, vision (and its derivatives) forms the opposite pole. . . . Where the need for the maintenance of the steady state is intimate contact, the visual gives way to the tactile. *Where* on the contrary *the need is to avoid dangerous contiguity but still maintain some sort of contact, the tactile gives way to the visual*" (my italics). Wilbur, however, does not relate this to the problems being considered above; he relates it only to the problem of achieving a visual "*mastery of the universe*" (p. 190, my italics).
   I take the opportunity of mentioning that the argument in the text does not deny other functions of vision as well as the defensive one. These are very important but not relevant to the present theme.
   [1] French, *Op. cit.*, p. 562.   [2] *Id.*, p. 566.
   [3] *Id.*, p. 568.   [4] *Id.*, p. 569.   [5] *Id.*, p. 570.

It is seldom that case reports bear directly on this, since they are not written with this distinction in mind, but some useful remarks are to be found. The remarks quoted from French, for instance, occur in an immediate context of organic disorder. Thus the dream representing muscular activity and being beaten on an anvil was followed two days later by lumbago. Again in the dream in which castration was projected and denied, the sequel was a headache. Though his principle of explanation is that there is a physiological change in the quantity of energy directed to the organ that is most under stress at the time of the conflict, he also surmises with regard to the anvil dream that

the violent activity in the dream may be reflecting some intense excitation in the muscles or in the associated nervous pathways corresponding to the wish to beat or be beaten of which the dream is an expression. The subsequent muscular and arthritic pains would in this case be at least in part the result of this intense functional excitation.[1]

This, if expanded, would seem to conform with Hypothesis V and others to be given later.

Wilson[2] reports a case in which a man dreamt that he was to have an abdominal operation and that he was dead or would die. He awoke with severe diarrhoea. With this kind of manifest content of a dream it would be unlikely that the conflict could be confined to visual imagery; one would expect it to arouse painful tactile sensations.

Daniels[3] gives one of the fullest reports of a psychosomatic case. He incidentally mentions images—the patient who had diabetes could not "focus images except at distant objects"[4]— but unfortunately no further information is given about them. Several instances are to be found in this paper, in which tactile and kinaesthetic sensations became replaced by dreams or attributed to physical traumas.[5] For example,[6] the patient dreamt of

[1] Id., p. 563.
[2] G. W. Wilson, "Typical Personality Trends and Conflicts in Cases of Spastic Colitis", The Psychoanalytic Quarterly, New York, 1934, Vol. III, No. iv, p. 562.
[3] G. E. Daniels, Op. cit.
[4] Id., p. 515.
[5] Id., pp. 522-3, 527, 529, 530-1, 533-4, 534-5, 535-6.
[6] Id., p. 532.

someone with dark glasses. Here we can tell that the content was visual imagery. In this dream he goes on to complain to a nurse about injections in his leg that had made it become hard. This could only be tactile. The nurse rubbed him and he felt better. This again is tactile. In such an example perhaps one reason why the painful tactile sensations were allowed to appear in the dream is that it was possible to obtain some tactile relief. These examples are reported from cases of patients suffering from such disorders and are interesting in the context; but they give no real confirmation of the view that psychosomatic disorders are conflicts in the kinaesthetic and tactile domain. A more direct connexion can be found from other cases.

Thus Hambling[1] describes a case of hypertension, in which the patient rushed about and 'boiled up inside' but could never let fly, and this is clearly kinaesthetic. Some of Hambling's views are in conformity with Hypothesis V (without, however, necessitating it); after stressing that hypertensives suffer from fear of giving way to rage, he continues[2]:

Muscle tension, stiff necks, headaches, palpitations and painful flushings seemed particularly related to this inner battle to prevent the outburst of destructive rage. One feels that arterial hypertension is a somatic expression of this inner rage.*

Wilson[3] gives a somewhat similar example in connexion with diabetes. To this might be added the interesting, if isolated, example given by Wolf and his colleagues[4]: a patient who suffered from hypertension ended a quarrel with his brother-in-law with whom he was on bad terms by successfully beating him up; after this his blood pressure was found to be normal. Here the frustrated kinaesthetic itch to strike his brother-in-law is to be interpreted as manifested in hypertension.

[1] John Hambling, "Emotions and Symptoms in Essential Hypertension", *The British Journal of Medical Psychology*, London, 1951, Vol. XXIV, Pt. iv, p. 248.

[2] *Id.*, p. 250.

* Fenichel previously expressed a similar opinion, put somewhat vaguely (Fenichel, *Op. cit.*, p. 306).

[3] Wilson, *Op. cit.*, pp. 525–6.

[4] Stewart Wolf *et al.*, "Hypertension as a Reaction-Pattern to Stress: Summary of Experimental Data on Variations in Blood Pressure and Renal Blood Flow", *Annals of Internal Medicine*, Lancaster (Pa.), 1948, Vol. XXIX, No. vi, p. 1071.

Gottschalk and his colleagues[1] set out to investigate the relation between conflict and muscular activity by comparing groups consisting of patients with rheumatoid arthritis and of hypertension with a control group. While the results tend to confirm that in both types of disorder there is an abnormal degree of muscular tension, they are not decisive.

From another type of disorder, confirmation appears to be forthcoming. As a result of Cannon's work on physiology[2] we know that the mastication of food, before the food enters the stomach, stimulates in particular the secretion of hydrochloric acid and sets the whole digestive process going. Now, if the foregoing hypothesis is correct, to imagine a meal and imagine food in the mouth in visual terms would not start the digestive process going; but, if the food is imagined in tactile and kinaesthetic terms, *i.e.* sensations are imagined in the mouth (lips, gums, jaws, tongue), this would be sufficient to bring about secretion of hydrochloric acid in the stomach. The question, then, whether a person with an unrecognised greed for maternal milk and a (permanent) phantasy of having it would develop some purely psychological disorder or a psychosomatic disorder such as duodenal ulcer symptoms, would depend on whether his conflict was conducted in terms of visual food or tactile and kinaesthetic sensations connected with eating. Can any confirmation be obtained for this?

Commenting on the stomach of a person who develops this kind of psychosomatic disorder, Alexander says:

Such a stomach behaves all the time as if it were taking or were about to take in food. . . . My present notion is that the stomach under this permanent chronic stimulation behaves constantly as it does during digestion. . . . The empty stomach is thus constantly exposed to the same physiologic stimuli to which, under normal conditions, it is exposed only periodically when it contains or is about to receive food.[3]

[1] L. A. Gottschalk *et al.*, "Psychologic Conflict and Neuromuscular Tension", *Psychosomatic Medicine*, Philadelphia, 1950, Vol. XII, No. v, pp. 315–19.

[2] W. B. Cannon, *Bodily Changes in Pain, Hunger, Fear and Rage*, New York, 1929, pp. 4–5.

[3] Alexander, "The Influence of Psychologic Factors", as cited.

In line with this is the interesting work by Szasz,[1] in which he has found evidence that patients with an ulcer or ulcer symptoms exhibit hypersalivation (and he has also found the significant condition that hypersalivation occurs where the oral phantasy is predominantly sadistic rather than receptive by which he appears to mean 'active rather than passive').[2] These views make it intelligible that ulcer symptoms might be caused by a phantasy, *i.e.* by something both mental and permanently resident in the mind. But, unless some further consideration is adduced, we should expect everyone with such a phantasy to succumb to psychosomatic disorder; and this does not happen. So far, therefore, the experimentation has not been crucial. Carefully prepared experiments on gastric hunger contractions have been carried out under hypnosis by Lewis and Sarbin.[3] The subject was offered 'fictitious' food and went through the usual motions of eating; as a result hunger contractions ceased. The effectiveness of such an experiment, however, as a test of the present hypothesis would depend on the wording of the offer of the 'fictitious' food. It would be necessary in one experiment to say, "You will not see or smell or imagine seeing or smelling the food I am now going to give you, but you will feel it with your hands and mouth and tongue", and in the other to say, "You are seeing some food but not smelling it, and you can see yourself putting it into your mouth but you cannot feel it with your hands or mouth or tongue." What we wish to know is whether in the second experiment there would be salivation and gastric secretion. If this should be found to occur, it would, I think, constitute conclusive evidence against the present theory.

It is perhaps worth mentioning that in childbirth painful delivery may come under the heading of a psychosomatic disorder in the sense of a kinaesthetic form of conflict. Read,[4]

---

[1] T. S. Szasz, "Psychoanalytic Observations concerning Hypersalivation", *Psychosomatic Medicine*, Philadelphia, 1950, Vol. XII, No. v, pp. 320–31.

[2] *Id.*, p. 326.

[3] J. H. Lewis and T. R. Sarbin, "The Influence of Hypnotic Stimulation on Gastric Hunger Contractions", *Psychosomatic Medicine*, Philadelphia, 1943, Vol. V, No. iii, pp. 205–10.

[4] G. D. Read, *Natural Childbirth*, London, 1933, p. 12; *Childbirth without Fear*, London, 1951, pp. 20–2.

according to whom delivery can be both painless and enjoyable, points out that pain when it occurs is due to two opposing groups of muscles working one against the other, when the contractions of the uterus are opposed by failure to relax on the part of the muscles at the outlet; and that this inability to relax is set up by fear. And he holds that, by allaying fear and by giving suitable exercises in relaxing the muscles, resistance at the outlet is not induced; hence no pain is then experienced. His theory about the painless deliveries under his care therefore would seem to involve the contraction of muscles through the psychological agency of kinaesthetic tension (it also involves that fear intensifies the activity of the sympathetic nervous system).

One misunderstanding that might arise may now be mentioned (another will be dealt with later). It might appear that, according to the foregoing hypothesis, a person who has visual imagery cannot be one who conducts his imagination in terms of sensations. This is not intended. What is intended is that a person who conducts his conflicts in terms of sensations will, if he feels ill, succumb to a psychosomatic disorder and not a purely psychological one, *because his attempts to conduct them in projective terms do not succeed*: his imagery may exist but fail in its function. Another way of putting the matter would be that, though the domain of imagery is open to him, the active source of his conflicts lies in the domain of sensation.

A modification to Hypothesis V must now be made. The underlying idea has been that projective images are defences against tactile and kinaesthetic sensations because the projection represents an attempt to get away from something unendurably painful. This would suggest that sensation is always correctly located, either on the body-boundary or inside. This of course is not always true. Thus when a person has had a leg amputated and has the well-known experience of possessing a phantom limb, he in a sense wrongly locates his sensations; indeed he may also wrongly orient his phantom, in that it may not exactly coincide with the position the physical limb would have occupied. This can happen even without amputation. Now if a person can imagine tactile and kinaesthetic sensations in a place where they normally do not occur, he can adopt a more subtle defence against 'raw' sensations by displacing them. Hence the hypothesis needs modification:

Hypothesis VI: In certain circumstances, displaced tactile and kinaesthetic sensations can occur as a defence against having them in an undisplaced position.

Moreover, well-known psychological experiments show that certain sensations are wrongly located by normal people: if touched by two pins fairly close together only one contact will be experienced (the interval varying according to the part of the body touched). This would seem to produce a complication; but it need not do so. We can establish with reasonable accuracy what is a normal amount of lack of discrimination in any one area; only in relation to that would deviations be said to occur and be regarded as defensive displacements from the 'normal'.

For the more ample presentation of the hypothesis thus modified, it is necessary to relate it to the concept of 'body-schema', that important psychological concept introduced by the well-known neurologist, Head,[1] and developed at length under a different name by Schilder.[2] The body-schema includes sense of posture and sense of relative positions of tactile and kinaesthetic sensations; but visual and other projective images of the body are also involved. For present purposes it is convenient to draw a dividing line between two schemata or components of the body-schema. We may then speak of the 'sensation-schema' and 'image-schema', where the one refers to the interrelationships of bodily sensations and the other to the interrelationships of projective images of the physical body. Thus our main hypothesis takes the form that psychosomatic disorders involve the sensation-schema and purely psychological ones the image-schema. The reason for bringing in these schemata is that the disorders can hardly be regarded as conflicts involving just a pair of sensations without regard to their location, relationship to other sensations, and general sense of posture.

If one attempted to use the hypothesis in practice, it would

---

[1] Henry Head and Gordon Holmes, "Sensory Disturbances from Cerebral Lesions", *Brain*, London, 1911–12, Vol. XXXIV, Pts. ii and iii, p. 187.

[2] Paul Schilder, *The Image and Appearance of the Human Body*, New York, 1935.

probably be necessary to go below such schemata to the basal 'body-scheme' introduced by Clifford Scott,[1] as is evidenced by the work of Dennis Scott.[2]

Another possible misunderstanding leads to certain supplementary hypotheses. There is an obvious ambiguity about "tension": there is the inner experience of tension or amount of felt need, which becomes associated with the muscles; and there is physical tension in a muscle which can be measured in a physiological laboratory. It may have seemed that these were confused above. In fact I was dealing throughout with psychological tension, the experience of tension, though some of the literature cited meant physical tension. Now, once this distinction is made, the whole problem, which had an air of being at any rate partially solved, seems to have been left fundamentally untouched; for, if we assert merely that certain patients conduct their conflicts in terms of felt tensions, there is nothing extra-psychological about this and it does not explain the presence of organic dysfunction. Here we are in fact up against the general problem of the mind-body relationship; and to deal with it we have to introduce additional hypotheses:

Hypothesis VII: A tactile or kinaesthetic sensation that is imagined is approximately equivalent to one produced by an extraneous cause.

In the limit, when the imagining is hallucinatory, there would be complete equivalence.* Thus the hallucinatory sensation of being bitten by a rat would be fully equivalent to the sensation of being bitten by a real rat.

In addition we need:

Hypothesis VIII: Tactile and kinaesthetic sensations produce physiological changes.

The force of these two hypotheses is that a neurological circuit is activated by a sensation and, moreover, that the same circuit is activated by an imagined sensation or by one due to an extraneous cause. In other words they assert the approximate physio-

---

[1] Scott, *Op. cit.*

[2] R. D. Scott, "The Psychology of the Body Image", *The British Journal of Medical Psychology*, London, 1951, Vol. XXIV, Pt. iv, pp. 254–66.

* The following stronger hypothesis could be offered instead: *There is no difference between a sensation induced by the imagination and a sensation excited by an extraneous cause.* This may indeed be true; but in the absence of definite knowledge of its truth it is preferable to adopt the weaker hypothesis.

logical equivalence of an imagined and an extraneously caused sensation. Moreover, whatever physiological correlate of images there may be has to be presumed to be different from the physiological correlate of sensation and to be secondary to it as regards capacity to initiate dysfunction. Thus we require:

Hypothesis IX: The physiological correlates of sensations can produce dysfunction directly (when the sensations are involved in mental conflict); *the physiological correlates of images can do so only indirectly by influencing the sensation-areas.*

This suggests that the parietal lobes, the areas bordering on Rolando's fissure, and the cerebellum would play an indispensable rôle in initiating dysfunction, whereas the occipital and temporal lobes would not (except possibly for the parts of the temporal lobes that are associated with smell and taste), or would do so only indirectly through the other areas.

Hypothesis VIII is very widely assumed, but it cannot be regarded as established; it must therefore be made explicit. The point involved may easily be missed. What the hypothesis asserts is not that physical stimuli induce organic changes, but that felt sensations do—which is not at all the same thing. The neurologist (and philosophical epiphenomenalist) officially holds the former and denies the latter; but everyone in practice holds the latter. The hypothesis may appear to be trivial, but it is far from being so, for it denies the official neurological doctrine, which has proved of enormous importance both in promoting understanding of physiological mechanisms and in blocking understanding of functional disorders. Moreover, if the hypothesis is false, that would undermine the present, and indeed, every theory of psychosomatic disorder. It is not part of my purpose to support this hypothesis here. I mention it mainly because I wish to make it explicit as an assumption, and to make clear that the solution of the mind-body problem depends on it; elsewhere I have put forward a model for the mind-body relationship,* which permits of two-way interaction, so

* J. O. Wisdom, "A New Model for the Mind-Body Relationship", *The Brit. Journal for the Philosophy of Science*, Edinburgh, 1952, Vol. II, No. viii, pp. 295-301. I find that the main idea had been mentioned by Day in a letter to *The Lancet* (George Day, *The Lancet*, London, Sept. 14, 1946, pp. 397-8; *cf.* "P.P.S.: Pneuma, Psyche, and Soma", *Op. cit.*, Oct. 11, 1952).

that mental changes can produce physiological changes as required by the above hypothesis. Here what I aim at is to reduce the mind-body problem to the problem of the relation between bodily sensations, *i.e.* felt sensations of the body, conceived as part of a sensation-schema, excluding projective imagery, on the one hand and physiological changes on the other. But it should be stressed that such a reduction of the terms of the problem does nothing whatever to eliminate either the concept of the mind or that of the body, nor does it fall in with the widespread tendency in psychosomatic writings to seek a fused mind-body concept; this tendency is understandable but it is based on the belief that psychosomatic problems can be solved only by a unified concept, and for this there is no evidence. For present purposes it is not necessary to consider whether an 'amalgam' concept might be the best description for the human organism in the first few weeks of life. The point is that such a concept is useless in connexion with psychosomatic problems as we meet them. What we meet with apparently is organic disorder brought about by mental conflict. Hence if we did have an 'amalgam' concept we should have new problems to shoulder, namely its relation to mental conflict on the one hand and to organic disorder on the other. Moreover, if an 'amalgam' concept is the proper one to describe a person, then the concept of psychosomatic becomes otiose—there would be no psychosomatic cases cases and no psychosomatic problems. On the contrary, the present theory is dualistic: it asserts that a psychological sensation in a sensation-schema can produce changes in the physiological system.

We come now to a major question: why does one person conduct his conflicts in projective terms and another in terms of sensation? The first step in the answer is that everyone does imagine to some extent in projective terms. The question should therefore be a different one: why does one person succeed in conducting conflicts in projective terms and another not? Our problem thus comes to be one of mechanism: in what ways can projective imagination fail? We may consider:

(*Mechanism*) *Hypothesis X: A person could fail to imagine in projective terms by having strong introjective needs (such as greed).*

This may be illustrated as follows. When an infant suffers intense dissatisfaction with a breast and his destructiveness (kin-aesthetic) is aroused, he may try to get rid of his destructiveness by attributing it to the breast, *i.e.* by projecting it and imagining it in projective terms. The breast is now dangerous and to be kept at a safe distance. But greed for the breast may tempt him to bring the breast with its projected destructiveness back towards himself and thus arouse the kinaesthetic destructiveness once more.[1] In other words the projective attempt could not be sustained. Again there is the possibility:

(*Inhibition*) *Hypothesis XI: Environmentally caused inhibition of projective imagination would deprive a person of an alternative to tactile and kinaesthetic conflict.*

Thus punishment for looking at certain things might prevent the projective mechanism from developing into a stable defence. Thus Ziwar[2] describes a case of glaucoma in which inhibitions about looking played a dominant rôle. Such an inhibition could come about whether the projection was pleasure-seeking or destructive.

The difference between these two mechanisms is that the first is one in which projection is overwhelmed while the second is one in which the projection is nipped in the bud.

We may ask where it is that guilt and anxiety go to in psycho-somatic disorders, for there seems little doubt that they are experienced to a far less degree in this field than in the field of purely psychological disorders—that is to say, they do not occur in a psychosomatic syndrome though this does not mean that a patient with such a disorder is free of them. A remark of Hambling's points the way:

It was impossible for any of these hypertensives to *feel* angry without becoming anxious lest he lost control of himself, or to *express* anger without suffering remorse and fear of punishment.... Muscle tension, stiff necks, headaches, palpitations and painful flushings seemed particularly related to this inner battle to prevent the outburst of destructive rage.[3]

[1] *Cf.* Melanie Klein, *The Psycho-Analysis of Children*, London, 1937, pp. 248 f.; *Contributions to Psycho-Analysis*, London, 1948, pp. 282 f., 327 f.

[2] Moustafa Ziwar, "Psychanalyse des principaux syndromes psycho-somatiques", *Revue française de psychanalyse*, Paris, 1948, Tome XII, No. iv, pp. 505–40.

[3] Hambling, *Loc. cit.*

This would suggest that guilt and anxiety are obviated because there occurs instead a kinaesthetic tension leading to pain or dysfunction.*

In this connexion another phenomenon is relevant. Some patients in analysis suddenly develop somatic pains during actual treatment when psychological resistances are being partially undermined. It seems likely that this is an escape into a psychosomatic disorder to avoid a purely mental conflict to avoid anxiety or guilt. It would seem, therefore, that where a psychosomatic disorder obviates either of these it must be secondary to a primary disorder of a purely psychological kind, involving anxiety or guilt (and by contrast a psychosomatic disorder would be primary if it did not arise to obviate anxiety or guilt). But this leads to the problem of explaining guilt and anxiety. Can they be interpreted in turn as a projective defensive against tactile and kinaesthetic pain? This would seem to be possible; but discussion of it would take us into problems of detail outside the scope of the present enquiry.

We come now to the general question of testing the theory. It could be refuted by a certain result in the experiment in hypnosis described above; it would be false if the official neurological theory should turn out to be true without the restriction that it seems to require at present; it would be false if the occipital or temporal lobes could initiate dysfunction directly; and it could be tested by its consequences in clinical practice. We know that psycho-analysis can alleviate or arrest the development of psychosomatic disorders and in some cases achieve more striking results than this; but the prognosis is in general uncertain. From the present theory it would follow that a psychosomatic disorder would be unlikely to be radically affected under

* The question of the location and nature of phantasy is of interest here. In the sense used by Klein, Isaacs (Susan Isaacs, "The Nature and Function of Phantasy", *The International Journal of Psycho-Analysis*, London, 1948, Vol. XXIX, Pt. ii) and others, it is a permanent feature of the mind. If we may interpret it in terms of sensations, tactile and kinaesthetic, then it would follow that phantasies are always present as Klein and Isaacs hold. But it would not follow that they were always expressed in visual terms; in deep sleep it may be that no projection from tactile and kinaesthetic sensation takes place; and, if that is true, then, in so far as dreams consist of projective imagery, there would be phantasy throughout but not necessarily a dream.

psycho-analysis unless the analysis were carried out in terms of tactile and kinaesthetic sensations. Some techniques, however, are not very far off this. Thus in accordance with her theory of 'internal objects', Klein[1] does not in general frame interpretations to patients solely in terms of wishes and fears felt towards external objects but frames them in terms of internal objects as well. Now all analysis must refer by implication to felt sensations, but most interpretations do so *only* by implication. It seems extremely likely, however, that interpretations in terms of internal objects make the implication more nearly explicit. The presumption here is that it would be an advantage to make it wholly explicit. To take an example: Alexander was treating a peptic ulcer patient who had a dream of a doctor grabbing his testicles.[2] Since most dreams are visual, this one probably took place in visual terms. If this is so, it would have a significant bearing on the confirmation or refutation of the present theory to know the consequences of alternative interpretations. It would be of moment to the present theory to know, for example, what would happen if the dream were interpreted first as an attempt to avoid the sensation of having the testicles grabbed, this being followed perhaps by an interpretation of the reason, whatever it might be in the context, expressed in terms of sensations, *e.g.* sensations of muscular activity aiming at destroying someone. All the usual types of interpretation could be used, even though constantly framed with reference to the difference between projective imagery and tactile and kinaesthetic sensation. It would also be desirable to give special attention to the patient's projective mechanisms. All this would require an exploration into the patient's method of imagining.

Thus it would be possible to seek a test for the theory in clinical practice.

The last matter for discussion is the relation between the present theory and those of Alexander, Deutsch, and Selye. The present one seems to be in general agreement with that of Deutsch; this is difficult to decide exactly, because his theory is

[1] Klein, *Op. cit.*

[2] Franz Alexander, "Treatment of a Case of Peptic Ulcer and Personality Disorder," *Psychosomatic Medicine*, Philadelphia, 1947, Vol. IX, No. v, p. 327. (Reprinted in Alexander and French, *Op. cit.*)

much less definite. It seems to me that, when he (and Alexander) speak of personality-type as a determinant, it is necessary to qualify this by saying that the personality-type must be one in which projective imagery is not a very effective defence. As regards the claim made by Deutsch that a physical trauma must always have occurred in childhood if a psychosomatic disorder is to occur, I venture no opinion; if it is so, I should suppose that the trauma, in setting up a conflict, always interfered with the projective mechanism of imagery.

What is to be said about the threefold classification given by Alexander? There is nothing in the present theory that is incompatible with it. All that is held here is that conflicts fought out in terms of imagined sensations act as stimuli in exactly the same way as would sensations caused by extraneous factors. Thus the kinaesthetic phantasy of chewing would bring about both a normal physiological accompaniment such as toughness in jaw muscles and a derivative dysfunction consisting of ulcer symptoms. On the present theory, however, it would be unnecessary to insist upon the distinction between 'conversion' disorders and those in which the dysfunction is the normal concomitant of a conflict, for both are explained in the same way here. There may be greater symbolic reinforcement in the one than in the other; but recently Garma[1] has argued that conversion symbolism is to be found even in disorders that are under the control of the autonomic nervous system. Although the present theory seems to bear on all three of the types of disorder distinguished by Alexander, it is not worth while speculating on its applicability to them all unless it survives testing in the field of the neuro-muscular and perceptual systems; for there would be a considerable problem in explaining how a dysfunction of, say, the pancreas could arise as a consequence of a dysfunction in the neuro-muscular system.

It is at this point that Selye's theory comes in, for it renders possible almost any physiological consequence. This may well have diagnostic rather than theoretical importance; for it may be that chains of organic dysfunctions and lesions that might be

[1] Angel Garma, "On the Pathogenesis of Peptic Ulcer", *The International Journal of Psycho-Analysis*, London, 1950, Vol. XXXI, Pts. i and ii, pp. 53–72.

expected to follow a conflict involving tactile and kinaesthetic sensations would be modified in a great variety of ways by target-organ weakness and the like, as Selye indicates.

In short, the relation to Deutsch's theory is that the complete generality of it is not accepted in the one here put forward; and the doubtful early physical trauma is not postulated.

Alexander's theoretical formulations do not constitute a theory in the same way. He has a theory of classification; and this is in part acceptable; but it is descriptive, not explanatory. His directional analysis is not in fact a theory of a certain class of disorders but a correlation between mental and physiological trends.

As regards the question of personality-type, the present theory has not been concerned with it in the form in which it is used by Alexander and Deutsch. Nonetheless the chief feature of the present theory is that it makes a highly general characterisation of personality-types into those that use projective imagery successfully and those that fail.

Selye's theory of the target-organ would seem to provide reasons why mixed types of disorder should be more clinically familiar than the ideal types that over-simplified theory might lead one to expect.

Chapter 23

THE MECHANISM IN BERKELEY'S
PSYCHOSOMATIC DISORDER

THE reason for introducing the foregoing theory is that it has a direct application to Berkeley, for in his first major publication, *An Essay towards a New Theory of Vision* (1709), he drew a fundamental distinction between vision and touch.

The core of his thesis is this. In visual perception, *i.e.* when one sees what Berkeley called "ideas", the ideas seen do not exist in physical space but only in the mind. Thus they do not exist at any distance from the percipient, they have no size, and they have no orientation—all with reference to physical space. They are not what he called "without the mind", which for brevity we may replace by "external". Now in this work Berkeley wrote of certain objects that do exist externally in a certain sense. These are 'tangible' objects: tangible objects exist at a distance, have a size, and have an orientation, physical space is therefore no more than tangible space. Hence his doctrine was that visual ideas have no distance, size, or orientation in tactual space; visual ideas are in the mind and tangible objects are external. By association of ideas a percipient learns to use his visual ideas to judge the distance, size, and orientation of tangible objects. Kinaesthetic ideas come in also, for the percipient learns to judge from visual ideas the distance of a tangible object by learning how far he would have to move to reach the tangible object.

The next step is to elucidate the conception of 'tangible object'. To speak of tangible objects is not to speak literally; it is simply a way of saying that tactile ideas obtainable—*if* a percipient moves in such and such a way he *will have* a certain tactile idea (or sensation). In other words the 'tangible object' is not an actual object but a potentiality—a potentiality for the occurrence of an actual tactile idea. And tactile ideas are *not* external but are 'in the mind'.

Thus Berkeley's theory is that visual ideas, which exist only

in the mind and which in an important sense are at no distance
and have no size or orientation, suggest tangible objects, *i.e.*
suggest obtainable tactile and kinaesthetic ideas, which also
exist only in the mind but which do have the properties of distance, size, and orientation.

We are now in a position to interpret 'external'. One usage
is equivalent to 'in Matter'. In this sense Berkeley held throughout his published work, including the essay on vision, that
nothing is external. The other usage, according to which tangible
objects are external, is simply a way of saying that obtainable
tactile ideas have the properties of distance, size, and orientation, which visual ideas do not have. That is to say, "external"
in this sense would mean 'having the properties of distance, size,
and orientation' while "internal" would mean not having
them.*

Now everything, whether 'external' or 'internal' in the last
senses described, is in another sense internal or 'in the mind'.
This phrase is the most difficult in all Berkeley's writing. It is
usually interpreted in the sense of "mind-dependence". Berkeley himself never used this expression, but it would in fact be
more appropriate for his considered philosophy than would "in
the mind". The use of such a strange phase needs explanation;
let us see whether we can interpret it.

To do this we must pay special attention to the conception
of the body-boundary, the importance of which has been
greatly stressed by Scott.[1] On Berkeley's theory, the tactile idea
of his teeth is inside the tactile idea of his body-surface. Now
visual ideas, say of a distant tower, are not outside the visual
ideas of the body-boundary; nor are they inside. Likewise visual
ideas of the body-boundary are not outside tactile ideas of the
teeth. Thus visual ideas of the body-boundary do not coincide
with tactile ideas of it. Put generally, all visual ideas must be
inside all tactile ideas, even those of the inside of the body. This

* Berkeley's theory was perfectly consistent with the philosophical doctrine of *Esse percipi* according to which all ideas—and therefore tactile
ones as well as visual—are in the mind. Nonetheless, consistency is
established only if the above distinctions are made plain.

[1] W. Clifford M. Scott, "The 'Body Scheme' in Psychotherapy",
The British Journal of Medical Psychology, London, 1949, Vol. XXII, Pts.
iii and iv, p. 142.

assertion is, of course, no more than a particular application of Berkeley's theory. (Nonetheless visual ideas, in so far as they can by association lead to correct judgments of tactile ideas, can be regarded as having an order, though not an order in a spatial volume of a tactile kind.) Add to this that for Berkeley a mind seems to have been a collection of ideas perceived from a certain perspective, and we arrive at the following. A visual mind was a sort of point-mind or monad (possessing an internal order), in relation to which all tactile ideas, even those inside the body-boundary, were external. Here is what we might call a "contraction-effect", in that the visual universe was contracted to a point. By contrast with this, tactile ideas extended through the entire volume of the body including its boundary. Kinaesthetic ideas, which are also mentioned in Berkeley's theory, may be bracketed with these. But what is to be said about ideas outside the body-boundary? Visual there are none; but neither are there tactile. By moving one may obtain a tactile idea of a chair that was a short distance away, but there is no tactile idea of it until it is obtained by actual contact. Hence the tactile idea is on the body-boundary, and there are no tactile ideas outside it. Outside there are *possibilities* of tactile ideas and nothing else. These results may be expressed as follows:

Interpretation LII: Berkeley introjected the visual universe and contracted it to a point, locating his visual mind at this point; his tactual and kinaesthetic mind extended over the inside of his body to its boundary, though not outside. Outside, possibilities alone existed.

It is worth noting in passing that Berkeley, when he was considering the problem of identity, held that the thing one sees is not the same as the thing one touches, so that he was concerned with linking sights and touches and concerned also with the relation between an object and two unconnected ideas associated with it. Now this theme will concern even a person who believes that what he sees is located at a distance from himself in the neighbourhood of what he touches. But it would seem that there was an additional stress in the problem of identity for Berkeley, because of the lack of congruence on his view between the visual and tactual mind.

Let us now consider something passing across the body-boundary, whether inwards or outwards. In particular consider something consisting of tactile ideas passing outwards. Once it is outside the boundary it ceases to consist of tactile ideas. It is therefore either nothing or visual ideas or tangible possibilities. But the visual ideas are not outside. In the process of passing through the boundary the tactile ideas give place to visual ones which are at once introjected to the visual point-mind; by association they tell what tactile idea could be obtained by moving the body; that is to say, visual ideas are 'cashed' for further experience only by obtaining further tactile ideas, which are within the tactual mind. Hence nothing except bare possibilities can pass outside the body-boundary. In this way we reach:

Interpretation LIII: "*In the mind*" *means 'being a tactile or kinaesthetic idea on or within the body-boundary or being a visual idea at a point inside the body':* (*And Immaterialism signifies that nothing exists except bare possibilities outside the tactile body-boundary*).

What happens now if the principle of *Esse percipi* breaks down or is not felt to be fully effective? Matter would exist outside the mind; the existence of bad faeces would be recognised; and visual and tactile ideas of poison would become possible. In such an eventuality, would any defence have been open to Berkeley?

The scotomisation of Matter was Berkeley's most prominent defence; but the foregoing interpretation of the theory of vision suggests that there was a more primitive defence as well, consisting of the contraction-effect. Even though Matter should become allowed through failure of the *esse-percipi* defence (and likewise if it had been recognised to exist before this defence had developed), *i.e.* even though bad faeces were admitted to exist in the external world, the contraction-effect would enable Berkeley to protect himself by restricting the perception of the poison to the domain of vision; for visual ideas of Matter would not have distance, size, or orientation and would be withdrawn to a point, to his visual mind, inside his tactual mind, and well away from Matter itself. This process, of course, both presupposes and works only on the condition that Matter is a tangible object, *i.e.* a potentiality; for then the visual ideas of it merely suggest possible, obtainable tactile ideas of it—actual tactile ideas would be avoidable.

Psychogenetically this defence would have been earlier than that of *Esse percipi*: so long as he only saw and did not touch bad faeces he would feel safe.

That this defence against Matter underlay the *New Theory of Vision* may be discerned from the critical aim of that essay. The received theories, which he attacked, explained the visual perception of distance, size, and orientation by means of geometrical lines and angles. In this way vision was intimately connected with mathematics and therefore with Matter (thus even in this work Berkeley was opposing Matter). In offering his new theory, he was replacing those that were founded on Matter by one in which Matter was kept literally out of sight. And the contraction-effect served this purpose. Thus we have:

(*Defence*) *Interpretation LIV: Berkeley's contraction of his visual mind was designed to confine poison to the domain of vision.*

(*Defence*) *Interpretation LV: The visual perception of poison was made safe by removing visual ideas to the maximum possible extent from the poison.*

Our remaining problem then is to understand exactly why the theory of vision provided an insufficiently strong defence: *i.e.* why it had to be supplemented by later ones, notably *Esse percipi*, and therefore why it broke down when deprived of an auxiliary defence.

The weakness of the defence would lie in the tax it put on Berkeley's control over incorporation. Seeing was an introjection; we presumed in the childhood reconstructions that greed to incorporate could compel him to incorporate despite the danger from the object; and visual incorporation cannot be effective for more than a short time, since nothing is thereby incorporated, so that in the end tactile and kinaesthetic incorporation is the only alternative to the last available defence against hunger. The presumption of a strong need for food or great greed would help to explain not only the Solipsism but the method of contracting visual ideas instead of the more usual procedure of projecting them outwards. Clearly the only remaining way of dealing with such a situation was to deny the existence of Matter altogether, so that it could not even be seen, and thus remove the visual temptation to incorporate it.

Interpretation LVI: The introjective nature of vision for Berkeley could only lead to frustration and thence to tactile and kinaesthetic incorporation.

The application of the theory put forward in the previous chapter is evident. Berkeley attempted to deal with his conflict about bad faeces by conceiving them in visual terms alone and not in tactile and kinaesthetic terms, by separating off visual ideas and withdrawing them from the tactual field. The introjective nature of this defence led to its defeat and therefore to tactile and kinaesthetic incorporation. Consequently, the sensations of poisonous faeces became imagined in their 'natural' or undisplaced position inside his body. The conception of poison has to be taken, of course, not as a chemical poison but as a sensation of some pain, such as gripe, something gnawing, or burning. Hypotheses VII and VIII connect this sensation with intestinal dysfunction.

The one point of apparent divergence with the theory should not be overlooked. The theory was framed mainly in terms of projective images functioning as a protection against sensation. In Berkeley, however, visual images were not projected but introjected to a point: projection of visual ideas would have put them in contact with Matter; introjection avoided this. Nonetheless this unusual mechanism segregated visual from tactile and kinaesthetic ideas, and hence would not directly arouse tactile and kinaesthetic sensations. Thus the introjection mechanism would serve the same purpose as the projection mechanism, of protecting him from having unwelcome sensations.

There is therefore a very close fit between the theory and its application to Berkeley.

Chapter 24

CONCLUSION

DOES an analysis such as the foregoing imply that the subject treated was a grossly abnormal man? This may or may not be so. It would be most misleading, however, to suggest that Berkeley was very abnormal. A great deal of his activity and behaviour indicate the contrary. This means that he was able to keep his fundamental conflict under some control; even when at its height it did not swamp his whole life; and at other times it was more or less confined to his writings and his psychosomatic symptoms. Nor is such an analysis in the least derogatory. There is nothing, save perhaps his handling of the deists, to detract from Bishop Atterbury's sincere eulogy. There is no known ground for doubting that Berkeley was a really fine character.

And what of the truth of the analysis? On being presented with an analysis of a person from his writings, the reader may ask if there is any reason to accept it. The question is: what sort of tests are available?

(1) The interpretations offered should be internally coherent.

(2) There should be no known fact about the subject analysed that conflicts with these interpretations.

(3) The analysis should throw light on some problem. In a certain sense it does not constitute the *explanation* of anything, in that we cannot deduce, given the childhood structure and the environment, say, that Berkeley would create a philosophy. Psycho-analytic interpretations do not describe causes whose effects can be uniquely predicted—they do not in general work forwards. They describe causes of some known effect—they work backwards. This limitation is not absolute. One may be able to predict that one or other of a small group of effects will occur. And it is possible sometimes to go a little farther. Given the childhood structure, it would be possible, if the psychosomatic theory in Chapter 22 is correct, to make a conditional prediction of mental disorder and to specify whether it would be psychosomatic or purely psychological. Such a pre-

diction is conditional, for it would not materialise unless certain environmental circumstances were to arise in the course of the subject's life. It should be possible to specify such circumstances in general terms—such as a serious setback of a kind that would have an intimate connexion with the fundamental defence mechanisms. I do not think it likely, for instance, that, if Berkeley's friend, Tom Prior, had let him down and made off with his funds, he would have developed a mental disorder; for such an occurrence would not have revealed any fundamental weakness in his projective defence system.

The possibility may be mentioned that a person with an 'unstable' mental structure in early childhood will somehow engineer circumstances that will wreck his defences and bring about an overt disorder. That this is true in certain cases is very likely. I would doubt its being true generally; but the point is obviously a difficult one to settle. Berkeley helped to bring failure on himself. But with a little 'luck', that is to say had Walpole been more scrupulous, this might very well not have happened; and it is probable that Berkeley would have lived an active life in Rhode Island in good health for many years. This, however, is speculative.

(4) Interpretations should be of a clinical type, preferably widely used in clinical practice. Almost all those used in the analysis of Berkeley satisfy this condition. The few exceptions are numbers XV and XLIX, according to which he projected himself into God and his father for certain special purposes, and numbers LII to LV, to do with introjecting the visual universe to a point. I do not know of their ever having been made; but they are of a clinical type and could be used.

(5) The most important test is, of course, the effect of the interpretations upon a patient; and this is totally lacking in an investigation of the present kind.

In this connexion it should perhaps be noted that the clinical test of interpretations is not that a patient becomes 'cured'. Psycho-analysts find 'cure' a complex and vague concept by comparison with the degree of definiteness that attaches to clinical concepts. This does not mean that improvement in a patient is not a criterion at all. Improvement certainly suggests that there is a *prima facie* case for the interpretations, so that one will entertain a somewhat unspecific hypothesis to the effect that the interpretations have some value which may require sifting but which should be looked into. The fundamental tests for interpretations are largely independent of improvements in the patient's state and lie in the day-to-day work of understanding the flux in his subsequent associations. It would be out of place, however, to enter into this very complex matter here. The purpose of making these few remarks is simply to emphasise —what is usually overlooked by readers who take analytic interpretations to be pure speculation—that such analyses as the present one are rooted in clinical practice. It should perhaps be added that, contrary to what is widely supposed, interpretations are not simply bizarre statements that somehow illuminate and have a good effect upon neurotic people; analysts mean them literally, and the final stage of an analysis might be described as the discovery that the interpretations after all mean what they say.

Psycho-analysis has often been applied outside the clinical field, to the elucidation, for instance, of problems in literature, art, politics, religion, folklore, and so on. It has rarely been applied to philosophers in relation to their philosophy. There have been a few examples in the field of social and political philosophy and ethics. Of the most abstract part of the subject, metaphysics, the only instances known to me are the analyses given by Hitschmann on Schopenhauer,[1] by von Winterstein on the history of philosophy,[2] by Roeder on Aristotle,[3] and by myself on Schopenhauer[4] and on Descartes.[5] To these should perhaps be added a forerunner of all of them, which is intermediate between myth and metaphysics: Freud's celebrated

[1] Eduard Hitschmann, "Schopenhauer", *Imago*, Leipzig, 1913, Bd. II, Heft ii, S. 101–74.
[2] Alfred von Winterstein, "Psychoanalytische Anmerkungen zur Geschichte der Philosophie", *Loc. cit.*, S. 175–237.
[3] Egenolf Roeder, "Das Ding an Sich", *Imago*, Leipzig, 1923, Bd. IX, Heft iii, S. 273–99.
[4] J. O. Wisdom, "The Unconscious Origin of Schopenhauer's Philosophy", *The International Journal of Psycho-Analysis*, London, 1945, Vol. XXVI, Pts. i and ii, pp. 44–52.
[5] J. O. Wisdom, "Three Dreams of Descartes", *The International Journal of Psycho-Analysis*, London, 1947, Vol. XXVIII, Pt. i, pp. 11–18.

analysis of the Schreber case.[1] Here a former President of the Dresden Senate became a lunatic; he remained socially charming and erudite, but developed a mystical system of thought according to which he would bear a new race of men begotten by the divine rays of the sun.

Philosophy is the last refuge open to myth (though not necessarily every kind of philosophy is impregnated with it). Nonetheless the analysis of a philosopher does not in itself refute the philosophy. This I have discussed elsewhere.[2] The value of such analyses would seem to lie in several different consequences. (i) They give a new angle from which one can approach intellectual problems and contributions: one recognises more easily a phantastic system for what it is, though more ready to see the possibility of a grain of truth hidden in a system that might otherwise be written off. (ii) One is less concerned with arguments about the truth or falsity of such a system when it obviously depicts a phantasy. (iii) Such systems are seen to have a meaning and not to be nonsense as Logical Positivism has asserted. And (iv) the nature of the meaning brought out by an analysis may provide a good practical indication of whether or not there is something objective present.

Berkeley tried to cure men's minds of evil by the therapeutic strength of *Esse percipi*. He tried to cure men's bodies of poison by the therapeutic strength of tar-water. In a sense his approach was psychosomatic in this attempt. If I have followed him in only one thing it is in this approach. His measures unfortunately were founded largely on myth or magic. The much practised procedures that I have relied upon are founded on realities. Whether or not the same can be said of the unconfirmed psychosomatic theory that I have put forward must await the possibility of trial and the test of clinical experience.

It is perhaps fitting to end a work on Berkeley with certain quotations of his ideals which were no idle boast, even though

[1] Freud, *Collected Papers*, London, 1925, Vol. III, "Psycho-Analytic Notes upon an Autobiographical Account of a Case of Paranoia" (1911), pp. 387–470.
[2] J. O. Wisdom, *The Metamorphosis of Philosophy*, Cairo (Al-Ma'aref and Basil Blackwell), 1947, Pt. III.

he wished to preach his philosophy, and have others accept it
rather than find their own path. They are worthy ideals for the
philosopher and scientist. He was fortunate in that, unlike certain other philosophers, he was never made to suffer for them;
but he was not the less sincere about them on this account. To
his opponents who bowed to the authority of Newton he wrote
in his *A Defence of Freethinking in Mathematics*:

§ 13   I shall never say of him as you do, *Vestigia pronus adoro*. This
same adoration that you pay to him, I will pay only to truth.

§ 19   The only advantage I pretend to is that I have always
thought and judged for myself.

And the last word comes from his last writing, *Siris*:

§ 368   Truth is the cry of all, but the game of a few. . . . He that
would make a real progress in knowledge must dedicate his age as
well as youth, the later growth as well as first fruits, at the altar of
Truth.

Appendix

BERKELEY'S WILL

BERKELEY's will contains a curious stipulation:

Item, that my body, before it is buried, be kept five days above ground, or longer, even till it grow offensive by the cadaverous smell, and that during the said time it lye unwashed, undisturbed, and covered by the same bed clothes, in the same bed, the head being raised upon pillows.[1]

Some five years before there had appeared in the Press some alarming tales of people being buried while still alive, substantiated apparently by an eminent physician. It was stated that

there is scarce any Case in which the common Appearances of Death may be safely rely'd on.[2]

Even surgical tests were not considered sufficient. Fantastic claims were made about the length of time—days and even weeks—that people had lain in water and yet recovered. Then comes the assertion that there is "no Sign infallible but the beginning of Putrefaction".

Evidently Berkeley took all this seriously, and he adopted the putrefaction safety-measure. It struck some chord within him.

Two points are obvious. He feared being buried alive; and he felt that there was the possibility that though alive he might show all the signs of death. The first means that he feared being unable to move while still wanting to move (it is also likely to be associated with the struggle for breath, but we do not know whether he had any asthmatic or other difficulties in breathing). The second is interesting, for it amounts to the fear, so to speak, of a psychosomatic 'death-syndrome', *i.e.* that he might for psychological reasons become motionless, without breath, with-

---

[1] A. A. Luce, *The Life of George Berkeley*, Edinburgh, 1949, p. 222.

[2] "A Dissertation on the Uncertainty of the Signs of Death", *The Dublin Journal*, Aug. 1–4, 1747, No. 2127, citing the *Gentleman's Magazine*.

out pulse, and display pallor and fixity of eye. Such symptoms would be the acme of repudiation of kinaesthetic sensation and the most intense reaction against motility. It would seem that, just as he began life with fluidity of bowel and bladder, which became intolerable, so he expected to end life with constipation become absolute. The precaution that he was not to be buried till he stank means that his body was to become faecal and to be recognised as offensive faeces by others. Then and only then would the poison inside him have permeated his whole body. Total poisoning would seem to be what death meant to him.

BIBLIOGRAPHICAL NOTE

FOR bibliography the student of Berkeley must turn to Jessop's incomparable work devoted to this alone (T. E. Jessop, *A Bibliography of George Berkeley*, Oxford, 1934). It lists with extraordinary completeness and accuracy Berkeley's works, translations, and works on Berkeley in the several languages in which they have appeared. Hardly any other works have come to light since. Professor Jessop has noted Smith's *Optics* and I have come upon Robertson's discussion of *Alciphron* and Cajori's study of the mathematical controversy. All these works are important. In addition, Leyburn has found another edition of one of Berkeley's pamphlets. Details are as follows:

1731. George Berkeley, *Queries Relation to a National Bank, Extracted from the Querist. Also the Letter Containing a Plan or Sketch of such a Bank*, Dublin.

This tiny pamphlet was discovered by Prof. E. D. Leyburn in the Sterling Library at Yale University. It contains queries about the bank which were omitted from the second and all subsequent editions of *The Querist*. It should appear after No. 29b in Jessop's *Bibliography*.

1738. Robert Smith, *A Compleat System of Opticks*, Cambridge.

He does not mention Berkeley in the index. He refers to the "acute and judicious author of the *Theory of Vision*" (Vol. II, § 161), "a Work highly entertaining and useful to all that are duly qualified to consider it" (Vol. II, § 217). He quotes Berkeley at length and with approval; and also criticises. See Vol. I, Bk. i, Ch. 5; Vol. II, §§ 160–2, 171–7, 209–46, 321–43.

1906. J. M. Robertson, *A Short History of Freethought*, London, second edition.

Vol. II, pp. 138–41, contains a terrific indictment of Berkeley's lack of toleration towards the deists; reproduced with small additions of the same intensity in subsequent editions: Vol. II, 1915, pp. 162–4; Vol. II, 1936 ("Short" deleted from title), pp. 733–5.

1919. Florian Cajori, *A History of the Conceptions of Limits and Fluxions in Great Britain from Newton to Woodhouse*, Chicago.

This traces the history of the *Analyst* controversy in full.

Since 1934 an increasingly large amount has been written about Berkeley, and a valuable, though incomplete, supplement to Jessop's *Bibliography*, covering the years 1934–52, has appeared in the Belgian journal:

1953. Jean Lameere, "Bibliographie", *Revue internationale de philosophie*, Bruxelles, VII⁰ année, No. xxiii–xxiv: George Berkeley, 1685–1753.

An entire issue of this journal, as well as of the two following, was devoted to Berkeley for the bicentenary of his death:

1953. *Revue philosophique de la France et de l'étranger*, Paris, Nos. iv–vi: Bicentenaire de la Mort de Berkeley.

1953. *The British Journal for the Philosophy of Science*, Edinburgh, Vol. IV, No. xiii: George Berkeley Bicentenary.

The first two journals devote themselves to all aspects of Berkeley's philosophy. The last-mentioned restricts itself to Berkeley's four contributions to science and its philosophy.

INDEX

Aaron, R. I. 29, 30
abstract ideas. *See* ideas, abstract
aetiology 140, 196
Alexander, F. 194, 195, 197, 198,
 209, 218, 219, 220
'amalgam' concept 215
ambivalence 150, 151, 156-8
annihilation. *See* creation
archetypes & ectypes 16, 18n, 48,
 51, 57, 60
Aristotle 11, 26, 51, 229
'Athens of the World' 151
Atterbury, Bishop 104, 227
authority, independence of 33,
 231

Baladi, N. 53
Baldwin 5n
Balfour, A. J. 100
Bell, J. 79
Berkeley, an Anglican 5
 and Irish language 117n
 as preacher 102-3
 importance of 22, 40, 96, 97,
 99, 102
 traditional interpretation of 1,
 16, Ch. 4; Ch. 5; 80, 101
Berkeley, Mrs. 98, 110f, 176-7
Berkeley, Thomas 109-10
Berkeley's American project Ch.
 11; 132, 151, 154, 155, 169
 aggressiveness 105-8, 157-8,
 165, 167, 176, 180, 182,
 184, 185, 186, 189, 193
 apparel 175
 career Ch. 9
 caution vis-à-vis the Church
 34, 156

considered philosophy 2, Ch.
 2; 42, 51, 53, 55, 154, 167.
 See also Phenomenalism,
 Theocentric
contributions to economics 2,
 80, 88-94, 122-3
contributions to mathematics
 2, 80, 86-8, 99, 157
contributions to philosophy of
 physics 2, 80, 85-6, 97
contributions to psychology 2,
 80, 81-5, 96, 99, 102
criticism of mathematics 32-3,
 35-6, 86-8
family life, 110f
generosity 119-20
health 98, 100, 112, 121, 123,
 Ch. 12; 136, 139, 140, 155,
 167, 169, 174
important contributions 2, 80
independence of mind 34,
 156, 231
interest in architecture 101, 102
lost treatise 97
marriage 98, 135-6, 152, 177,
 190
national feeling 35-6, 113-18
nominalism & positivism 36
parentage 95
personal appearance 103
personal losses 98, 100, 113
personal qualities 3, 33-5, 39,
 40, 98, Ch. 10; 151, 152, 156,
 227, 231
philosophical hopes, 27
philosophy criticised 28
Platonism Ch. 5
poem 102, 127, 152-3

dirt. *See* faeces as poison *and* tar-
water & poison
disorder, functional 136, 167,
214. *See* dysfunction
dreams 137, 142, 143, 217n
Dublin 101, 102, 128
Dunlop, R. 89n, 93
dysfunction 167, 195, 196, 198,
213, 214, 217, 219, 226

Egmont. *See* Percival, Sir J.
Epiphenomenalism 214
Esse causari 18, 19, 21, 58, 148
Esse concipi 9, 21n, 46, 47
Esse percipere 8
Esse percipi 7, 8, 9, 10, 11, 13n,
17, 19, 19n, 28, 34, 41, 46,
47, 55, 58, 61, 88, 121, 124,
136, 137, 148n, 151, 154,
161, 169, 170, 174, 176,
177, 222n, 230
Esse percipi & introjection 171
Esse percipi causari 22, 25, 27, 60
Esse percipiposse. See ideas, possible
Esse percipi, psychological rôle of
142–4, 149, 164, 166, 169,
172, 180, 181, 187, 188,
191, 193, 224, 225
Esse velle (*agere*) 18
experiment proposed 210, 217
Ezriel, H. viii

faeces & food 178, 187–8, 192
& mathematics 160
& money 162–3
as destructive power 181
as poison 149, 161, 178, 179,
224, 226
faeces, derivatives of 178
good & bad 149, 161, 164,
165, 178–9, 180, 181, 182,
186, 192

liquid 183, 233
fathers 181–3
Fenichel, O. 171, 176, 196, 208n
Ferenczi, S. 162
flux 131, 132, 133, 134, 159, 161,
183
Fraser, A. C. 29, 44n, 45n, 100,
132, 174
Frazer, J. G. 201
freethinkers. *See* deists
French, T. 198, 206, 207
Freud 161, 162, 170n, 179, 194,
201, 229
'furniture of the earth' 8, 27

Garma, A. 219
God & existence 5, 15–16, 17, 42,
59
& Mammon 147n
& Matter 38, 39, Ch. 15; 159,
182, 184, 185
& mother 185
as cause 16–19, 19–22, 24, 48,
49, 59, 60, 145, 154, 155,
181, 183
as disembodied 16
Gottschalk, L. A. 209
guilt & anxiety in psychosomatic disorder 216–17

hallucination 203, 204, 205, 213
Hambling, J. viii, 208, 216
Head, H. 212
Hicks, G. D. 44–5, 47
Hitschmann, E. vii, 229
hoarding 164
Home Guard & Local Security
Force 106
hormones 168, 196
Hume 19, 19n, 37, 39, 43, 44, 46,
80, 94, 96

DATE DUE

APR 3 1992		FEB 2 7 1998	
APR 06 1992		MAY 0 2 1999	
APR 1 1 1994			
APR 2 6 1994		APR 1 3 1999	
		APR 0 3 2000	
NOV 2 7 1995			
MAR 0 2 1996			

Lightning Source UK Ltd.
Milton Keynes UK
UKHW010728140223
416966UK00007B/92

9 781013 402753